SPARKNOTES®

WORKOUT in FRENCH

SPARK PUBLISHING

Contributing writers: Suzanna G. Carr, Melanie Martinho, Pierre-Alexandre Scott
Illustrations by Christina Berg Renzi.

SPARKNOTES is a registered trademark of SparkNotes LLC.

Spark Publishing
A Division of Barnes & Noble
120 Fifth Avenue
New York, NY 10011
www.sparknotes.com

ISBN-13: 978-1-4114-9678-1
ISBN-10: 1-4114-9678-7

Library of Congress Cataloging-in-Publication Data

Workout in French: practice for the tricky rules of French grammar.
    p. cm.—(Workout in)
  ISBN-13: 978-1-4114-9678-1 (pbk.)
  ISBN-10: 1-4114-9678-7 (pbk.)
  1. French language—Textbooks for foreign speakers—English. 2. French language—Problems, exercises, etc. 3. French language—Self instruction.

PC2129.E5W665 2007
448.2'421—dc22

                                                            2007028605

Please submit changes or report errors to www.sparknotes.com/errors.

Printed and bound in Canada

10 9 8 7 6 5 4 3 2 1

A Note from SparkNotes

There's a saying that goes, *if you can speak three languages, you're trilingual; if you can speak two languages, you're bilingual; and if you speak only one language, you're American.* If you're a student who dreams of bilingual fluency—or who just dreams of passing that French final exam—you've come to the right place.

We've designed the *Workout In* series to be the hammer that helps you nail down your studies. The 100 workouts you're holding in your hands cover all of the trickiest grammar rules. Whether you're taking your first course in a language, moving from a beginner to an intermediate level, or coming back for a little refresher course, these bite-size lessons and power-packed exercises will give you the help you need.

This book is organized by subject, some of which include Nouns, Verbs, Adjectives, and Adverbs. Sample sentences show you how to apply these rules, and English translations and bolded text help you zero in on the words being discussed.

The following additional features make it easy to navigate around trouble spots that are likely to cost you points on a test:

→ ***Attention!* boxes** provide tips and strategies to solidify your learning and alert you to potential pitfalls.

→ ***L'Exception* boxes** call out exceptions to the rules.

→ ***La Langue Vivante* boxes** explain some of the quirkier rules of grammar, or point out where a rule may differ from colloquial usage.

This format makes it easy for you to get the information you need most. But reading a bunch of rules on grammar will get you only so far. The key to learning any language is practice—and you'll get lots of practice with this book. To go with all the rules and fancy features, each workout includes several sets of exercises in a variety of formats, from fill-ins, translations, and matching questions to crossword puzzles, writing prompts, and personal profiles.

We've also included a glossary of irregular and special usage words, as well as a handy reference for general grammar terms (just in case you don't know your preterite from your past participle). So dig in. Whether you thumb through and find help in the areas you need it most or read it cover to cover, this book will give you what you need to get to the next level.

Contents

An Introduction to French

More than 300 million people worldwide speak French today. It's an official language in forty-one countries, and many people across the globe learn French as a second language. With such a broad international reach, it is prominent as an official and administrative language in many important agencies, including the United Nations, the World Trade Organization, and the European Union.

French is one of the Romance languages, along with languages such as Spanish, Italian, Portuguese, and Romanian. All Romance languages originated from Vulgar Latin, the common language of the Roman Empire (not to be confused with Classical Latin, the language of the Roman elite). As regional languages were constantly evolving and changing (due primarily to contact with separate language groups, such as Arabic or Germanic), Vulgar Latin morphed into several distinct languages. Their shared origin led to many similarities among these languages in both sound and structure.

Though French was only made the official language of France in 1992, its origins as a unique language date back much further. Ancient French was partially influenced by the Celtic dialects of Northern France, as well as those of the northern tribe called the Franks (from which the name French, or *Français,* is derived). Throughout its development, several other languages made their mark on French, such as English (from the Norman conquerors) and Arabic (from the spice traders). Words from these cultures were incorporated into French centuries ago and are now part of the accepted vocabulary.

When France joined the rest of Europe in world exploration in the fifteen century, the French language was transmitted to far-flung colonies from Guyana to Madagascar to Tahiti to Canada. While this common colonial history enables people from distant regions to communicate in a universally understood language, spoken French varies from region to region across the globe. Accents are the most noticeable difference, but the meaning of many words and expressions varies as well. For example, *écraser* (to crush) in French is *écrapoutir* in Québécois. Still, most grammatical structures and vocabulary are identical in the various French-speaking countries, so differences might result in only slight misunderstandings. A good grasp of the basics will gain you entry into conversations with French speakers all over the world.

In 1593, under the unified monarchy of King Francis I, modern French overtook the various regional dialects and was made the official language of the country. During France's period of international dominance in the seventeenth, eighteenth, and nineteenth centuries, the French language came to be seen as the *lingua franca* (commonly used language) of all educated classes of Europe, spreading the language beyond its borders.

L'Académie Française was established in 1634 by a group of scholars with the mission of keeping the French language pure from the invasions of other linguistic influences. Many of France's most esteemed literary figures, including Balzac, Flaubert, and Molière, have been a part of the elite circle of academy scholars. The prestige associated with membership in this group has kept the academy culturally relevant for the 400 years that have elapsed since its founding. Though frequently the source of humor and derision, the academy holds serious influence over French grammar and often oversees modernizations brought on by changes in society. For example, their suggestion of the French noun *baladeur* (literally, portable one) effectively prevented the term *walkman* from infiltrating the French language. L'Académie Française is also charged with accepting or rejecting new words proposed for the official French language. Slang words, such as recent inductees *boulot* (job) and *bagnole* (car), only become official when l'Académie Française gives its nod of approval.

But despite the best attempts of purists, modern English does creep into spoken French. *Un barman* will serve you your drink, which you can use to wash down *un cheeseburger.* During *le weekend,* you may *faire le jogging* or *faire le shopping.* But to rely too heavily on English to get you through French can be a mistake—there are many examples of false cognates (*faux amis*), words that seem the same in French and English but that have entirely different meanings. *Sensible,* for example, actually means *sensitive* in French, not *sensible.*

Because of their different origins, French operates by rules unfamiliar to English speakers. For example, adjectives usually come *after* the noun in French (*un chapeau rouge*), where they usually come *before* the noun in English (*a red hat*). The fact that every French noun has a gender can also pose a problem to non-native speakers. While not many people could tell you what makes water (*l'eau*) feminine and fire (*le feu*) masculine, knowing gender is necessary for clear communication. And, unfortunately, the numerous exceptions to grammar rules, such as word gender, make memorization a necessary part of learning the language. Luckily, with practice and time these grammatical differences become second-nature, even to native English speakers.

Definite articles point out something specific. The definite articles in French are *le, la,* and *les.* Their English equivalent is *the,* as in *the bottle* or *the students.*

Definite articles agree in gender and number with the nouns they accompany.

	Singular	Plural
Masculine	*le*	*les*
Feminine	*la*	*les*
Before a vowel or silent *h*	*l'*	*les*

le garçon (**the** boy)	*les* garçons (**the** boys)
la fille (**the** girl)	*les* filles (**the** girls)
*l'*oiseau (**the** bird)	*les* oiseaux (**the** birds)
*l'*homme (**the** man)	*les* hommes (**the** men)

Le and *la* become *l'* before a noun starting with a vowel or a silent *h.* This is called an *elision,* or *élision* in French.

la + *eau* = *l'eau* (**the** water)
le + *ange* = *l'ange* (**the** angel)
le + *hiver* = *l'hiver* (**the** winter)

The definite article is used to specify a particular person, place, or thing, as opposed to an unspecified person, place, or thing.

*Est-ce que tu as vu **la nouvelle série belge**?*
Have you seen **the new Belgian TV show**?

***Le professeur** est en colère.*
The teacher is angry.

***Les élèves** disent qu'ils sont sages.*
The students say they are well behaved.

The definite article accompanies the noun when expressing broad generality. In English, an article is not used for this purpose.

***Le cancer** est grave.*
Cancer is serious.

The definite article is also used to express preference.

*J'aime **la danse classique**.*
I like **classical dance.**

*Je n'aime pas **les fruits**.*
I don't like **fruit.**

Definite articles are also used to indicate that an event occurs habitually; for example, on a certain day of the week or at a certain time of day.

***Le lundi** je vais à Montréal.*
Every Monday I go to Montreal.

***L'après-midi,** je travaille.*
Every afternoon, I work.

Definite articles are used to identify specific groups of people.

*À plus tard, **les mecs**!*
See you later, **guys**!

Attention!

Le and *les* combine with the prepositions *à* and *de* to form contracted articles.

à + *le* = *au*		*de* + *le* = *du*
à + *les* = *aux*		*de* + *les* = *des*

*Il va **au** supermarché.*
He is going **to the** supermarket.

*Je viens **des** États-Unis.*
I am **from the** United States.

Exercise 1

Provide both the singular and plural forms of the definite articles for the following sets of words.

1. _____ bibliothèque, _____ bibliothèques

2. _____ café, _____ cafés

3. _____ oeil, _____ yeux

4. _____ os (singular), _____ os (plural)

5. _____ lune, _____ lunes

6. _____ église, _____ églises

Exercise 2

Correct the mistakes in the following sentences so that the definite articles agrees with their nouns. Note: Not all sentences have mistakes.

1. La filles sont canadiennes.

Les filles sont canadiennes

2. Mme. Roche est le professeur de biologie.

3. J'ai grillé les poisson.

4. Le oreilles sont très sensibles.

Les oreilles sont très sensibles

5. Nous avons vu la nouveau film de Luc Besson.

We

Exercise 3

Translate the following sentences into French using the correct articles.

1. I met the president.

2. The post office is closed.

3. My mother made the cookies.

Ma mère a fait les biscuits

4. The actress is beautiful.

L'actrice est belle

5. He swam at the pool.

Il a nagé à la piscine

6. I ate at the restaurant.

J'ai mangé au restaurant

1

Indefinite articles refer to something in a general sense, such as *a book*. Indefinite articles in French are *un, une,* and *des.* Their English equivalents are *a, an,* and *some.*

Definite articles agree in gender and number with the nouns they accompany.

	Singular	Plural
Masculine	un	des
Feminine	une	des

un chien (**a** dog) — *des* chiens (**some** dogs, or **dogs** in general)

une vache (**a** cow) — *des* vaches (**some** cows, or **cows** in general)

The singular definite article can also refer to the number one.

une chaise (**a** chair or **one** chair)

In a negative sentence in which the indefinite article follows the negative verb, the indefinite article is replaced by *de.* When the indefinite article precedes the negative verb, it doesn't change to *de.*

*Il a **un** chat.*
He has **a** cat.

*Il **n'a pas de** chat.*
He **doesn't have** a cat.

Une fille est déjà assez.
One girl is already enough.

*Une fille **n'est pas** assez.*
One girl **is not** enough.

L'Exception

When the verb *être* (to be) is used in a negative sentence, the indefinite article is not replaced by *de.*

*C'est **une** blague.*
It's **a** joke.

*Ce **n'est pas une** blague.*
It **is not a** joke.

The plural indefinite article changes from *des* to *de* when preceding a plural adjective modifying a plural noun. If the adjective follows the plural noun, *des* is used.

de vieux livres
some old books

de jolies maisons
some beautiful houses

*Il a **de** beaux **yeux**.*
He has beautiful **eyes**.

*Il a **des yeux** bleus.*
He has blue **eyes**.

Exercise 1

Provide both the singular and plural indefinite articles for the following sets of words.

1. _____ chambre, _____ chambres
2. _____ enfant, _____ enfants
3. _____ pays, _____ pays
4. _____ vélo, _____ vélos
5. _____ maison, _____ maisons
6. _____ avocat, _____ avocats

Exercise 2

Fill in the blanks in this recipe for quiche with the proper indefinite articles.

1. _____ épices
2. _____ tranche de jambon
3. _____ oeufs
4. _____ demi-kilo de farine
5. _____ poivron

Exercise 3

Translate the following sentences into French using the correct indefinite articles.

1. I live in a house.

   Je vis dans une maison

2. She has a cat.

   Elle a un chat

3. I would like a coffee with milk.

   Je voudrais un café avec du lait

4. They bought a shirt and a gift.

5. We bought some clothes and some gifts.

6. I have problems.

   J'ai des problèmes

Exercise 4

Circle the correct definite or indefinite articles in parentheses to complete each of the following sentences.

1. Il y a (les/des) livres à la bibliothèque.

2. J'ai aimé (le/un) repas que j'ai mangé chez Cédric samedi soir.

3. Ils cherchent (la/une) maison à acheter.

4. Ils cherchent (la/une) maison de Lucie.

5. J'ai (la/une) soeur et (les/des) frères.

Exercise 5

Make the following sentences negative using the correct form of the indefinite article.

1. Je suis une pessimiste.

2. J'ai une voiture.

3. Il a une amie.

4. Il a des amis.

5. C'est une sorcière.

2

3 Articles *Partitive Articles*

Partitive articles express a quantity that is uncountable or suggest part of a whole. The closest equivalent in English is *some*, but this word is frequently omitted in English where it would be included in French.

Partitive articles agree in gender with the nouns they accompany.

Masculine	*du*
Feminine	*de la*
Before a vowel and silent *h*	*de l'*

du pain	**some** bread
de la farine	**some** flour
*de l'*intelligence	**some** intelligence

When discussing a specific noun, the definite article is used instead of the partitive article. The definite article can also imply that something is all gone, while the partitive article either accentuates the fact that there is some remaining or that only a part of the whole is being discussed.

Partitive Article	Definite Article
*Il a bu **de la** bière.* He drank **(some)** beer.	*Il a bu **la** bière.* He drank **the (specific)** beer.
*Elle a mangé **du** riz.* She ate **(some)** rice.	*Elle a mangé **le** riz.* She ate **the (specific)** rice.

When quantity is known or specified, either the indefinite article or a number is used. When quantity is not known or not specified, the partitive article is used.

Partitive Article	Indefinite Article
*Je bois **du** Coca tous les jours.* I drink **(some)** Coke every day.	*Je bois **un** Coca tous les jours.* I drink **one** Coke every day.

In a negative sentence expressing quantity, the partitive article changes to *de* regardless of the gender of the noun it precedes.

*Elle boit **du** thé.* She drinks **(some)** tea.	*Elle **ne boit pas de** thé.* She **doesn't drink (any)** tea.
*Il y a encore **de la** moutarde.* There is **some** mustard left.	*Il **n'y a plus de** moutarde.* There **isn't any** mustard left.

La Langue Vivante

The partitive article is often used when discussing food, since the nature of food lends itself to discussing uncountable quantities. For example, **du** *beurre*, or **some** butter, is used as opposed to *a specific amount of* butter or *one* butter that is expressed in **le** *beurre*.

Exercise 1

Fill in the following blanks with the correct partitive article.

1. Il ne reste pas _____ quiche, mais il reste _____ pain.

2. Julie a mangé _____ glace artisanale.

3. Je n'ai pas bu _____ vin rosé.

4. Est-ce que vous voulez _____ eau?

5. Pour la sauce, il faut ajouter _____ huile.

Exercise 2

Make the following sentences negative using the correct form of the partitive article.

1. Je vais acheter du café.

   _____

   _____

2. Qui boit de l'eau?

   _____

   _____

3. Il a commandé du pâté.

   _____

   _____

4. Ce soir je mange du thon.

   _____

   _____

5. Vous faites du sport demain.

   _____

   _____

6. Il a mangé du fromage.

   _____

   _____

Exercise 3

Choose from the following articles to complete each sentence. Use each article only once.

des, un, au, les, la, du

1. _____ chambre de Françoise est belle.

2. Elles adorent _____ bonbons.

3. Je cuisine avec _____ recettes typiques.

4. Antoine est _____ élève _____ Lycée Charles de Gaulle.

5. Je mange souvent _____ poisson.

3

Nouns *Gender*

Every French noun has a gender, either masculine or feminine. While memorization is the only sure way to know the gender of a noun, there are some guidelines that can help determine the gender of a noun.

Masculine nouns are often preceded by one of two articles: the masculine indefinite article *un* or the masculine definite article *le*.

un *stylo*	**a** pen	***le*** *stylo*	**the** pen
un *crayon*	**a** pencil	***le*** *crayon*	**the** pencil

Feminine nouns are often preceded by one of two articles: the feminine indefinite article *une* or the feminine definite article *la*.

une *bouteille*	**a** bottle	***la*** *bouteille*	**the** bottle
une *cerise*	**a** cherry	***la*** *cerise*	**the** cherry

Attention!

Both the masculine and feminine definite article changes to *l'* when preceding a noun that starts with a vowel or a silent *h*. In these cases, they cannot be used in determining gender.

un *océan*	an ocean	***l'****océan*	the ocean
une *écharpe*	a scarf	***l'****écharpe*	the scarf
un *homme*	a man	***l'****homme*	the man

Some nouns have both a masculine and feminine form depending on the subject. In many cases, an *-e* is added to the end of the masculine noun to form the feminine.

un ami	*une ami**e***
a (*male*) friend	a (*female*) friend
*Paul est **un ami**.*	*Carole est **une amie**.*
Paul is **a friend**.	Carole is **a friend**.

A variety of other ending changes are used to form the feminine for some nouns.

	Masculine	Feminine
no change:	*un élève*	*une élève* (a student)
eur/eure:	*un serv**eur***	*une serv**euse*** (a waiter, waitress)
teur/trice:	*un direc**teur***	*une direc**trice*** (a director)

*Sebastien est **un élève**.*	*Anaïs est **une élève**.*
Sebastien is **a student**.	Anaïs is **a student**.

Nouns referring to males are masculine.

le roi	the king	*le parrain*	the godfather
le coq	the rooster	*le père*	the father
l'oncle	the uncle	*le frère*	the brother

Nouns referring to females are feminine.

la reine	the queen	*la marraine*	the godmother
la poule	the hen	*la mère*	the mother
la tante	the aunt	*la soeur*	the sister

Attention!

Only nouns referring to male and female beings have both a masculine and a feminine form. For example, a *guest* can be male (**un** *invité*) or female (**une** *invitée*). Most inanimate objects are either masculine or feminine and have only one form, such as the feminine **une** *chaise* (a chair).

Attention!

Past participles must agree with direct-object pronouns and can therefore indicate noun gender. If the past participle ends in an *-e* or *-es*, the noun object is feminine singular or feminine plural, respectively. If it ends in an *-s*, it is masculine plural or mixed-gender plural.

*Les artistes? Je les ai vu**s** ce matin.*	The (male or mixed gender) artists? I saw them this morning.
*Les artistes? Je les ai vu**es** ce matin.*	The (female) artists? I saw them this morning.

Verbs that take the auxiliary *être* in the passé composé must also agree with the past participle. That agreement can hint at the noun's gender.

*Les artistes sont parti**s**.*	The (male or mixed gender) artists left.
*Les artistes sont parti**es**.*	The (female) artists left.

Exercise 1

Use the article to determine whether each of the following nouns is masculine (M), feminine (F), or not obvious (N).

1. _____ une ceinture

2. _____ la salade

3. _____ un genou

4. _____ l'étoile

5. _____ le sel

6. _____ une brosse

7. _____ un livre

8. _____ l'échelle

9. _____ la main

10. _____ un timbre

Exercise 3

Give the appropriate indefinite article (*un* or *une*) for each of the following nouns.

1. _____ duc

2. _____ ami

3. _____ neveu

4. _____ princesse

5. _____ amie

6. _____ femme

7. _____ vache

8. _____ cousin

9. _____ étudiant

10. _____ fille

Exercise 2

Based on their gender, sort the following words into each column.

prince, fils, cousine, niece, taureau, homme, jumelle, garcon, jumeau, duchesse, étudiante

Masculine	Feminine

4

Some guidelines can help determine a noun's gender when it is not clear.

The ending of a noun often indicates its gender. There are many endings generally associated with masculine nouns.

Masculine Ending	Example	Translation
-c	un éche**c**	a defeat
-cle	un mira**cle**	a miracle
-d	un nigau**d**	a gullible person
-eau	un cad**eau**	a gift
-et	un fil**et**	a net
-f	un el**f**	an elf
-i	un cr**i**	a cry
-isme	un sé**isme**	an earthquake
-l	le se**l**	salt
-m	un essai**m**	a swarm
-ment	un élé**ment**	an element
-oir	un mir**oir**	a mirror
-ou	un ch**ou**	a cabbage
-ysme	un catacl**ysme**	a cataclysm

There are many endings generally associated with feminine nouns.

Feminine Ending	Example	Translation
-ace	une r**ace**	a race
-ainte	une pl**ainte**	a complaint
-ance	la ch**ance**	luck
-anse	une d**anse**	a dance
-ée	la matin**ée**	the morning
-einte	une empr**einte**	a fingerprint
-elle	une p**elle**	a shovel
-ence	l'abs**ence**	absence
-ense	la déf**ense**	defense
-esse	une maît**resse**	a school teacher
-ête	la t**ête**	the head
-ie	la v**ie**	life
-ique	la mus**ique**	music
-ise	une surpr**ise**	a surprise
-mme	une fe**mme**	a woman
-nne	une couro**nne**	a crown
-sion	la discus**sion**	the discussion
-son	une chan**son**	a song

-tié	l'ami**tié**	friendship
-tion	l'ac**tion**	action
-té	la beau**té**	beauty
-tte	l'assie**tte**	the plate
-ue	la v**ue**	the view
-ure	la voit**ure**	the car

L'Exception

Numerous exceptions exist for each of these noun endings. For example, despite their endings, the common nouns *une boucle* (buckle), *la peau* (skin), *l'eau* (water), *la soif* (thirst), *la foi* (faith), *la loi* (law), and *la faim* (hunger) are feminine. The common nouns as *le silence* (silence), *un lycée* (high school), *un musée* (museum), *un incendie* (fire), *le parapluie* (umbrella), *un graphique* (graph), *un dilemme* (dilemma), *un gramme* (gram), *un blouson* (blouse), *le comté* (the country), *le côté* (side), *un été* (summer), *un squelette* (skeleton), and *le dinosaure* (dinosaur) are all masculine. However, these endings can still prove useful for determining noun gender in most cases.

Some masculine endings change in regular patterns to form the feminine noun.

Ending		Example	
Masculine	Feminine	Masculine	Feminine
-deur	-drice	un ambassa**deur** (ambassador)	une ambassa**drice** (ambassador)
-e	-esse	un maît**re** (master)	une maît**resse** (mistress)
-eau	-elle	un cham**eau** (male camel)	une cham**elle** (female camel)
-el	-elle	un colon**el** (colonel)	une colon**elle** (colonel's wife)
-er	-ère	un fromag**er** (cheese seller)	une fromag**ère** (cheese seller)
-eur	-eresse	un enchant**eur** (magician)	une enchant**eresse** (magician)
	-euse	un ment**eur** (liar)	une ment**euse** (liar)
-f	-ve	un veu**f** (widower)	une veu**ve** (widow)
-n	-nne	un chie**n** (male dog)	une chie**nne** (female dog)
-p	-ve	un lou**p** (male wolf)	une lou**ve** (female wolf)

-teur	-trice	un ac**teur** (actor)	une ac**trice** (actress)
-x	-se	un épou**x** (spouse, husband)	une épou**se** (spouse, wife)

Some nouns change their meaning with a change in gender.

Masculine	Feminine
un livre (a book)	une livre (a sterling pound)
le mode (the mode, the manner)	la mode (fashion)
un hymne (a national anthem)	une hymne (a religious song)
un voile (a veil)	une voile (a sail, for a boat)

Exercice 1

Based on their gender, sort the following nouns into each column.

chance, natation, genou, cyclisme, ambiance, hibou, cerise, cerf, renard, tendresse

Masculine	Feminine

Exercise 2

Provide examples of masculine words using the following endings.

1. -oir _____

2. -cle _____

3. -c _____

4. -eau _____

5. -ou _____

6. -ment _____

Exercise 3

Provide examples of feminine words using the following endings.

1. -ure _____

2. -té _____

3. -nne _____

4. -ace _____

5. -ête _____

6. -sion _____

Exercise 4

Change the following nouns from masculine to feminine.

1. un serveur _____

2. un lion _____

3. un coiffeur _____

4. un directeur _____

5. un laitier _____

5

6 Nouns *Number*

In French, a plural noun is usually formed by adding an -s to the end of the singular noun. The article changes as well.

Singular	Plural
un verre (a glass)	*des verres* (glasses)
une lettre (a letter)	*des lettres* (letters)

L'Exception

Most nouns ending with *-ou* form the plural by adding an *-s*. The following are examples of some exceptions that take an *-x* at the end in the plural form: *bijou, caillou, chou, genou, hibou, joujou,* and *pou.*

Singular	Plural
un bijou (a jewel)	*des bijoux* (jewelry)
un chou (a cabbage)	*des choux* (cabbages)

Singular nouns ending in -s, -x, and -z do not change to form the plural.

Singular	Plural
une fois (one time)	*des fois* (more than one time, sometimes)
un nez (a nose)	*des nez* (noses)

Attention!

The following nouns also remain invariable in the plural form.

numbers used as nouns:

*trois **une** de suite*   three **ones** in a row

interjections:

*Il poussait **des** oh et **des** ah.*   He exclaimed profusely. (Literally: He was emitting **ohs** and **ahs**.)

letters of the alphabet:

*des A et **des** B*   **As** and **Bs**

acronyms:

***Les** CD sont des disques compacts.*   **CDs** are compact disks.

proper family names:

les Dupont   the **Duponts**
les Miller   the **Millers**

Nouns ending in -al, -eau, and -au in the singular take the ending -aux when forming the plural. Nouns ending in -eu take the ending -eux in the plural.

Singular	Plural
un cadeau (a gift)	*des cadeaux* (gifts)
un cheveu (a hair)	*des cheveux* (hair)

L'Exception

Some nouns ending in *-al* do not take *-aux* in the plural. Instead, these nouns simply add an *-s* to the singular form. Some examples are *bal, cal, carnaval, chacal, festival, récital,* and *régal.*

Singular	Plural
un bal (a ball, a formal dance)	*des bals* (balls)
un carnaval (a carnival)	*des carnavals* (carnivals)

L'Exception

The following eight words ending with *-ail* take the ending *-aux* when forming the plural: *bail, corail, émail, fermail, soupirail, travail, vantail,* and *vitrail.*

Singular	Plural
un corail (a piece of coral)	*des coraux* (coral)
un vitrail (a stained-glass window)	*des vitraux* (stained-glass windows)

Some French nouns undergo irregular changes when forming the plural.

Singular	Plural
un oeil (an eye)	*des **yeux*** (eyes)
Madame (Mrs., Ma'am)	*mesdames* (ladies)
Monsieur (Mr., Sir)	*messieurs* (gentlemen)
Mademoiselle (Miss)	*mesdemoiselles* (young ladies)

La Langue Vivante

In spoken French, singular nouns often sound the same as their plural forms. Sometimes, the only way to tell if a noun is plural is by listening to the preceding article or determinant. If you hear *des filles* as opposed to *une fille,* you know that several girls are being discussed, rather than just one.

Some words that are singular in English are typically plural in French.

French Plural	English Singular
des asperges	asparagus
des bagages	luggage
des cheveux	hair
des coordonnées	personal information
des déchets	waste, trash
des devoirs	homework
des informations	information
des maths	math
des médicaments	medicine
des meubles	furniture
des renseignements	information
des vacances	vacation
des vêtements	clothing

Certain adjectives can be used as nouns when referring to groups of people. These also are plural in French, though singular in English.

French Plural	English Singular
les jeunes	the young
les malades	the sick
les vivants	the living

Exercise 1

Provide the plural form for each of the following singular nouns.

1. genou _____

2. souris _____

3. drapeau _____

4. festival _____

5. journal _____

6. message _____

Exercise 2

Provide the singular form for each of the following plural nouns.

1. mains _____

2. mesdemoiselles _____

3. clous _____

4. récitals _____

5. coraux _____

6. bijoux _____

Exercise 3

Complete the following crossword puzzle by providing the French word for each English clue.

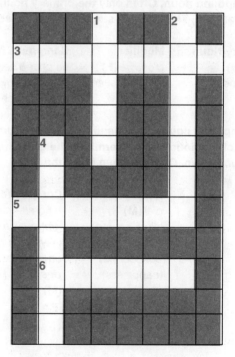

Across:
3. vacation
5. trash
6. chess

Down:
1. hair
2. pasta
4. homework

6

A compound noun, or *composé,* is a noun composed of two other words, frequently separated by a hyphen. Though most compound nouns are masculine, this is not always the case, and rules for determining the gender of a compound noun can be complicated.

For compound nouns composed of two nouns, the gender of the primary (first) noun often determines the gender of the compound noun. Both nouns take the plural form.

Primary Noun		Secondary Noun		Compound Noun
pause **(F)** (pause, break)	+	*café* **(M)** (coffee)	=	*une pause-café/**des** pauses-cafés* **(F)** (coffee break/s)
chou **(M)** (cabbage)	+	*fleur* **(F)** (flower)	=	*un chou-fleur/**des** choux-fleurs* **(M)** (cauliflower/s)

For compound nouns composed of a primary noun + noun modifier (which is often accompanied by a preposition), the primary noun determines the gender of the compound noun. Often only the primary noun takes the plural form. The modifier stays in the singular form.

Primary Noun		Modifier		Compound Noun
chef **(M)** (head/boss)	+	*d'oeuvre* **(F)** (of work, of art)	=	*un chef-d'oeuvre/**des** chefs-d'oeuvre* **(M)** (masterpiece/s)

For compound nouns composed of a verb + noun, the gender of the noun often determines the gender of the compound noun. Only the noun takes the plural form.

Verb		Noun		Compound Noun
gratter (to scratch)	+	*ciel* **(M)** (sky)	=	*un gratte-ciel/**des** gratte-ciels* **(M)** (skyscraper/s)
porter (to bring)	+	*bonheur* **(M)** (happiness)	=	*un porte-bonheur/**des** porte-bonheurs* **(M)** (lucky charm/s)

For compound nouns composed of an adjective + noun, the gender of the noun determines the gender of the adjective and the compound noun. Both the adjective and the noun take the plural form.

Adjective		Noun		Compound Noun
chauve **(F)** (bald)	+	*souris* **(F)** (mouse)	=	*une chauve-souris/**des** chauves-souris* **(F)** (bat/s)
petite **(F)** (little)	+	*fille* **(F)** (girl)	=	*une petite-fille/ **des** petittes-filles* **(F)** (granddaughter/s)

A compound noun composed of adjective + adjective are generally formed with two words of the same gender. Both adjectives will take the plural form.

Adjective		Adjective		Compound Noun
douce **(F)** (sweet)	+	*amère* **(F)** (bitter)	=	*une douce-amère/**des** doux-amères* **(F)** (bittersweet/s)

L'Exception

Regardless of the gender of their components, some compound nouns are always masculine. Common examples include:

un brise-glace	icebreaker
un en-tête	heading
un garde-pêche	fish warden
un porte-monnaie	coin purse
un rouge-gorge	robin
un tête-à-tête	private talk

Some compound nouns are made up of complete sentences or phrases. These compound nouns are invariable and do not change in their plural form.

un je-ne-sais-quoi	*des je-ne-sais-quoi* (something indefinable; literally: I-don't-know-what/s)
un je-m'en-fichisme	*des je-m'en-fichisme* (couldn't-care-less attitude/s)

Exercise 1

Label the parts of speech that make up each of the following compound nouns. Note masculine or feminine, if applicable, for each component.

1. porte-avions

porte-	avions

2. arc-en-ciel

arc-	en-	ciel

3. sourd-muet

sourd-	muet

4. station-service

station-	service

5. oiseau-mouche

oiseau-	mouche

6. l'après-midi

après-	midi

7. le chou-fleur

chou-	fleur

8. un haut-parleur

haut-	parleur

9. une contre-offensive

contre-	offensive

10. un cessez-le-feu

cessez-	le-	feu

Exercise 2

Determine the gender (M or F) of the following compound nouns from the previous exercise.

1. _____ porte-avions

2. _____ arc-en-ciel

3. _____ sourd-muet

4. _____ station-service

5. _____ oiseau-mouche

Exercise 3

Provide the plural form for each of the following compound verbs. Include the article in your answer.

1. l'après-midi _____

2. le chou-fleur_____

3. un haut-parleur_____

4. une contre-offensive_____

5. un cessez-le-feu_____

Adjectives *Number and Gender Agreement*

As with articles, adjectives also agree in gender and number with the nouns they modify. Adjectives undergo predictable spelling changes in order to agree with their nouns.

Most adjectives form the feminine by adding an -e to the end of the masculine form.

Masculine	Feminine
un **petit** chat (a **little** cat)	une **petite** voiture (a **little** car)
un **joli** vélo (a **pretty** bicycle)	une **jolie** maison (a **pretty** house)

L'Exception

While most adjectives ending in *-ot* add an *-e* in the feminine form, not all do. The exceptions are *pâlot* (pale), *sot* (stupid), and *vieillot* (quaint), which add the ending *-otte* in the feminine.

Masculine	Feminine
un refrain **idiot** (an **idiotic** refrain)	une personne **idiote** (an **idiotic** person)
garçon **sot** (a stupid boy)	une histoire **sotte** (a **stupid** story)

L'Exception

Some adjectives whose masculine form ends in *-s* add the ending *-sse* to form the feminine.

Masculine	Feminine
un coups **bas** (a **low** hit)	une marrée **basse** (a **low** tide)
un mur **épais** (a **thick** wall)	une planche **épaisse** (a **thick** board)

Some adjectives follow specific patterns to form the feminine, depending on their masculine endings.

Ending Masculine	Ending Feminine	Example Masculine	Example Feminine
-c	-che	fran**c**	fran**che** (frank, straightforward)
-eil	-eille	par**eil**	par**eille** (similar)
-el	-elle	cru**el**	cru**elle** (cruel)
-er	-ère	lég**er**	lég**ère** (light)
-et	-ette	coqu**et**	coqu**ette** (stylish)
-f	-ve	neu**f**	neu**ve** (new)
-ien	-ienne	anc**ien**	anc**ienne** (old, former)
-on	-onne	b**on**	b**onne** (good)
-ul	-ulle	n**ul**	n**ulle** (stupid)

L'Exception

Some adjectives whose masculine forms end in *-et* do not form the feminine with *-ette*. Instead the *-et* ending changes to *-ète* in the feminine.

Masculine	Feminine
compl**et**	compl**ète** (complete)
désu**et**	désu**ète** (obsolete)
discr**et**	discr**ète** (discreet)
inqui**et**	inqui**ète** (worried, anxious)

L'Exception

Certain adjectives whose masculine form ends in *-x* have irregular feminine forms.

Masculine	Feminine
dou**x**	dou**ce** (soft, gentle)
fau**x**	fau**sse** (false, fake)
rou**x**	rou**sse** (redheaded)

Adjectives whose masculine form ends in -e have only one form and do not change when modifying feminine nouns.

Masculine	Feminine
un examen **facile** (an **easy** test)	une chanson **facile** (an **easy** song)
un bâtiment **solide** (a **sturdy** building)	une maison **solide** (a **sturdy** house)

Some common adjectives undergo irregular changes from their masculine to feminine forms. These changes do not follow a specific pattern and must be memorized.

Masculine	Feminine
beau	belle (beautiful)
nouveau	nouvelle (new)
fou	folle (crazy)
frais	fraîche (fresh)
mou	molle (soft)
vieux	vieille (old)

Attention!

Some of these irregular adjectives take on a new form when used before a masculine noun beginning with a vowel. They are pronounced like the feminine form.

nouveau + *appartement* = *un nouvel appartement*
(a new apartment)
fou + *amour* = *un fol amour* (a crazy love)

Exercise 1

Provide the feminine form for the following masculine adjectives.

1. fier _____

2. magnifique _____

3. réel _____

4. vieux _____

5. excéllent _____

6. fou _____

7. pâle _____

8. inquiet _____

Exercise 2

Circle the correct adjective in the parentheses to complete each of the following descriptive phrases.

1. une (beau/belle) maison

2. un (grand/grande) lit

3. une tarte (délicieux/délicieuse)

4. une (beau/belle) fille

5. un imperméable (léger/légère)

Exercise 3

Complete the descriptions of the people in the following examples by providing two adjectives in the correct form.

1. Ma mère est _____

et _____.

2. Ma dentiste est _____ et

_____.

3. Mon chien/chat est _____ et

_____.

4. Le proviseur du lycée est _____

et _____.

5. Madonna est _____ et

_____.

Demonstrative adjectives describe a specific noun. They are equivalent to *this, that, these,* and *those* in English.

Like in English, demonstrative adjectives in French agree in number with the noun they modify. Unlike in English, singular demonstrative adjectives in French also agree in gender with the noun they modify.

Masculine	Feminine	Plural (M and F)
ce, cet	cette	ces

Demonstrative adjectives precede the nouns they modify.

Cet homme lit ces livres.
This man reads **these** books.

Ce train est le plus rapide du monde.
This is the fastest train in the world.

Ce garçon aime cette fille.
This boy likes **this** girl.

A demonstrative adjective can be reinforced by placing -ci or -là after the noun to provide further precision. The difference between -ci and -là is similar to the difference between *this* and *that* in English.

J'aime ce cours-ci.
I like **this** class.

Je déteste ce cours-là.
I hate **that** class.

To emphasize comparison, -ci and -là can be used with two nouns in succession.

Veux-tu ce livre-ci ou ce livre-là?
Do you want **this** book or **that** book?

Souhaites-tu prendre ce croissant-ci ou ce croissant-là?
Do you want **this** croissant or **that** croissant?

When used in reference to time, -ci indicates an event that happened more recently than -là.

A cette heure-ci, je travaille.
At **this** hour (recent), I'm working.

A cette heure-là, je travaillais.
At **that** hour (farther in the past), I was working.

When two nouns are mentioned by name, then referred to again in the same sentence or discussion, -ci often refers to the first noun and -là refers to the second.

Voici une rose et une tulipe.
Here are **a rose** and **a tulip**.

Je préfère cette fleur-ci à cette fleur-là.
I prefer **this** flower (the tulip) to **that** flower (the rose).

Voici une Mercedes et une Ferrari.
Here are **a Mercedes** and **a Ferrari**.

Je préfère cette voiture-ci à cette voiture-là.
I prefer **this** car (the Mercedes) to **that** car (the Ferrari).

Exercise 1

Provide the correct demonstrative adjective for each of the following words.

1. _____ chausettes

2. _____ radio

3. _____ pantalon

4. _____ porte

5. _____ bagages

6. _____ lunettes

7. _____ aileron

Exercise 2

Complete the following dialogue between a vendor and a client at a cheese market using the appropriate demonstrative adjectives.

Le fromager: Bonjour. Que désirez-vous?

Le client: Quel est_____ fromage-_____ ?

(*Pointing directly to the cheese in front of him.*)

Le fromager:_____ fromage-_____ est

un Époisses de Bourgogne.

Le client: Et quel est_____ fromage-_____ ?

(*Pointing to a cheese farther away.*)

Le fromager:_____ fromage-_____ est

un Ami du Chambertin.

Le client: Lequel me conseillez-vous?

Le fromager: Entre l'Époisses et le Chambertin je vous

recommande_____ fromage-_____ à

_____ fromage-_____ .

Le client: Bon, je prends 500g d'Époisses. Merci de votre

conseil.

Exercise 3

Translate the following sentences into French.

1. This morning it rained.

   _____

   _____

2. This afternoon it was sunny.

   _____

   _____

3. Tonight it is cloudy.

   _____

   _____

4. These sentences are difficult.

   _____

   _____

5. Do you prefer this shirt or that tank top?

   _____

   _____

6. Between them I prefer that tank top.

   _____

   _____

9

Possessive adjectives are used in place of an article to indicate the owner or possessor of an object.

mon *mari*	**my** husband
ta *tante*	**your** aunt
nos *projets*	**our** plans

Like possessive adjectives in English, possessive adjectives in French generally refer back to the object's possessor. However, French possessive adjectives must agree with the *object* modified, both in gender and number. This is especially important for the third-person singular, in which there is no distinction between a female possessor and a male possessor.

Subject	Masculine	Object Feminine	Plural
je	mon	ma	mes
tu	ton	ta	tes
il, elle	son	sa	ses
nous	notre		nos
vous	votre		vos
ils, elles	leur		leurs

Il (third-person singular subject) *aime* **son** *chien* (third-person masculine singular object).
He loves **his** dog.

Il aime **son** *chien et* **sa** *fille.*
He loves **his** dog and **his** daughter.

Ils aiment **leur** *chien et* **leurs** *filles.*
They love **their** dog and **their** daughters.

Attention!

Because possessive adjectives agree in gender with the object, rather than the subject, the gender of the object must always be taken into account. For example, because *nom* (name) is a masculine noun, it will always be preceded by *mon, son, ton, votre, notre, or leur,* even if referring to a female's name. Similarly, feminine nouns, such as most flowers, fruits, and vegetables, will always be preceded by *ma, ta, sa,* and so on, even if possessed by a male.

Son *nom est Jessica.*	**Son** *nom est Léo.*
Her name is Jessica.	**His** name is Léo.

Attention!

Before a vowel sound, the feminine possessive adjectives (*ma, ta,* and *sa*) take the masculine form (*mon, ton,* and *son*).

Ma *mère* (feminine) *est aussi* **mon** *amie* (feminine).
My mother is also **my** friend.

When more than one object is used in a sentence, each noun is accompanied by a possessive adjective.

Il a invité **sa** *mère et* **son** *père.*
He invited **his** mother and **his** father.

Objects that express a collective meaning are usually presented in the singular and take a singular possessive adjective, even when they refer to something plural.

Mêmes les criminels aiment **leur** *mère.*
Even criminals love **their** mothers.

Attention!

Occasionally, singular collective nouns can create confusion in a sentence. Context must be used to determine the exact meaning of the possessive adjective.

Luc et Léa prennent **leurs voitures** (plural object) *pour venir.*
Luc and Lea take **their cars** to come.

Luc et Léa prennent **leur voiture** (object may be singular or plural) *pour venir.*
Luc and Lea take **their car(s)** to come.

La Langue Vivante

While English uses possessive adjectives to refer to body parts, French uses definite articles, most often with a reflexive verb.

Je me suis cassé **le** *bras.*
I broke **my** arm. (Literally: I myself broke **the arm.**)

Exercise 1

Match the following French phrases in column A to the correct English translations in column B.

	A		B
_____	**1.** son stylo		a. their grandmother
_____	**2.** sa chambre		b. their garden
_____	**3.** notre chat		c. my friends
_____	**4.** mes amis		d. his pen
_____	**5.** leur grand-mère		e. your dogs
_____	**6.** vos chiens		f. his bedroom
_____	**7.** leur jardin		g. our cat

Exercise 2

Circle the nouns that each possessive adjective below can modify.

1. **mon:** appartement, livre, calculatrice, vêtements, serviette

2. **ta:** chemise, règle, sacs, chaussures, jupe, livre

3. **ses:** montre, oncle, scooters, devoirs, balcon

4. **vos:** idées, vélo, colliers, chambres, portable

5. **sa:** chien, manteau, fourchette, amis, mère, voyage

6. **notre:** ordinateur, assiettes, cahier, maison, pitié

Exercise 3

Fill in the blanks below with the correct possessive adjectives.

1. Je vais chez _____ (my) mère à Noël.

2. Mélissa a donné _____ (her) couteau à _____ (her) cousin.

3. Lucas a dit à Émilien, "J'aime _____ (your) voiture."

4. Ils passent _____ (their) vacances à _____ (their) maison à la plage.

5. J'ai prêté _____ (my) maillot de bain à _____ (my) soeur.

6. "_____ (your) efforts ne sont pas sérieux," a dit le professeur à tous _____ (her) élèves.

10

Unlike adjectives in English, most French adjectives are placed after the noun they modify. However, there are a number of adjectives that are placed before the noun. The rules governing placement should be memorized.

The following adjectives are always placed after the noun they modify:

Adjectives	Example
describing nationality	*la langue française* (the **French** language) *le chocolat suisse* (the **Swiss** chocolate)
describing shape	*une fenêtre carée* (a **square** window) *un ballon rond* (a **round** ball)
describing color	*la peinture verte* (the **green** paint) *les murs jaunes* (the **yellow** walls)
derived from the past participle	*une ville perdue* (a **faraway** town) *un fait accompli* (an **accomplished** deed/fact)
describing taste	*une sauce piquante* (a **spicy** sauce) *un gâteau sucré* (a **sweet** cake)
describing religion	*un temple juif* (a **Jewish** temple) *une messe catholique* (a **Catholic** mass)
describing mood	*un enfant heureux* (a **happy** child) *un étudiant fatigué* (a **tired** student)
describing social status	*une idée bourgeoise* (an **upper-class** idea) *une famille aristocratique* (an **aristocratic** family)
describing personality	*un homme patriotique* (a **patriotic** man) *une fille studieuse* (a **studious** girl)

Certain descriptive adjectives are placed before the noun the modify.

Adjectives	Example
describing beauty	*une jolie fleur* (a **pretty** flower) *une belle fleur* (a **beautiful** flower)
describing age	*un vieux machin* (an **old** thing) *une nouvelle maison* (a **new** house)
describing goodness	*un mauvais garçon* (a **bad** boy) *une bonne idée* (a **good** idea)
describing size	*un petit pont* (a **little** bridge) *une grande tache* (a **big** stain)

Attention!

Several adjectives change meaning depending on where they are placed. Some of the more common include:

vrai:	*des faits vrais* (**true** facts) *la vraie raison* (the **real** reason)
grand:	*un grand président* (a **great** president) *un président grand* (a **tall** president)
premier:	*la première raison* (the **first** reason) *la raison première* (the **primary** reason)
dernier:	*le dernier mois* (the **last/final** month) *le mois dernier* (**last** month)
seul:	*un seul homme* (a **lone/single** man) *un homme seul* (a **lonely** man)

Multiple adjectives may be used to describe one noun. When the adjectives are placed after the noun, they are joined by *et* (and). When the adjectives are placed before the noun, they are seldom joined by *et*.

une femme intelligente et douce
an **intelligent, gentle** woman

une belle jeune femme
a **beautiful, young** woman

un fromage crémeux, onctueux, et coulant
a **creamy, smooth, and melty** cheese

Exercise 1

Decide if the adjective placement is correct in each case below. If incorrect, fix the mistake.

1. des produits laitiers _____

2. une noire valise _____

3. une bouteille verte _____

4. un nouveau lecteur DVD _____

5. le affreux bruit _____

2. _____

Exercise 2

Translate each of the following phrases into French, placing the adjective in the proper position.

1. Catholic school _____

2. young calves _____

3. a big heart _____

4. hot, salty water _____

5. fat men _____

3. _____

4. _____

Exercise 3

Use at least three adjectives in the proper position to describe the people in the following pictures.

5. _____

1. _____

11

12 Adverbs *Using -ment*

Adverbs modify, or describe, the verbs they accompany. There are several kinds of adverbs in French. The easiest to recognize are those that end in *-ment,* which functions similarly to the ending *-ly* in English.

In many cases, the adverb is formed by adding the *-ment* ending to the masculine form adjectives that end with a vowel.

vrai + ment = vraiment
true + ly = truly

poli + ment = poliment
polite + ly = politely

*Il m'a **poliment** demandé sa question.*
He **politely** asked me his question.

For adjectives whose masculine forms end in a consonant, the *-ment* ending is added to the feminine form of the adjective to form the adverb.

doux (masculine) → *douce* (feminine) + *ment =*
doucement (softly)
lent (masculine) → *lente* (feminine) + *ment =*
lentement (slowly)
franc (masculine) → *franche* (feminine) + *ment =*
franchement (frankly)

*Il a roulé **lentement** dans le quartier.*
He drove **slowly** in the neighborhood.

*Le candidat parle **franchement.***
The candidate speaks **frankly.**

Attention!

Some adjectives take an accent mark (*é*) before taking the *-ment* adverb ending.

précis	→	*précisément*	precisely
profond	→	*profondément*	profoundly
énorme	→	*énormément*	enormously

Attention!

Not all words ending in *-ment* are adverbs; some are nouns.

un ligament	ligament
un fondement	basis
un enterrement	burial
un médicament	medicine

To form an adverb from an adjective ending in *-ent,* remove the ending and add *-emment* to the stem.

récent (recent)
réc + emment = récemment (recently)

fréquent (frequent)
fréqu + emment = fréquemment (recently)

*Je fais **fréquemment** les bêtises.*
I **frequently** make mistakes.

To form an adverb from an adjective ending in *-ant,* remove the ending and add *-amment* to the stem.

méchant (mean)
méch + amment = méchamment (meanly)

suffisant (sufficient)
suffis + amment = suffisamment (sufficiently, enough)

Il lui a répondu méchamment.
He responded meanly (rudely) to him.

L'Exception

Some adjectives undergo form changes before adding the adverb ending.

gentil (masculine) → *genti + ment = gentiment* (kindly)

Exercise 1

Form adverbs from the following adjectives.

1. lent(e) _____

2. probable _____

3. fréquent _____

4. amoureux _____

5. suffisant _____

Exercise 2

Correct the errors in the following sentences. Note: Not all sentences contain errors.

1. J'aime vraiement Camus.

   _____

   _____

2. Il parle brillamment.

   _____

   _____

3. Elles sont absoluement correctes.

   _____

   _____

4. Nicolas et Jacques chantent merveilleuxment.

   _____

   _____

5. Julie porte fréquemment une jupe.

   _____

   _____

Exercise 3

Respond to the following questions, changing the adjectives in parentheses into adverbs in your answer.

1. Est-ce que Marie est jolie? Oui, elle _____

   _____. (extraordinaire)

2. Est-ce que tu aimes la glace? Oui, j' _____

   _____. (énorme)

3. Comment est-ce que tu manges ta glace? Je _____

   _____. (lente)

4. Comment est-ce qu'elle t'a invité? Elle _____ .

   _____. (gentille)

5. Est-ce qu'il va à Dijon? Oui, il _____ .

   _____. (sûr)

Exercise 4

Some of the following -*ment* words are actually nouns. Determine which words are nouns and which are adverbs. For the nouns, place the appropriate article in front.

appartement, crissement, uniquement, traitement, apparemment, traitement, équipement, finalement, franchement, honnêtement, justement

Adverbs	Nouns

12

Adverbs of manner describe how something happens. Most French adverbs of manner end in *-ment*. Some common examples include:

absolument	absolutely
apparemment	apparently
couramment	fluently
énormément	enormously
patiemment	patiently
précisément	precisely
rapidement	rapidly
sérieusement	seriously
spontanément	spontaneously

*Il attendait **patiemment** à l'arrêt de bus.*
He waited **patiently** at the bus stop.

*Elle sait **précisément** ce qu'elle veut.*
She knows **precisely** what she wants.

*J'étudie **sérieusement** pendant l'année scolaire.*
I study **seriously** during the school year.

*Ils parlent **couramment** le français.*
They speak French **fluently.**

Some adverbs of manner have irregular forms that do not end in *-ment*.

ainsi	thus, in this way
bien	well
debout	standing up
exprès	on purpose
mal	poorly, badly
mieux	better
pire	worse
vite	quickly
volontiers	gladly

*Ça peut **mal** finir.*
It could finish **badly.**

*Ça peut **vite** finir.*
It could finish **quickly.**

*Il chante **mieux** qu'avant.*
He sings **better** than before.

Bon is an adjective meaning *good*. Just like *good* in English, *bon* cannot be used as an adverb to describe the manner in which something is done. Instead, the adverb *bien* (well) is used.

*Il chante **bien**.*
He sings **well**.

Adverbs of place describe where something happens. Adverbs of place do not end in *-ment*. Some common examples include:

ailleurs	elsewhere
autour	around
dedans	inside
dehors	outside
derrière	behind
dessous	below
dessus	above
devant	in front
en bas	down (or downstairs)
en haut	up (or upstairs)
ici	here
là	there (or here)
là-bas	over there
loin	far away
n'importe où	anywhere
nulle part	nowhere
partout	everywhere
près	near
quelque part	somewhere

*Mon voisin fait du bruit **en haut**.*
My neighbor makes noise **upstairs.**

*Il pleut **ici**.*
It's raining **here.**

*Nous sommes **loin** de chez nous.*
We're **far** from our house.

Some adverbs of place can function as prepositions rather than adverbs.

*J'habite **devant** un supermarché.*
I live **in front of** a supermarket.

Exercise 1

Match the following English adverbs in column A with their French equivalents in column B.

	A		B
_____	**1.** inside		a. ailleurs
_____	**2.** better		b. dedans
_____	**3.** around		c. autour
_____	**4.** on purpose		d. mieux
_____	**5.** profoundly		e. bien
_____	**6.** in front		f. vite
_____	**7.** quickly		g. exprès
_____	**8.** well		h. profondément
_____	**9.** elsewhere		i. devant

Exercise 2

Choose the correct adverb from the following list of words to complete each sentence. Use each adverb only once.

derrière, debout, loin, apparemment, précisément, ainsi

1. Je reste _____toute la journée au boulot parce que je suis caissier.

2. Elle est partie _____de chez ses parents, elle voulait voir l'Australie.

3. Il est _____huit heures du matin.

4. Je pense que le chien est _____la maison et non pas devant.

5. Il a fait beaucoup d'économies et _____ il a pu acheter son billet d'avion.

6. Je crois qu'il s'est _____trompé d'heure pour notre rendez-vous.

Exercise 3

Translate the following sentences into French using the correct adverb of manner or place.

1. You should do your homework.

_____

_____

2. Here it's always nice weather.

_____

_____

3. It would be better to leave now.

_____

_____

4. I would prefer to live elsewhere.

_____

_____

5. I really like it.

_____

_____

13

Adverbs of quantity describe how much or how often.
Common adverbs of quantity include:

assez	quite, fairly, enough
autant	as much, as many
beaucoup	a lot, many
bien	quite a few
combien	how many, much
encore	more
la majorité	the majority of
la minorité	the minority of
moins	less, fewer
un nombre	a number of
pas mal	quite a few
(un) peu	few, little, not very
la plupart	most
plus	more
une quantité	a lot of
tant	so much, so many
très	very
trop	too much, too many

*Je l'aime **bien**.*
I like it **a lot.**

*Ils ne travaillent pas **autant que** moi.*
They don't work **as much as** I do.

*Il a **très** faim.*
He is **very** hungry.

Adverbs of quantity are often used as quantifying pronouns, modifying nouns rather than verbs. In these cases, with the exception of the adverb *très* **(very), they are always followed by the preposition** *de* **(of).**

*J'ai **encore des** choses à faire.*
I have **more** things to do.

*J'ai **beaucoup de** choses à faire.*
I have **many** things to do.

*J'ai **un nombre de** choses à faire.*
I have **a number of** things to do.

When the preposition *de* **follows a quantifier, the article is not used.** *De* **is invariable in these cases, and does not change to agree with a plural noun. Exceptions are** *la plupart de* **(most) and** *bien de* **(many), which are always followed by the definite article.**

***Beaucoup de** médecins sont très respectés.*
Many doctors are very respected.

L'Exception

When the noun following *de* refers to a specific ensemble of things or persons, the article must be used. *De* is variable in these cases and combines with the article as it normally would.

***Beaucoup des** médecins à l'hôpital où je travaille sont très respectés.*
Many of the doctors at the hospital where I work are very respected.

Adverbs of time describe when something happens.

actuellement	currently
alors	then
après	after
aujourd'hui	today
auparavant	previously, beforehand
aussitôt	immediately
autrefois	formerly, in the past
avant	before
avant-hier	the day before yesterday
bientôt	soon
d'abord	first, at first
de bonne heure	early
déjà	already, ever, yet
demain	tomorrow
depuis	since
dernièrement	lately
désormais	from now, from then on
enfin	at last, finally
ensuite	next, then
hier	yesterday
il y a	ago
immédiatement	immediately
longtemps	for a long time
maintenant	now
n'importe quand	anytime
précédemment	previously
récemment	recently
tard	late
tôt	early
tout à l'heure	a little while ago, in a little while
tout de suite	immediately, right away

*Il faut que j'aille à l'hôpital **tout de suite**.*
I must go to the hospital **right away.**

*Quand il a des rendez-vous le soir il mange **tard**.*
When he has meetings at night he eats **late.**

Exercise 1

Match the French adverbs in column A with their English equivalents in column B.

A		B
_____ **1.** assez		a. before
_____ **2.** hier		b. most
_____ **3.** beaucoup		c. quite, fairly, enough
_____ **4.** avant		d. very
_____ **5.** la plupart		e. yesterday
_____ **6.** depuis		f. since
_____ **7.** trop		g. too much
_____ **8.** enfin		h. a lot, much
_____ **9.** très		i. finally

Exercise 2

Choose the correct adverb from the following list to complete each sentence. Use each adverb only once.

autrefois, trop, assez, bientôt, après

1. Tu en a fait_____ pour aujourd'hui.

2. J'ai_____ mangé de pizza, six tranches et j'ai mal au ventre.

3. Veux-tu aller au cinéma_____ avoir fait tes devoirs?

4. Les français vivaient_____ différement.

5. Je vais_____ terminer. Il ne me reste pas grand chose à faire.

Exercise 3

Translate the following sentences into French using the appropriate adverb.

1. I've had enough of your mistakes.

_____

_____

2. You ask me again to help you.

_____

_____

3. I'm too hot!

_____

_____

4. You must never say it's impossible.

_____

_____

5. Don't come home too late!

_____

_____

14

Placement of an adverb is often dictated by conventional usage, rather than by set rules. Adverb placement in French often differs from that in English.

An adverb normally follows the conjugated verb that it modifies.

> Je **cours vite** le matin.
> I **run fast** in the morning.

> Il **mange beaucoup.**
> He **eats a lot.**

When used with a compound verb tense, the adverb normally follows the auxiliary verb but comes before the participle.

> J'**ai vite fait** mes devoirs.
> I **did** my homework **quickly.**

> Il **a beaucoup mangé** au restaurant hier.
> He **ate a lot** at the restaurant yesterday.

An adverb usually precedes the infinitive verb it modifies; however, it can also follow.

> **Beaucoup parler** n'est pas **bien parler.**
> **Parler beaucoup** n'est pas **parler bien.**
> To speak **a lot** is not to speak **well.**

An adverb generally follows the gerund or present participle it modifies.

> Il mange en **parlant beaucoup.**
> He eats while **talking a lot.**

> J'étais assise à côté d'un homme **parlant beaucoup.**
> I was sitting next to a man (who was) **talking a lot.**

An adverb usually follows a past participle that is not accompanied by an auxiliary verb (which is being used as an adjective). However, the adverb can also precede the past participle in these cases.

> Un chien **souvent battu** est d'habitude méchant.
> An **often-beaten** dog is usually mean.

An adverb precedes an adjective it modifies.

> Louis XIV était un roi **souvent bavard.**
> Louis XIV was an **often talkative** king.

> Léa mange **souvent plus** que Luc.
> Léa **often** eats **more** than Luc.

> Léa mange **plus souvent** que Luc.
> Léa eats **more often** than Luc.

Most adverbs can be used as interjections at the beginning, middle, or end of a sentence.

> Il a parlé de Léa, **naturellement,** et de Luc.
> He has spoken of Léa, **naturally,** and of Luc.

> **Naturellement,** il a parlé de Léa et de Luc.
> **Naturally,** he has spoken of Léa and of Luc.

L'Exception

The adverbs *jusque, où, en,* and *y*, as well as most adverbs expressing quantity or intensity, cannot be separated from the sentence by commas.

Il a parlé **beaucoup** de Léa et Luc.
He talked **a lot** about Léa et Luc.

Exercise 1

Decide whether the following rules regarding adverb placement are true (*vrai*) or false (*faux*).

1. _____ Most adverbs expressing time, space, or manner can be placed in apposition.

2. _____ In a compound tense the adverb usually comes after the auxiliary verb.

3. _____ An adverb precedes the present participle it modifies.

4. _____ The adverb usually goes after the verb it is modifying.

5. _____ An adverb comes after an adjective it modifies.

Exercise 2

Correct the mistakes in the following sentences.

1. Il parle beaucoup très fort.

_____

_____

2. Beaucoup il parle.

_____

_____

3. Ce livre est intéressant vraiment.

_____

_____

4. Cette fille est fatiguée très.

_____

_____

5. Ce jeu est passionnant super.

_____

_____

Exercise 3

Translate the following sentences into French.

1. I have a dog who is sometimes mean.

_____

_____

2. He drove too fast and, of course, was stopped by the police.

_____

_____

3. I have a house that is sometimes broken into.

_____

_____

4. He snores a lot while sleeping.

_____

_____

5. My new neighbor makes a lot more noise than the old one.

_____

_____

15

16 Prepositions À

The French preposition *à* is used before nouns referring to places and times. It has several meanings that would take a variety of prepositions in English.

À is placed before a place and translates as *at* or *to*.

Victor dort à la maison.
Victor is sleeping **at** home.

Attention!

À combines with the definite articles *le, la, l',* and *les*.

à + le = au	à + l' = à l'
à + la = à la	à + les = aux

Allons au casino.
Let's go **to the** casino.

À means *in* when used alone in front of cities or islands.

J'habite à Bordeaux.
I live **in** Bordeaux.

Ils sont à la Barbade.
They're **in** Barbados.

À means *at* when discussing time.

Rendez-vous à midi.
See you **at** noon.

Je me lève à huit heures.
I get up **at** eight.

À can translate as *away* when expressing distance, in terms of time or physical space, separating people or things.

Martine vit à trois heures de Paris.
Martine lives three hours **away** from Paris.

La plage est à un kilomètre de la maison.
The beach is one kilometer **away** from the house.

À means *with* when describing intrinsic features or physical traits of a person or thing.

C'est une omelette aux poivrons verts.
This is a green-pepper omelet./This is an omelet **with** green peppers.

Mon cousin est le garçon au piercing.
My cousin is the boy **with the** piercing.

Verbs followed by an infinitive, as in certain two-verb constructions, usually take either the preposition *à* or *de* before the infinitive. The first verb determines which preposition is used.

Le vent commence à souffler.
The wind is **starting to blow.**

Continue à chanter.
Keep singing.

Attention!

Following are some common verbs that specifically take the preposition *à*.

aider à	to help
apprendre à	to learn, to teach
commencer à	to start
continuer à	to continue
inviter à	to invite
réussir à	to succeed
s'intéresser à	to be interested in

À means *to* when used after verbs expressing transfer or communication. In these cases, *à* introduces an indirect-object pronoun referring to people or animals.

Nous parlons à mes parents.
We're talking **to my parents.**

Vous donnez du fromage à votre chien?
You give cheese **to your dog**?

Attention!

When *à* is followed by an indirect object, a pronoun can be used to replace both *à* and the object.

Elle parle à Marc.
She's speaking **to Marc.**

Elle lui parle.
She's speaking **to him.**

Exercise 1

Create a sentence to say where each of the following people is going by combining *à* with the given article and noun.

1. nous / le café

_____

_____

2. les enfants / la piscine

_____

_____

3. Madame Dumont / la poste

_____

_____

4. Oscar / le travail

_____

_____

5. Sylvie et Cynthia / les États-Unis

_____

_____

Exercise 2

What people or things do you wish for? Use the preposition *à* to indicate the specific features that you prefer for each of the following items.

Example: un gâteau <u>au chocolat</u>

1. des vêtements _____

2. une femme / un homme _____

3. une pizza _____

4. une confiture _____

5. un tableau _____

Exercise 3

Translate the following sentences into French using the preposition *à*.

1. His sisters live five minutes away from here.

_____

_____

2. I'd love to be in Madagascar.

_____

_____

3. My colleague invited me to play golf with him.

_____

_____

4. I go to bed at ten.

_____

_____

5. Let's give this pineapple to Nadège.

_____

_____

16

17 Prereneeeeee*Prepositions De*

De can mean *of* or *from* and is used for many purposes in French.

De means *from* when used before nouns referring to places.

*Il revient **de** chez lui.*
He's coming back **from** his place.

Attention!

De combines with the definite articles *le*, *la*, *l'*, and *les*.

de + le = du   de + l' = de l'
de + la = de la   de + les = des

In front of a vowel, *de* becomes *d'*.

*Ils viennent **d'**Alsace.*
They come **from** Alsace.

De is used to express possession or relationship, similar to *of* or *belonging to*. In English, many of these situations would use the possessive *'s*.

*Voici le château **de** sa mère.*
Here is her/his mother**'s** castle.
(Literally: Here is the castle **of** his/her mother.)

*Le frère **de** ma mère est mon oncle.*
My mother**'s** brother is my uncle.
(Literally: The brother **of** my mother is my uncle.)

De is used to indicate what things or people are composed of.

*C'est une confiture **de** fraises.*
It's a strawberry jam.
(Literally: It's a jam **of** strawberries.)

*Elle aime ce collier **de** perles.*
She likes this pearl necklace.
(Literally: She likes this necklace **of** pearls.)

*C'est une personne **de** grande sagesse.*
She/He is a person **of** great wisdom.

De means *from* when discussing the origin of a person or a thing.

*Eva est **de** Madagascar.*
Eva is **from** Madagascar.

*Cette confiture vient **d'**Arménie.*
This jam comes **from** Armenia.

Attention!

When discussing origin, feminine countries (for the most part, those ending in -e) take *de*. Masculine countries take *du*. Countries with plural names, such as *the United States*, take *des*.

*Je suis **de** France, il est **du** Maroc, et elle est **des** États-Unis.*
I am **from** France, he is **from** Morocco, and she is **from the** United States.

De is used to indicate measurement.

*Notre famille a un terrain **de** 20 pieds.*
Our family has a 20-foot piece of land.

*Il a une cicatrice **de** dix centimètres à la jambe.*
He has a ten-centimeter-long scar on his leg.

Verbs followed by an infinitive, as in certain two-verb constructions, usually take either the preposition *à* or *de* before the infinitive. The first verb determines which preposition is used.

*Il **accepte de tourner** le film.*
He **accepts to shoot** the movie.

*Dis**-lui d'écrire**.*
Tell him/her **to write**.

Attention!

Following are common verbs that take the preposition *de*.

accepter de	to accept
arrêter de	to stop
choisir de	to choose
demander de	to ask
dire de	to say
écrire de	to write to
essayer de	to try
finir de	to stop
oublier de	to forget
refuser de	to refuse to
regretter de	to regret
suggérer de	to suggest

Exercise 1

Use *de* and the verb *venir* to express where the following things are from.

1. cette voiture / Italie

_____

_____

2. ce chocolat / Belgique

_____

_____

3. ce champagne / France

_____

_____

4. ce saké / Japon

_____

_____

5. cet ordinateur / Chine

_____

_____

6. cette fusée / États-Unis

_____

_____

Exercise 2

Choose from the list of nouns to express what each of the following things is made of. Write complete sentences.

bois, papier, metal, plastique, sucre

1. Un bonbon_____

_____

2. La Tour Eiffel_____

_____

3. Une table ancienne_____

_____

4. Un verre_____

_____

5. Une feuille_____

_____

Exercise 3

Translate the following sentences into French using the preposition *de*.

1. A three-foot-long monster was there.

_____

_____

2. He stopped smoking last year.

_____

_____

3. My grandmother's cake is the pride of my family.

_____

_____

4. I regretted not attending the show.

_____

_____

5. From my window, I saw everything.

_____

_____

17

A pronoun replaces a noun in a sentence. A subject pronoun replaces a noun that is the subject of a sentence.

Subject pronouns are almost always followed by the verb indicating the action being performed by the subject.

Antoine aime des hamburgers.
Antoine likes hamburgers.

Il aime des hamburgers.
He likes hamburgers.

Subject pronouns agree with the noun they replace in person, gender, and number.

Singular		Plural	
je	I	*nous*	we
tu	you	*vous*	you (formal or plural)
il	he	*ils*	they (masculine)
elle	she	*elles*	they (feminine)
on	one (impersonal)		

Attention!

Before a vowel or silent *h*, the subject pronoun *je* becomes *j'*.

The second-person plural pronoun *vous* can be used to represent more than one person. *Vous* can also be used as a singular second-person pronoun in formal situations, as when addressing an elder or a person in authority.

Vous êtes fatigués tous les deux?
Are **you** both tired?

Comment allez-**vous,** Monsieur le Maire?
How are **you,** Mr. Mayor?

There is no French equivalent for the English *it*. Because each noun is either masculine or feminine, even objects are referred to as *il* or *elle*. Plural objects are referred to as *ils* and *elles*.

Regardez la forêt. **Elle** est immense.
Look at the forest. **It** is huge.

J'aime les crêpes. **Elles** sont délicieuses.
I love crepes. **They** are delicious.

The pronoun *il* can be used in impersonal construction, similar to the English *it*. In these cases, *il* does not refer to a specific noun.

Il pleut.
It is raining.

Il est tard.
It is late.

The masculine plural pronoun *ils* is used to represent a group of mixed gender.

Ils sont gentils, ton fils et ta fille.
They are nice, your son and daughter.

Attention!

The singular *je* and *tu* are always subject pronouns, but the plural *nous* and *vous* can function as subjects, as direct or indirect objects, or as reflexive or reciprocal pronouns.

Nous (subject pronoun) *l'appelons.*
We call him.

Il ***nous*** (direct-object pronoun) *appelle.*
He calls **us.**

Il pense à ***nous*** (indirect-object pronoun).
He thinks about **us.**

Nous ***nous*** (reflexive pronoun) *habillons.*
We dress **ourselves.**

Nous ***nous*** (reciprocal pronoun) *appelons.*
We call **each other.**

Attention!

The masculine *il* and *ils* are always subjects, but the feminine *elle* and *elles* can be either subject pronouns or indirect-object pronouns.

Elle (subject pronoun) *pense à lui.*
She thinks about him.

Il pense à ***elle*** (indirect-object pronoun).
He thinks about **her.**

Exercise 1

Provide the French equivalent for each of the following English pronouns.

1. _____ he

2. _____ I

3. _____ she

4. _____ you (singular, informal)

5. _____ us

6. _____ you (singular, formal)

7. _____ they (masculine)

8. _____ they (feminine)

9. _____ you (plural)

10. _____ they (masculine and feminine together)

Exercise 2

Which subject pronoun would you use for the following situations?

1. talking about yourself _____

2. talking about your brother to someone else _____

3. talking to your brother _____

4. talking to your boyfriend/girlfriend's mother _____

5. talking about your family members _____

6. talking to a group of your family members _____

Exercise 3

Would you use *tu* or *vous* with the following people? Sort the people below into the appropriate columns.

your professor, your father, your younger cousin, a classmate, the bus driver, your elderly neighbor

Tu	Vous

Exercise 4

Use the subject pronouns to construct answers to the following questions.

1. Est-ce que je suis en retard?

   _____

   _____

2. Est-ce que tu aimes chanter?

   _____

   _____

3. Quand est-ce que les filles vont à l'école?

   _____

   _____

4. Qu'est-ce qu'Élizabeth a mangé à midi?

   _____

   _____

5. Vous êtes les nouveaux élèves?

   _____

   _____

18

Possessive pronouns indicate possession or ownership. They replace a noun that is preceded by a possessive adjective, like *mon, ta,* or *ses.* The equivalents in English are *mine, yours, his, hers, ours,* and *theirs.*

A possessive pronoun agrees in person with the possessor and in gender and number with the noun it replaces (the object possessed). The possessive pronoun is always accompanied by the definite article, which agrees with the replaced noun in gender and number.

| | Masculine | | Feminine | |
	Singular	Plural	Singular	Plural
mine	*le mien*	*les miens*	*la mienne*	*les miennes*
yours	*le tien*	*les tiens*	*la tienne*	*les tiennes*
his, hers, its, one's	*le sien*	*les siens*	*la sienne*	*les siennes*
ours	*le nôtre*	*les nôtres*	*la nôtre*	*les nôtres*
yours (formal or plural)	*le vôtre*	*les vôtres*	*la vôtre*	*les vôtres*
theirs	*le leur*	*les leurs*	*la leur*	*les leurs*

J'aime **mon stylo** (M).
I like **my pen.**

J'aime **le mien.**
I like **mine.**

J'aime **le stylo** (M) **de Luc/Léa.**
I like **Luc's/Léa's pen.**

J'aime **le sien.**
I like **his/hers.**

J'aime **notre stylo.**
I like **our pen.**

J'aime **le nôtre.**
I like **ours.**

J'aime **notre radio** (F).
I like **our radio.**

J'aime **la nôtre.**
I like **ours.**

J'aime **nos projets.**
I like **our plans.**

J'aime **les nôtres.**
I like **ours.**

Attention!

When used with the prepositions *de* and *à*, the definite article accompanying the possessive pronoun will merge to form *du/des* and *au/aux.*

du mien	of mine
au mien	to mine
des leurs	of theirs
aux leurs	to theirs

Attention!

A circumflex accent (ˆ) differentiates the possessive pronouns *nôtre* and *vôtre* from the adjectives *notre* and *votre.* The pronoun and adjective *leur(s)* are identical.

J'aime **leur stylo.**
I like **their pen.**

J'aime **le leur.**
I like **theirs.**

L'Exception

Possessive pronouns do not take an article when they are used as an adjective in a figurative sense. This use is only typical in a romantic context.

Tu es **mien.**
You are **mine.**

Possessive pronouns are commonly used in sentences with the demonstrative pronoun *ce* (this/it).

C'est **mon stylo.**
This/it is **my pen.**

C'est **le mien.**
This/it is **mine.**

La Langue Vivante

Possessive pronouns are often replaced by indirect-object pronouns in spoken French.

Ce stylo est **à moi.**
This pen is **mine.**

C'est **à moi.**
It's **mine.**

Exercise 1

Match the English possessive pronouns in column A to the French equivalents in column B.

	A		B
_____	**1.** ours (plural, masculine)	a. le mien
_____	**2.** yours (plural, feminine, formal)	b. les nôtres
_____	**3.** his (plural, feminine)	c. le tien
_____	**4.** mine (singular, masculine)	d. les tiennes
_____	**5.** yours (singular, masculine, informal)	e. les vôtres
_____	**6.** yours (plural, feminine, informal)	f. les siennes

Exercise 2

Circle the correct possessive pronoun for each of the following nouns.

1. son (her) livre
   a. la sienne
   b. le sien
   c. le mien

2. notre télévision
   a. le nôtre
   b. la vôtre
   c. la nôtre

3. leurs claviers
   a. les leurs
   b. les leur
   c. le leur

4. vos calendriers
   a. les vôtre
   b. le vôtre
   c. les vôtres

5. ma poupée
   a. la mienne
   b. le mien
   c. la tienne

Exercise 3

Jessica and Dave are comparing various things in their lives. Replace each italicized word in their dialogue with the correct possessive pronoun.

1. Jessica: *Mon père* est ingénieur.

   Dave: _____ est homme d'affaires.

2. Jessica: *Ma mère* est infirmière.

   Dave: _____ est médecin.

3. Jessica: *Mes soeurs* sont belles.

   Dave: _____ sont très, très belles.

4. Jessica: *Mes amis* sont généreux.

   Dave: _____ aussi.

5. Jessica: *Nos vies* sont belles.

   Dave: C'est clair. _____ sont belles.

19

Pronouns *Reflexive and Reciprocal Pronouns*

Reflexive pronouns are used when the subject performs an action on itself. Reciprocal pronouns are a form of reflexive pronoun in which an action or feeling is shared among plural subjects. French reflexive pronouns are used more frequently than their English equivalents, though their meaning does not always translate exactly into English.

In English, reflexive pronouns are those with *-self* or *-selves* at the end, and reciprocal pronouns are represented by *each other* or *one another*. In French, both are expressed by the same pronouns.

Singular		Plural	
Subject	**Reflexive Pronoun**	**Subject**	**Reflexive Pronoun**
je	*me*	*nous*	*nous*
tu	*te*	*vous* (formal and plural)	*vous*
il, elle, on	*se*	*ils, elles*	*se*

*Nous **nous** amusons.*
We enjoy **ourselves.**

*Ils **se** soutiennent.*
They support **each other.**

Attention!

Me, *te*, and *se* shorten to *m'*, *t'*, and *s'* before a vowel sound.

*Je **m'**appelle Anne-Sophie.*
My name is Anne-Sophie.
(Literally: I call **myself** Anne-Sophie.)

In French, the third-person reflexive pronoun *se* does not express the gender or number of the person or persons completing the action.

*Il **s'**amuse.*
He enjoys **himself.**

*Elle **s'**amuse.*
She enjoys **herself.**

*Ils **s'**amusent.*
They enjoy **themselves.**

*Ils **s'**aiment.*
They love **each other.**

Attention!

The subject pronoun and the reflexive pronoun may be the same word in French, and they may follow each other in a sentence. These two pronouns, however, do not have the same meaning.

***Vous** (subject pronoun) **vous** (reflexive pronoun) couchez?*
Are you going to sleep?
(Literally: Are **you** putting **yourself** to sleep?)

Attention!

The first- and second-person reflexive pronouns (*me, te, nous,* and *vous*) are the same as the direct-object and indirect-object pronouns. However, all of these pronouns express a slightly different meaning which can be deduced from the context.

Emphatic reflexive pronouns are used in addition to the reflexive pronoun for added emphasis, even when it is clear that the verb is reflexive. Emphatic reflexive pronouns are added to the end of a sentence or clause.

Singular		Plural	
Pronoun	**English Equivalent**	**Pronoun**	**English Equivalent**
moi-même	myself	*nous-mêmes*	ourselves
toi-même	yourself	*vous-mêmes*	yourselves
vous-même (formal)	yourself		
lui-même	himself	*eux-mêmes*	themselves (masculine)
elle-même	herself		
soi-même	itself, oneself	*elles-mêmes*	themselves (feminine)

*Nous **nous** parlons à **nous-mêmes**.*
We talk to **ourselves.**

*Je **m'**interroge **moi-même**.*
I ask **myself** questions.

The emphatic reflexive pronoun *soi-même* is frequently shortened just to *soi*.

*On aime tous parler de **soi**.*
People (in general) like to talk about **themselves.**

*C'est difficile d'habiter loin de chez **soi**.*
It's difficult to live far from **one's** home.

La Langue Vivante

Emphatic reflexive pronouns can also be used for emphasis in sentences that do not contain reflexive verbs and therefore do not contain reflexive pronouns.

*Je le ferai **moi-même**.*
I will do it **myself.**

Exercise 1

Use context to determine the pronoun type for each of the following bolded words.

1. Je **vous** invite.

_____

2. Nous **nous** sommes perdus.

_____

3. **Je** me pose plein de questions.

_____

4. Tu **t'**es bien habillé.

_____

5. Je me suis posé(e) plein de questions, **moi-même.**

_____

Exercise 2

Translate the following sentences into French.

1. I look at myself in the mirror.

_____

_____

2. They are noticing each other. (feminine, plural)

_____

_____

3. They ask themselves questions. (masculine, plural)

_____

_____

4. I give myself permission.

_____

_____

Exercise 3

Add emphasis to each sentence using the emphatic reflexive pronouns.

1. Faites vos photocopies!

_____

_____

2. Ils font le ménage.

_____

_____

3. Elle cuisine.

_____

_____

4. J'apprend le karaté.

_____

_____

20

Variable demonstrative pronouns in French express both the gender and number of the noun they are replacing.

	Singular	Plural
Masculine	*celui*	*ceux*
Feminine	*celle*	*celles*

*Prends **celui** que tu veux.*
Take **the one** you want.

Variable demonstrative pronouns replace a demonstrative adjective plus noun, similar to *the one, that one, this one,* or *these and those* in English.

*C'est **l'homme** que j'aime.*　　*C'est **celui** que j'aime.*
It is **the man** I like.　　　It is **the one** I like.

*C'est **la fille** que j'aime.*　　*C'est **celle** que j'aime.*
It is **the girl** I like.　　　It is **the one** I like.

Demonstrative pronouns can be used in the following circumstances:

- In prepositional phrases (usually before the preposition *de*)

  *C'est **celui de gauche**.*
  It's **that one on the left.**

- Followed by a relative pronoun (*que, qui, dont*) and a dependent clause

  *C'est **celui que** je veux.*
  That's **the one (that)** I want.

  *C'est **celle dont** tout le monde parle en ce moment.*
  That's **the one about which** everyone is talking right now.

The suffixes *-ci* or *-là* can be added to the demonstrative pronouns to emphasize a contrast between objects or people, similar to their use with demonstrative adjectives.

*J'aime **cet homme-ci**.*　　*J'aime **celui-ci**.*
I like **this man.**　　　I like **this one.**

*J'aime **cette fille-là**.*　　*J'aime **celle-là**.*
I like **that girl.**　　　I like **that one.**

Attention!

Unlike *the one* in English, French demonstrative pronouns cannot stand alone. They must always be accompanied by a qualifying description, including *-ci* or *-là*.

*Montre-moi **celle qui te plaît**.*
Show me **the one that you like.**

*C'est **celui-ci**.*
It's **this one.**

*C'est **celui-là**.*
That's **the one.**

Attention!

Unlike in English, French demonstrative pronouns are never completed by an adjective. In these cases, the adjective replaces the noun in French.

*Je veux **le stylo bleu**.*　　*Je veux **le bleu**.*
I want **the blue pen.**　　I want **the blue one.**

Exercise 1

Match the variable demonstrative pronouns in English in column A to their French equivalents in column B.

A	B
_____ **1.** the one (feminine)	a. celui
_____ **2.** the one (masculine, singular)	b. ceux
_____ **3.** the ones (feminine)	c. celle
_____ **4.** the ones (masculine)	d. celles

Exercise 2

Correct the errors in the following sentences. The noun that each demonstrative pronoun replaces is in parentheses. Note: Not all sentences have errors.

1. C'est celui dans le placard. (la chemise)

_____

_____

2. Je veux les moins chers. (les verres)

_____

_____

3. C'est celle-ci qui s'est fait arrêter par la police. (Stéphane)

_____

_____

4. C'est celui qui part en vacances. (Bruno)

_____

_____

5. C'est celle de la Suisse. (la frontière)

_____

_____

Exercise 3

Translate the following sentences into French. Refer to the noun in parentheses to determine the appropriate variable demonstrative pronoun.

1. I like them, especially those that stink. (strong cheeses)

_____

_____

2. It's the one I like. (chair)

_____

_____

3. I like this one. (puppy)

_____

_____

4. I'll take the small one. (slice of pizza)

_____

_____

5. Do you want this one or that one? (puzzle)

_____

_____

21

Invariable demonstrative pronouns do not have a specific gender or number (they are only singular). They are similar to *this* (one), *that* (one), and *it* in English, though they have specific uses depending on context.

The invariable demonstrative pronouns *ceci*, *cela*, and *ça* refer to things that have no assigned gender, such as ideas, facts, statements, or actions that have been performed.

> *Pour avoir un jardin comme **ceci**, il faut en prendre soin tous les jours.*
> To have a garden like **this one**, you must take care of it every day.

> *Il est en prison maintenant. **Cela** est la conséquence de ses actes.*
> He is in prison now. **That**'s the consequence of his actions.

> *Tu ne devrais pas faire **ceci**, mais plutôt **cela**!*
> You shouldn't do **this**, but rather **that**!

The demonstrative pronoun *ça* replaces *ceci* and *cela* in informal spoken French.

> *J'aime **ça**.*
> I like **that**.

> *Lire? **Ça** me plaît.*
> To read? I like **that/it**.

La Langue Vivante

In formal French, *ceci* is used to introduce something that will be said, while *cela* or *ça* is used to introduce something that has already been said.

*N'oublie jamais **ceci**: je t'aime.*
Never forget **this**: I love you.

*Je t'aime; n'oublie jamais **ça (cela)**.*
I love you; never forget **that**.

The invariable demonstrative pronoun *ce* is primarily used in front of the verb *être* (to be), and functions similar to the English pronouns *it*, *this*, and *that*.

> ***C'est** vrai.*
> **This is** true./**That's** true.

> ***C'est** une très jolie région.*
> **This is** a really pretty region./**That's** a really pretty region.

Attention!

Though *ce* is a singular pronoun, it can be followed by a plural verb.

***Ce sont** de bons élèves.*
Those/These are good students.

L'Exception

If a pronoun other than the object pronoun *en* (*some*) comes before the verb *être*, a demonstrative pronoun such as *ceci*, *cela*, or *ça* is used.

***Ça m**'est arrivé.*
That has happened to **me.**

***Ça y** est.*
That's it.

Exercise 1

Explain why *ceci*, *cela*, and *ça* are all appropriate for the following sentence. Why can't *ce* be used as well?

Ceci/Cela/Ça me semble hors de prix.
(It seems really expensive to me.)

_____

_____

_____

_____

_____

_____

_____

_____

Exercise 2

Translate the following sentences into French using the invariable demonstrative pronouns.

1. They are loyal friends. (Those I'm talking about.)

_____

_____

2. It's payday.

_____

_____

3. It's winter.

_____

_____

4. That's a good idea.

_____

_____

5. It's crazy.

_____

_____

6. They are good singers. (Those that are already being discussed.)

_____

_____

7. It's me.

_____

_____

Exercise 3

Rewrite the following formal sentences so that they are less formal.

1. Dans l'avenir il faudra penser à ceci.

_____

_____

2. À propos de ce cartable, cela me semble un peu trop lourd pour toi.

_____

_____

3. Ceci me plaît.

_____

_____

4. Cela va bientôt faire quatre ans que je suis au collège.

_____

_____

5. Cela commence à être difficile.

_____

_____

22

Pronouns *Interrogative Pronouns Qui, Que, and Quoi*

The interrogative pronouns *qui, que,* and *quoi* are used in questions to replace people and things. They translate as *what, which, who,* or *whom,* depending on where they are used.

	Subject of Question	Object of Question	After Preposition
People	*qui, qui est-ce qui*	*qui, qui est-ce que*	*qui*
Things	*qu'est-ce qui*	*que, qu'est-ce que*	*quoi*

Attention!

Qui and *qui est-ce que* can be preceded by a preposition.

Avec qui est-ce que tu manges?
Who are you eating **with**?

Qui is used in questions to replace people and animals that are considered pets, equivalent to the English *who* or *whom.* When acting as the subject of the question, either *qui* or the longer form *qui est-ce qui* can be used.

Qui est-ce qui a mangé la pomme?
Who ate the apple?

Qui aimes-tu? Qui est-ce que tu aimes?
Whom do you love?

When acting as the object of the question, either *qui* or the longer form *qui est-ce que* can be used. The long form cannot be used with an inverted subject and verb in an interrogative form.

Qui cherchez-vous? Qui est-ce que vous cherchez?
Who are you looking for?

Que is used in questions to express an object or event (as opposed to a person or pet) and is equivalent to the English *what.* The expression *qu'est-ce qui* is used to replace a thing when it is the subject of the question.

Qu'est-ce qui se passe?
What is going on?

Attention!

The pronoun *que* shortens to *qu'* before a vowel.

Attention!

In affirmative statements questioning *what* a person is, rather than *who, ce que* is used instead of *qui.*

Je me demande qui c'est. Luc?
I wonder **who** this is. Luc?

Je me demande ce qu'il est. Français?
I wonder **what** he is. French?

When acting as the object of the sentence, either *que* or the longer form *qu'est-ce que* can be used.

Que veux-tu?
What do you want?

Qu'est-ce que tu veux?
What do you want?

When following a preposition, the pronoun *quoi* replaces a noun representing a thing.

De quoi parles-tu?
What are you talking **about**?

La Langue Vivante

Similar to English, questions are often formed in spoken French using an affirmative statement stressed to sound like a question. In these cases, the pronoun *quoi* is used as a direct object.

Tu veux quoi?
You want **what**?

Exercise 1

Match the interrogative pronouns in column A with their proper use in column B.

A	B
_____ **1.** qui *or* qui est-ce qui	a. subject of a question (thing)
_____ **2.** qu'est-ce qui	b. object of a question (person)
_____ **3.** *only* qui	c. subject of question (person)
_____ **4.** *only* quoi	d. object of a question (thing)
_____ **5.** que *or* qu'est que	e. object of a preposition (thing)
_____ **6.** qui *or* qui est-ce que	f. object of a preposition (person)

Exercise 2

Fill in the following blanks with the correct interrogative pronouns.

1. _____ est produit dans cette usine?

2. _____ est arrivé? Sidney ou Raoul?

3. _____ te déranges? C'est tes devoirs ou ton boulot?

4. _____ je cherche? J'oublie toujours au supermarché.

5. De _____ s'agit-il?

6. _____ vous avez vu au parc cet après-midi? Des amis?

7. Avec _____ est-ce que tu pars en vacances?

Exercise 3

Translate the following sentences into French using the correct interrogative pronouns.

1. What did you do?

_____

_____

2. Who do they study with?

_____

_____

3. Who do you (plural) know?

_____

_____

4. What do you (singular) want to eat?

_____

_____

5. What's not working?

_____

_____

6. What's happening?

_____

_____

7. Who is the prime minister of Canada?

_____

_____

23

Lequel (which) is a combination of the definite article *le* plus the relative pronoun *quel*. *Lequel* replaces *quel* when modifying a noun, similar to *which* or *which one* in English.

> *Quel film* *est-ce que tu préfères?*
> **Which film** do you prefer?

> *Lequel* *est-ce que tu préfères?*
> **Which one** do you prefer?

Lequel agrees in gender and number with the noun it replaces.

	Singular	Plural
Masculine	*lequel*	*lesquels*
Feminine	*laquelle*	*lesquelles*

Tu aimes ces bonbons?
You like these candies?

> *Lequel* *est-ce que tu préfères parmi eux?*
> **Which** one do you prefer among them?

> *Laquelle* *est ta préférée entre tes peluches?*
> **Which** is your favorite of your stuffed animals?

When the noun being discussed is obvious, *lequel* can entirely replace it in the sentence.

> *Lequel* *est-ce que tu préfères?*
> **Which** one do you prefer?

> *Laquelle* *est ta préférée?*
> **Which** one is your favorite?

> *Lesquelles* *souhaites-tu voir gagner?*
> **Which ones** do you want to see win?

Lequel is used with the prepositions *à* and *de* to mean *to which* and *of which*. *Lequel* changes form in all but the feminine singular when used with these prepositions.

	Singular	Plural
Masculine	*auquel* (to/at which) *duquel* (of/ about which)	*auxquels* (to/at which) *desquels* (of/about which)
Feminine	*à laquelle* (to/at which) *de laquelle* (of/ about which)	*auxquelles* (to/at which) *desquelles* (of/about which)

> *À laquelle* *d'entre elles avez-vous posé la question?*
> **To which one** of them did you ask the question?

> *Auquel* *souhaites-tu parler?*
> **Which one** do you want to talk **to**?

> *Ma tante?* *De laquelle* *est-ce que tu me parles?*
> My aunt? **Which one** are you talking to me **about**?

> *Mon oncle?* *Duquel* *est-ce tu me parles?*
> My uncle? **Which one** are you talking to me **about**?

Exercise 1

Place the following nouns into the correct square based on which form of *lequel* would replace them in a question.

une pomme	des chaussures	des poires
des serviettes	une chaise	des
un lecteur DVD	des portes	portefeuilles
une brosse	un radio-réveil	des lunettes
un mouchoir		des savons

lequel	lesquels
laquelle	**lesquelles**

Exercise 2

Replace the noun in the following questions with the appropriate form of *lequel*.

1. Quel DVD est-ce que tu veux louer?

_____

_____

2. Quelle voiture veux-tu prendre pour partir en vacances?

_____

_____

3. Quels rollers souhaites-tu acheter?

_____

_____

4. Quelles personnes t'ont fait un cadeau pour ton départ en retraite?

_____

_____

5. Quel jouet souhaites-tu acheter pour ton neveu?

_____

_____

6. Auquel restaurant penses-tu pour ce soir?

_____

_____

7. De laquelle copine parlez-vous?

_____

_____

Exercise 3

Two friends, Paul and Pierre, are at the market buying supplies for their New Year's Eve party. Use the following nouns to write a possible dialogue between the Paul and Pierre as they discuss what they need.

les gateaux apératif, les crackers, les apéricubes, du jus d'orange, du fois gras

Example: Pierre: Okay, Paul. Va me chercher des gateaux apératif.
Paul: Lesquels veux-tu que je prenne?

_____

_____

_____

_____

_____

_____

_____

_____

_____

_____

_____

_____

_____

24

The direct object of a sentence is the person or thing receiving the action of the verb. A direct object pronoun replaces a direct object noun.

Singular		Plural	
me	*me*	us	*nous*
you	*te*	you (formal or plural)	*vous*
him, it (masculine) her, it (feminine)	*le* *la*	them	*les*

Direct object pronouns precede the verb.

J'aime **Léa.**   Je **l'**aime.
I love **Léa.**   I love **her.**

J'emmène **mon cartable** à l'école.
I bring my **backpack** to school.

Je **l'**emmène à l'école.
I bring **it** to school.

Attention!

Before a vowel sound, *me* and *te* shorten to *m'* and *t'*, and *le* and *la* shorten to *l'*.

In a compound tense, like the *passé composé*, the direct-object pronoun precedes the auxiliary verb.

J'ai emmené **mon cartable** à l'école.
I brought my **backpack** to school.

Je **l'**ai emmené à l'école.
I brought **it** to school.

Attention!

When the direct object pronoun is used with a past participle, the past participle must agree with the gender and number of the direct object.

J'ai emmené **ma gomme** l'école.
I brought **my eraser** to school.

Je **l'**ai emmené**e** à à l'école.
I brought **it** to school.

J'ai emmené **mes gommes** à l'école.
I brought **my erasers** to school.

Je **les** ai emmené**es** à l'école.
I brought **them** to school.

The direct object pronoun can also be placed directly before an infinitive when the pronoun is the direct object of the infinitive verb rather than the conjugated verb.

Je vais emmener **mon cartable** à l'école.
I'm going to bring my **backpack** to school.

Je vais **l'**emmener à l'école.
I'm going to bring **it** to school.

In a negative command, or imperative, the direct-object pronoun takes its normal position in front of the verb. In an affirmative imperative, the direct object pronoun is attached to the verb with a hyphen. The pronouns *me* and *te* change to *moi* and *toi* in the affirmative imperative form.

Ne **me** regarde pas!   Regarde-**moi**!
Don't look at **me**!   Look at **me**!

Ne **vous** méfiez pas!   Méfiez-**vous**!
Don't be too cautious!   Be very careful!
(Literally: Don't be
distrustful!)

Direct objects can be simple nouns or noun phrases, which include articles or adjectives related to the noun. A direct object pronoun can be used to replace an entire noun phrase.

Je mange **les** (definite article) **bonbons bleus.**
I eat **the blue candies.**

Je **les** (direct-object pronoun) mange.
I eat **them.**

Direct objects can also be verbal phrases, either as an infinitive verb or as a clause introduced by a relative pronoun *que* or *qui*. Verbal phrases can be replaced by the neutral direct-object pronoun *le* (the feminine *la* is not used).

Je pense **que j'ai faim.**   Je **le** pense.
I think **(that) I am hungry.**   I think **it.** (I think so.)

Je veux **manger.**   Je **le** veux.
I want **to eat.**   I want **it.** (I want to.)

Exercise 1

Match the English direct object pronouns in column A with their French equivalents in column B.

	A		B
_____	**1.** me		a. nous
_____	**2.** you (plural)		b. vous
_____	**3.** them (masculine)		c. me
_____	**4.** her		d. les
_____	**5.** us		e. la

Exercise 2

Correct the errors in the following sentences. Note: Not all sentences contain errors.

1. Je leur encourage.

_____

2. Nous les trouvons beaux.

_____

3. Il lui ennuie.

_____

4. Ecoutez-me!

_____

5. Marine nous invitons.

_____

6. Tu me plaît.

_____

7. J'ai le mangé.

_____

Exercise 3

Answer the following questions using the direct object pronoun to replace the noun in your answer.

1. Est-ce que tu aimes la série *Les Experts* (*CSI*)?

_____

2. Est-ce que tu as vu l'accident sur l'autoroute?

_____

3. Est-ce que Juliette a bu le verre avec du poison à la fin de la pièce de Shakespeare?

_____

4. Est-ce que tes voisins font la fête souvent?

_____

5. Est-ce que tu va voir la mer cet été?

_____

Exercise 4

Convert the following sentences into imperatives.

1. Tu les manges.

_____

2. Vous m'embrassez.

_____

3. Tu te dépêches.

_____

4. Vous vous dépêchez.

_____

5. Tu ne le fais pas.

_____

25

An indirect object expresses a person or thing indirectly affected by the action of a verb and is often introduced by a preposition. An indirect object pronoun replaces an indirect object.

Singular		Plural	
me	*me*	us	*nous*
you	*te*	you (formal or plural)	*vous*
him, her	*lui*	them	*leur*

An indirect object is generally preceded by a preposition. An indirect object pronoun is always placed before the verb and does not take a preposition.

*Je parle **à Léa.***   *Je **lui** parle.*
I talk **to Léa.**   I talk **to her.**

*Je rend visite **à Marc.***   *Je **lui** rend visite.*
I visit **Marc.**   I visit **him.**

Attention!

Before a vowel sound, the indirect-object pronouns *me* and *te* shorten to *m'* and *t'*.

Attention!

Unlike the possessive adjective *leur*, the indirect-object pronoun *leur* never takes an *-s*.

*Je **leur** (pronoun) donne **leur** (adjective) livre.*
I give **them their** book.

*Je **leur** (pronoun) donne **leurs** (adjective) livres.*
I give **them their** books.

In a compound tense, like the *passé composé,* the indirect object pronoun precedes the auxiliary verb.

*J'ai rendu visite à **Marc.***   *Je **lui** ai rendu visite.*
I visited **Marc.**   I visited **him.**

The indirect object pronoun is placed directly before an infinitive when the pronoun functions as the indirect object of the infinitive verb rather than the conjugated verb.

*Je vais **lui** rendre visite.*
I am going to visit **him.**

Indirect objects can be nouns or noun phrases (a noun with articles and adjectives). An indirect object pronoun can be used to replace an entire noun phrase.

*Je parle **à ma jeune cousine.***   *Je **lui** parle.*
I talk **to my young cousin.**   I talk **to her.**

*Je parle **à la fille qui aime lire.***   *Je **lui** parle.*
I talk to **the girl who likes to read.**   I talk **to her.**

Attention!

Unlike direct-object pronouns, past participles do not agree with indirect-object pronouns.

*Je **lui** ai **envoyé** une lettre.*
I **sent** a letter to **her.**

Similar to the direct object pronoun, the indirect object pronoun takes the normal position in front of the verb in a negative imperative. In an affirmative imperative, the direct object pronoun is attached with a hyphen to the verb. *Me* and *te* change to *moi* and *toi* in the affirmative imperative form.

*Ne **me** donne pas!*   *Donne-**moi**!*
Don't give (it) to **me!**   Give (it) to **me!**

*Ne **lui** expliquez pas!*   *Expliquez-**lui**!*
Don't explain (it) to **him!**   Explain (it) to **him!**

Attention!

The first- and second-person direct object pronouns and indirect object pronouns have the same form and can be confused in the imperative. Context can be used to determine which pronoun is being used. For example, the verbs *donner à* and *expliquer à* include a preposition, indicating that they take an indirect-object pronoun.

*Ne **m'**expliquez pas!*   *Expliquez-**moi**!*
Don't explain (it) to **me!**   Explain (it) to **me!**

Exercise 1

Answer *vrai* (true) or *faux* (false) to the following statements about indirect object pronouns.

1. _____ The indirect-object pronoun *leur* usually has an -*s* at the end.

2. _____ An imperative with a direct-object pronoun and an indirect-object pronoun can appear to have the same structure with some subjects.

3. _____ Indirect objects usually follow prepositions.

4. _____ Past participles do not agree with the indirect-object pronoun that precedes them.

5. _____ Past participles do not agree with the direct-object pronoun that precedes them.

Exercise 2

Use the cues in parentheses to determine the appropriate indirect object pronoun for each of the following sentences.

1. Est-ce que vous _____ parlez? (to them)

2. N'oublie pas de _____ téléphoner! (me)

3. Qu'est-ce que tu _____ as dit? (to us)

4. Dis-_____! (to him)

5. Dis-_____! (to you, informal)

Exercise 3

Replace the indirect object with the appropriate indirect object pronoun for each of the following sentences.

1. Tu donnes la télécommande à moi.

_____

_____

2. Je parle à ma mère deux fois par semaine.

_____

_____

3. Marie a répondu à toutes mes questions.

_____

_____

4. Stéphane a téléphoné à sa soeur.

_____

_____

5. Nous avons donné un cadeau à notre grand-mère.

_____

_____

26

Disjunctive pronons, or stressed pronouns, refer back to a noun or a pronoun that has either already been mentioned or is obvious from the context.

Singular		Plural	
me	*moi*	us	*nous*
you	*toi*	you (formal or plural)	*vous*
him	*lui*	them (masculine)	*eux*
her	*elle*	them (feminine)	*elles*
it	*soi*		

Though they are similar to *me, you, him, her, us,* and *them* in English, disjunctive pronouns have a variety of uses in French that differ from their English equivalents.

Use	Example
To emphasize a statement	*Moi,* je suis en colère. **Me,** I'm angry. *Lui,* il ne chante pas. **Him,** he doesn't sing.
For emphasis when asking a question	*Est-ce que tu as faim, toi?* Do you have hunger, **you**?
In quick responses without a verb	*Qui part en vacances cette semaine? Eux.* Who is going on vacation this week? **Them.**
To follow the expressions *c'est* and *ce sont*	*C'est moi.* It's **me.**
After *que* (than), in comparisons	*Elle est plus petite que moi.* She is smaller **than me.**
After prepositions	*Je parle pour lui.* I talk **for him.** *Je parle de lui.* I talk **about him.**
After prepositions to indicate possession	*Ce sac est à elle.* This is **her** bag.
In sentences with a compound subject or object	*Ma soeur et moi,* nous allons au cinéma.* **My sister and I** are going to the movie theater.

Attention!

Disjunctive pronouns replace indirect objects introduced by the preposition *à*, in cases where *à* means *about*. Indirect pronouns are used to replace indirect objects introduced by the preposition *à* in cases where *à* means *to*. The different meanings for *à* depend on the verb used.

*Je **parle à Luc** (indirect object).*
I **talk to Luc.**

*Je **lui** (indirect-object pronoun) parle.*
I talk to **him.**

*Je **pense à Luc** (indirect object).*
I **think about Luc.**

*Je pense à **lui** (disjunctive pronoun).*
I think about **him.**

The disjunctive pronouns can be combined with -*même* to form emphatic reflexive pronouns, which add emphasis to a reflexive statement.

Moi-même, je pense que tu as raison.*
Myself, I think you're right.

Disjunctive pronouns are also used with the adverb expression *ne ... que* (only) and the negative conjunction *ne ... ni* (neither ... nor).

Tu n'aimes que moi. You love only **me.**	*Ni toi ni moi ne le ferons.* Neither **you** nor **I** do it.

Exercise 1

Complete each of the following sentences with the correct disjunctive pronoun.

1. C'est à _____, j'ai commandé la salade niçoise.

2. _____ et son frère vont tous les deux à l'école des garçons.

3. C'est à _____. Joanna a perdu son stylo hier.

4. On est mieux chacun chez _____.

5. Est-ce que tu as envie d'aller au cinéma, _____?

6. _____, je dis qu'il est important de voter.

7. Nous trouvons _____-mêmes que la vie en Espagne est moins chère.

Exercise 2

Indicate the role each disjuntive pronoun is playing in the following sentences.

1. Qui a faim? Moi!

_____

2. Nous et vous allons on va à la plage.

_____

3. Moi qui étais là, je sais ce qui s'est passé.

_____

4. C'est lui.

_____

5. J'ai construit le tabouret moi-même.

_____

6. Ni moi ni elle ne connaissons l'horaire pour la prochaine séance.

_____

7. Il est moins sérieux que moi.

_____

8. À quoi tu penses, toi?

_____

9. Ce billet est à elle.

_____

10. Tu ne penses qu'à elle.

_____

11. Tu le fais pour lui.

_____

Exercise 3

Translate the following sentences into French using the disjunctive pronoun.

1. They are going to do errands.

_____

_____

2. He decided to do painting.

_____

_____

3. I feel like talking to you.

_____

_____

4. We think it's going to be nice tomorrow.

_____

_____

5. You complicate life too much.

_____

_____

27

Indefinite pronouns replace a noun that is unspecified or vague.

quelqu'un	someone, somebody
quelque chose	something
personne	no one, nobody
rien	nothing
quelques-un(e)s	a few
chacun(e)	each one
aucun(e)	none, not one
tout(e)	all, everything
autre(s)	another, other(s)
n'importe qui	whoever, anybody
quiconque	whoever, anybody
n'importe quoi	whatever, anything
tel(le)(s)	such as, like
plusieurs	many, numerous, several
tout le monde	everybody
certain(e)(s)	certain ones

Personne *ne l'a vu.*
No one saw it.

Tout *va bien.*
Everything is going well.

Chacun *des spectateurs veut voir le film.*
Each one of the audience members wants to see the movie.

Quelques-uns *des passagers sont malades.*
Some of the passengers are sick.

N'importe qui *pourrait faire ce travail.*
Anyone can do this job.

Indefinite pronouns can act as the subject of a sentence, the object of a verb, or the object of a preposition.

Un autre (subject) *sera de trop.*
One more will be too much.

Tu n'as pas **quelque chose** (object) *à faire?*
Don't you have **something** to do?

J'ai envie de parler **à quelqu'un** (object of preposition).
I feel like talking **to someone.**

Attention!

Verbs that take an indefinite pronoun as a subject follow the standard conjugation rules according to the gender and number of the indefinite pronoun.

Quelqu'un *est venu ce matin.* (masculine, singular)
Someone came this morning.

Chacune *a pris de l'argent.* (feminine, singular)
Each one brought money.

Quelques- uns *sont partis avant.* (masculine, plural)
Some left before.

Quelques- unes *sont parties avant.* (feminine, plural)
Some left before.

Attention!

If *quelqu'un* (someone) or *quelque chose* (something) is followed by an adjective, the preposition *de* must be placed between them.

quelqu'un **de** *bien*
a good person, somebody good

quelque chose **de** *mal*
something bad

Attention!

The negative pronouns *personne* (no one), *rien* (nothing), and *aucun(e)* (none) must be accompanied by *ne* when used in a complete sentence.

Qui chante? **Personne.**
Who is singing? **No one.**

Je **ne** *connaissais* **personne.**
I did **not** know **anyone.**/I knew **no one.**

3. Elle a invité quelqu'un.

_____

_____

4. Elle a mangé.

_____

_____

5. Toutes les filles sont contentes.

_____

_____

Exercise 1

For each of the following setences, circle the appropriate indefinite pronoun in parentheses.

1. Elle a l'air de (tout / rien) savoir.

2. (Rien / Plusieurs) m'ont plu, je ne savais pas lequel choisir.

3. (Personne / Tout le monde) est content quand il fait beau.

4. (Personne / Chacun) a fait ses propres devoirs.

5. Est-ce que tu as envie de manger (quelque chose / rien)?

6. (L'autre / Les autres) arrivent à tout à l'heure.

Exercise 2

Make the sentences below negative using *rien, aucun(e),* and *personne.*

1. J'ai vu quelqu'un.

_____

_____

2. J'ai prévu beaucoup de choses.

_____

_____

Exercise 3

Translate the following sentences into French.

1. Is everything ready?

_____

_____

2. I haven't prepared anything.

_____

_____

3. Several candidates came for the debate.

_____

_____

4. Everybody left for the mall.

_____

_____

5. Some of them are going running later.

_____

_____

28

29 Pronouns *Que, Qui, Ce Que, and Ce Qui*

Relative pronouns limit repetition by linking the noun in a main clause with its antecedent. They create a subordinate clause that describes a noun in the main clause.

The relative pronoun *qui* functions as the subject of a sentence and is followed by a verb. The relative pronoun *que* functions as an object and does not take a verb.

*l'ami **qui** est là*
the friend **who** is there

*l'ami **que** j'aime*
the friend **(whom)** I like

*le livre **qui** est là*
the book **which/that** is there

*le livre **qu'**il aime*
the book **(which)** he likes

Attention!

Before a vowel, *que* shortens to *qu'*.

*la mangue **qu'**elle mange*
the mango **that** the girl eats

Attention!

With compound verbs, such as *le passé compose*, the verb must agree with the direct object that precedes it.

*le mangue **qu'elle** a mangée*
the mango **that** she ate

Qui is also used to replace an indirect-object pronoun after a preposition.

*le collègue **avec qui** j'ai parlé hier*
the colleague **with whom** I talked yesterday

*le voisin **à qui** j'ai prêté mes outils*
the neighbor **to whom** I lent my tools

L'Exception

Qui is not generally used with the preposition *de*. Instead, *dont* replaces the prepositional phrase *de qui*.

*la fille **dont** la voiture on a vu*
the girl **whose** car we saw

The relative pronouns *ce qui* and *ce que* are used to refer to an idea or something that is not specific or not stated. *Ce qui* functions as the subject of a clause, and *ce que* functions as a direct object of a clause.

*Il faut faire **ce que** t'a dit ton professeur.*
You must do **what** your teacher told you.

*J'adore tout **ce qui** est petit.*
I love everything **that** is little.

***Ce qui* and *ce qui* are often followed by *c'est* (it's, that's) for emphasis.**

***Ce qui** me plaît, **c'est** de voyager.*
What I like **is** to travel.

***Ce que** je veux, **c'est** de travailler au Canada.*
What I want **is** to work in Canada.

Exercise 1

Choose between *que* or *qui* to complete the following sentences.

1. C'est le vélo _____ j'ai prêté à mon frère.

2. C'est cette attraction _____ est la plus intéressante.

3. Je cherche le livre _____ se vend le plus en ce moment.

4. Le film _____ je préfère est *Le Seigneur des Anneaux*.

5. Le plat _____ j'aime manger en France est le poulet Gaston-Gérard.

Exercise 2

Choose between *ce que* or *ce qui* to complete the following sentences.

1. _____ je préfère, c'est de manger du chocolat.

2. _____ je redoute c'est le froid.

3. Gagner beaucoup d'argent, c'est _____ me motive.

4. Voir un bon film au cinéma, c'est _____ les gens recherchent.

5. Les douaniers cherchent tout _____ est illégal.

6. _____ j'aime chez toi, c'est ton écran plasma.

Exercise 3

Use the relative pronouns to link the two sentences in each of the following pairs.

1. Christine est très intelligente. Christine étudie les mathématiques.

   _____

   _____

2. Elle a trouvé dix euros. Elle a envie de dépenser les dix euros.

   _____

   _____

3. J'ai une belle moto. Elle me déplace vite en ville.

   _____

   _____

4. Le café m'énerve le plus.

   _____

   _____

5. J'ai un cousin. Mon cousin s'appelle Michel.

   _____

   _____

6. J'ai une belle moto. Tu peux acheter ma moto.

   _____

   _____

29

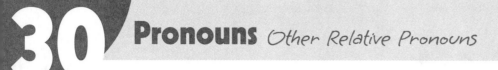
When the relative pronoun is the object of a preposition, *que* and *qui* are not used. Instead, there are different relative pronouns depending on the sentence: *dont, où, lequel, ce dont,* and *ce ... quoi.*

The relative pronoun *dont* indicates possession and usually translates as *that* or *whose.*

> *L'ingredient **dont** j'ai besoin est du beurre.*
> The ingredient **that** I need is butter.

***Ce dont* often replaces the person or thing that follows *de* in certain verbal expressions, such as *parler de* (talk about), *avoir besoin de* (to need), *avoir peur de* (to be afraid of), and *tenir de* (to take after).**

> *Est-ce que tu sais **de quoi il parle**?*
> Do you know **what he's talking about**?

> *Oui, je sais **ce dont** il parle.*
> I know **what** he's talking **about.**
> (Literally, I know **that of which** he speaks.)

***Ce dont* can refer to something that is unstated and unspecified and does not have an antecedent. *Ce dont* replaces *ce duquel* and can often be translated as *that of which* or *the one whose*. *Ce dont* is used when a subordinate clause requires an object introduced by the preposition *de*.**

> *Voici **ce dont** j'ai besoin.*
> Here is **what** I need.
> (Literally, here is **that of which** I have need)

> *J'ai vu la femme **celle dont** le mari est riche.*
> I saw the woman **whose** husband is rich.

> *J'ai doublé le skieur, **celui dont** les skis sont rouges.*
> I passed the skier, the one **whose** skis are red.

The relative pronoun *où* indicates physical location and usually translates as *where*. *Où* is often used to replace the prepositions *dans, à, sur,* and *sous*. *Où* can also be used with adverbs of time to mean *when*.

> *La place de la République, **où** j'ai vécu, est très jolie.*
> Place de la République, **where** I lived, is very pretty.

> *C'est **l'époque où** la vie était facile.*
> The **time when** life was easy.

***Lequel* is a combination of the definite article (*le, la*, and *les*) and the pronoun *quel*. Unlike *dont* and *où*, *lequel* changes form to agree in gender and number with the noun it is replacing.**

	Singular	**Plural**
Masculine	*lequel*	*lesquels*
Feminine	*laquelle*	*lesquelles*

> *C'est la voiture **avec laquelle** je vais au travail.*
> It is the car **with which** I go to work.

***Lequel* is used with the prepositions *à* and *de* to mean *to which* and *of which*. *Lequel* changes form in all but the feminine singular when used with these prepositions.**

	Singular	**Plural**
Masculine	*auquel* *duquel*	*auxquels* *desquels*
Feminine	*à laquelle* *de laquelle*	*auxquelles* *desquelles*

> *C'est la voiture **à laquelle** je pense.*
> That's the car **about which** I think.

> *C'est le pont **duquel** il a sauté.*
> That's the bridge **from which** he jumped.

Attention!

To avoid confusion, the forms of the composite relative pronoun *lequel* can be used to replace *qui* and *dont*.

> *Voici la moto de Luc, **qui** est rapide.*
> Here Luc's bike, **which/who** is fast.
> (*Qui* could refer to Luc or his bike.)

> *Voici la moto de Luc, **laquelle** est rapide.*
> Here is Luc's bike, **which** is fast.
> (*Laquelle* refers to Luc's bike.)

> *Voici la moto de Luc, **lequel** est rapide.*
> Here is Luc's bike, **who** is fast.
> (*Lequel* refers to Luc.)

The relative pronoun *ce à quoi* (or other prepsition replacing *à*) is used when a subordinate clause requires an object introduced by a preposition other than *de*.

Est-ce que tu sais à quoi il pense?
Do you know **what** he's thinking about?

Je sais ce à quoi il pense.
I know **what** he's thinking **about**.
(Literally: I know **that of which** he thinks.)

Exercise 1

Choose the appropriate relative pronoun to complete each of the following sentences.

1. Où est le train_____ j'ai besoin?
   a. dont
   b. où
   c. lequel
   d. laquelle

2. C'est là_____ je travaille.
   a. dont
   b. où
   c. lequel
   d. laquelle

3. Vous êtes la personne avec_____ je veux travailler.
   a. dont
   b. où
   c. lequel
   d. laquelle

4. Ce monument,_____ l'inauguration a eu lieu hier, est fermé aujourd'hui.
   a. dont
   b. où
   c. lequel
   d. laquelle

5. Voilà la chambre dans_____ je dors.
   a. dont
   b. où
   c. lequel
   d. laquelle

6. Voilà la chambre_____ je dors.
   a. dont
   b. où
   c. lequel
   d. laquelle

Exercise 2

Answer each of the following questions by replacing the noun with the appropriate form of the relative pronoun *lequel*, including composite forms with prepositions.

1. C'est l'oiseau_____ je pense.

2. Ce sont des amis_____ je pense.

3. _____ de ces deux glaces préfères-tu?

4. C'est la réponse à_____ je pensais.

5. C'est le taxi_____ il est sorti.

Exercise 3

Translate the following sentences into French using the appropriate relative pronouns.

1. What I need is a pencil sharpener.

   _____

   _____

2. It's what they dream about.

   _____

   _____

3. France is where it is nice to live.

   _____

   _____

4. L'Olympique Lyonnais is a soccer team that the Lyonnais are very proud of.

   _____

   _____

5. Did you ask her what she's thinking about?

   _____

   _____

30

The French pronoun *en* has many uses. At times it can be similar to *of, from there, some of,* or *any of* in English. The pronoun *y* translates as the English *there*. Both of these pronouns, however, precede the verb and function very differently from their English counterparts.

The pronoun *en* replaces a noun or an infinitive verb that is introduced by the preposition *de*.

*Je viens **de Paris**.*	*J'**en** viens.*
I come **from Paris**.	I come **from there**.
*Je rêve **de partir**.*	*J'**en** rêve.*
I dream **of leaving**.	I dream **of it**.

***En* also replaces a noun that is preceded by an expression of quantity, such as *beaucoup* (a lot) or *assez* (enough), or a specific number and the preposition *de*. In these cases, the expression of quantity remains after the verb while the preposition *de* and its objects are replaced by *en*, which precedes the verb.**

*J'ai **beaucoup de boucles d'oreilles**.*	*J'**en** ai **beaucoup**.*
I have lots **of earrings**.	I have **a lot of them**.
*J'ai **deux colliers**.*	*J'**en** ai **deux**.*
I have **two necklaces**.	I have **two of them**.

The pronoun *en* is also used to replace a noun introduced by an indefinite article (*un*, *une*, and *des*), similar to *some* or *any* in English.

*Je veux **des livres**.*	*J'**en** veux.*
I want **some books**.	I want **some**.

***En* can be used to replace the nouns that follow certain verb expressions using *de*.**

s'occuper de	to deal with
parler de	to speak of
remercier de	to give thanks for
revenir de	to come back from
venir de	to come from

*Merci de **vous occuper de ce problème**.*	*Merci de vous **en occuper**.*
Thank you for **dealing with this problem**.	Thank you for **dealing with it**.

The pronoun *y* replaces a noun or an infinitive verb introduced by the prepositions *à, en, dans, devant, derrière, sous,* and *sur*.

*Je vais **à Paris**.*	*J'**y** vais.*
I go **to Paris**.	I go **there**.

*J'étudie **à la Sorbonne**.*	*J'**y** étudie.*
I study **at the Sorbonne**.	I study **there**.
*Allons **à Montpellier**!*	*Allons-**y**!*
Let's go **to Montpellier**!	Let's go **(there)**!
*On va se retrouver **devant** l'hôtel de ville.*	*On **y** va se retrouver.*
We meet **in front of** the town hall.	We meet **there**.

***En* and *y* follow the same placement rules as the direct-object pronouns. They precede the verb, except in the affirmative imperative. In compound tenses, notably the *passé composé*, they precede the auxiliary.**

*Je suis déjà allé **à Montpellier**.*	*Je **y** suis déjà allé.*
I have already gone **to Montpellier**.	I have already gone **there**.

Attention!

When used with the expression *il y a* (there is, there are), *en* is placed between *y* and *a*.

*Est-ce qu'il y a **du pain**?*	*Oui, il y **en** a.*
Is there **any bread**?	Yes, there is **some**.

Attention!

The pronouns *y* and *en* are generally used to replace places, things, or abstract notions but can refer to people in informal speech. The disjunctive pronouns can also be used to replace nouns referring to people or pets.

*Il pense **à Luc**.*	*Il pense **à lui**.*
He thinks **about Luc**.	He thinks **about him**.
*Il pense **à sa voiture**.*	*Il **y** pense.*
He thinks **about his car**.	He thinks **about it**.

Attention!

The preposition *en* should not be confused with the pronoun *en*. A sentence containing the preposition *en* would take the pronoun *y*.

*Je voyage **en** train.*
I travel **by** train.

Exercise 1

Jean-François and Aurélie are having a discussion while eating dinner. Choose the correct pronoun for each of the following responses based on the context of the question.

1. Jean-François: Veux-tu du pain?

Aurélie: Oui, j'_____ veux, s'il te plaît.

2. Jean-François: Est-ce tu veux un verre de vin?

Aurélie: Non, je n'_____ veux pas.

3. Aurélie: Tu connais le café Le Chabrot?

Jean-François: Oui, on peut_____ aller après de

manger pour boire un verre.

4. Aurélie: As-tu regardé les desserts?

Jean-François: Non, pas encore. Mais, on peut s'

_____ intéresser.

5. Jean-François: Souhaites-tu prendre encore du fromage?

Aurélie: Non, j'_____ ai assez.

6. Jean-François: Penses-tu qu'il fera beau demain?

Aurélie: Je n'_____ crois pas.

7. Aurélie: Je n'ai pas payé l'addition. Peux-tu t'en occuper?

Jean-François: Je m'_____ occupe.

Exercise 2

Translate the following sentences into French using the correct pronoun.

1. Let's go (there).

_____

2. I'm going there this weekend.

_____

3. I have enough (of it).

_____

4. Take advantage of it.

_____

5. I don't believe it anymore.

_____

Exercise 3

Answer each of the following questions using either *y* or *en* in your response.

1. Est-ce que tu es déjà allé(e) à Toulouse?

_____

_____

2. Est-ce que tu t'intéresse à la science politique?

_____

_____

3. Est-ce que tu t'occupes de ton linge?

_____

_____

4. Est-ce que tu as des jeux vidéo?

_____

_____

5. Fais-tu attention à ton poids?

_____

_____

31

39 Pronouns On

The French indefinite subject pronoun *on* does not have an exact equivalent in English, but it does have a wide array of uses in French. *On* is mostly informal, and though it is used in writing, it is much more common in speech.

On can represent people in general, like the indefinite pronoun *one* or *you* in English. *On* can also represent people universally.

> *On* n'est jamais trop prudent.
> **One/You** can never be too careful.

> En France, **on** aime aimer.
> In France, **people** love to love.

Sentences using *on* are often translated into English using the passive voice. In these cases, *on* represents *one* or *someone* in general.

> *On* est en train d'apporter le dessert.
> The dessert is being brought.
> (Literally: **One** is in the process of bringing the dessert.)

On often replaces the subject pronouns *je* (I) and *nous* (we) in speech.

> *On* s'y fait.   *On* y va?
> **I**'m getting used to it.   Are **we** going?

Unlike other subject pronouns, *on* must be repeated before each verb in a sentence.

> *On* mange et **on** boit.
> **One** eats and drinks.

On remains third-person singular, regardless of the pronoun or noun it replaces. Verbs, auxiliaries, past participles, adjectives, adverbs, and reflexive or reciprocal pronouns should agree with *on* in the same way that they agree with the third person singular pronouns *il* or *elle.*

> *Nous* nous amusons.   *On* s'amuse.
> **We** enjoy ourselves.   **We** enjoy ourselves.

L'Exception

To be more explicit about the subject, the past participle and adjectives can be made to agree with the noun *on* refers to.

> *On* est bien **arrivées.**
> **We** (feminine) have **arrived** safely.

> *On* est **intelligentes** dans ma famille.
> **We** (feminine) are **smart** in my family.

La Langue Vivante

The expression *on dit* (people say) is a common expression that has become a composite noun: *on-dit* (rumor). It is masculine and invariable in the plural form.

> *On* le **dit** riche, mais ce ne sont que des **on-dit.**
> **People say** he's rich, but that's only a **rumor.**

Exercise 1

Rewrite the following sentences by replacing the subject pronouns with *on*.

1. Je suis contente.

_____

_____

2. Nous n'aimons plus cette série, *Lost.*

_____

_____

3. S'il fait froid, nous mangeons de la soupe.

_____

_____

4. Allons-y!

_____

_____

5. Nous sommes descendues les escaliers.

_____

_____

Exercice 2

Write two possible equivalents, each with a different subject pronoun, for each of the following sentences.

1. On aime chanter.

a. _____

b. _____

2. On aime danser.

a. _____

b. _____

3. On danse et on chante.

a. _____

b. _____

4. Au Canada, on joue souvent le hockey sur glace.

a. _____

b. _____

5. On s'habitue.

a. _____

b. _____

Exercice 3

Translate the following sentences into French using the pronoun *on*.

1. Italian is spoken here.

_____

_____

2. If we don't eat, we are hungry.

_____

_____

3. We are serious.

_____

_____

4. We are serious girls.

_____

_____

5. We arrived yesterday.

_____

_____

6. You never know.

_____

_____

7. I was told to come.

_____

_____

32

Pronoun placement varies greatly from French to English. Unlike in English, a French pronoun is seldom placed in the same position as the noun it replaces.

All pronouns, along with the verbal component and the negation adverbs *ne* and *pas,* follow a specific order.

1. subject pronoun
2. negative *ne*
3. the pronouns *me, te, nous, vous,* and *se*
4. the pronouns *le, la,* and *les*
5. the pronouns *lui* and *leur*
6. the pronoun *y*
7. the pronoun *en*
8. auxiliary verb
9. verb
10. inverted subject pronoun (linked to the verb by a hyphen)
11. negative *pas*
12. past participle
13. indirect-object pronoun (emphatic form)
14. reflexive pronoun (emphatic form)

Je (1) *me* (3) *le* (4) *dis* (9).
I tell it to myself.

Je (1) *le* (4) *lui* (5) *dis* (9).
I tell it to him.

Je (1) *ne* (2) *le* (4) *lui* (5) *dis* (9) *pas* (11).
I do not tell it to him.

Je (1) *me* (3) *parle* (9) *à moi-même* (14).
I talk to myself.

Je (1) *ne* (2) *me* (3) *parle* (9) *pas* (11) *à moi-même* (14).
I do not talk to myself.

Je (1) *lui* (5) *en* (7) *parle* (9).
I tell him about it.

Je (1) *lui* (5) *parle* (9) *d'elle* (12).
I tell him about her.

Je (1) *l'* (4) *y* (6) *ai* (8) *envoyé* (12).
I have sent it there.

En (7) *ai* (8) *-je* (10) *envoyé* (12)?
Have I sent any?

N' (2) *en* (7) *ai* (8) *-je* (10) *pas* (11) *envoyé* (12)?
Have I not sent some?

Attention!

Use the subject and the verb as anchors around which to place the pronouns. Avoid using the pronouns *y* and *en* in the same sentence. Also, watch for confusion when using the first- and second-person plural forms, which are the same for all personal pronouns.

Nous nous *parlons.*
We talk to each other.

Il **nous** *parle de* **nous.**
He tells us about us.

L'Exception

Pronouns do not follow the standard placement rules in the affirmative imperative form. In these cases, the pronoun is linked to the end of the verb by a hyphen.

*Tais-***toi***!*
Be quiet!

*Prenez-***le***!*
Take **it**!

Exercise 1

Correct any mistakes in pronoun placement in the following sentences. Note: Not all sentences include mistakes.

1. Les mangez!

   _____

2. J'y suis allée.

   _____

3. Il n'y a que ma mère pour faire ça!

   _____

4. Il a les posées. (some questions)

   _____

5. Ne les mangez pas!

   _____

6. J'ai en assez.

   _____

Exercise 2

Translate the following sentences into French. Pay close attention to the order of the pronouns.

1. She talks to him about herself.

_____

_____

2. Mine is the best. (feminine object)

_____

_____

3. I cut my hair myself.

_____

_____

4. I cut it (myself).

_____

_____

5. Do you prefer this one or that one? (masculine object)

_____

_____

6. I like that.

_____

_____

7. Don't forget it! It's important.

_____

_____

8. After fifteen minutes, I had enough.

_____

_____

Exercise 3

Put the following parts of speech in the order in which they should appear in a sentence.

1. elle-même débrouillée est elle se

_____

_____

2. ne pas ai en je

_____

_____

3. a pas lus il ne les

_____

_____

4. moi-même me débrouille je

_____

_____

5. les vus vous avez

_____

_____

33

34 Verbs Stems and Endings

Every French verb is composed of a stem and an ending. For example, the word *manger* (to eat) is composed of the stem *mang-* and the ending *-er*.

French verbs are split into three groups, depending primarily on the ending of their infinitive form. Each of these groups includes verbs with irregular forms.

	Infinitive Ending	Examples	Sentence
Group 1	*-er*	*manger* (to eat)	*Je mange.*
Group 2	most *-ir* verbs	*finir* (to finish)	*Je finis.*
Group 3 (mostly irregular verbs)	some *-ir* verbs	*ouvrir* (to open) *dormir* (to sleep) *mettre* (to place)	*J'ouvre.* *Je dors.*
	-re	*mettre* (to place)	*Je mets.*
	-oir	*vouloir* (to want)	*Je veux.*

Attention!

The auxiliary verbs, *être* (to be) and *avoir* (to have), are irregular and are not considered part of a specific verb group.

Verbs are conjugated according to the person and number of the subject, as well as the mood and tense of the sentence. For regular verbs, the ending changes to reflect conjugation, while the stem of the verb remains the same.

*Il **mang**e.* He eats. | *Ils **mang**ent.* They eat. | *Ils **mang**eront.* They will eat.

The ending of a verb changes to express mood, tense, and person.

Mood/Tense/Person	Example
indicative present, second-person singular	*Tu mang**es**.* You eat.
indicative present, third-person plural	*Ils mang**ent**.* They eat.
indicative future, third-person singular	*Il mang**era**.* He will eat.
conditional present, third-person singular	*Il mang**erait**.* He would eat.

Some verb endings that indicate different tenses, moods, and persons can be very similar. Context is often used to determine proper meaning.

indicative present, first-person singular	*Je mang**e**.* I eat.
indicative present, third-person singular	*Il mang**e**.* He eats.
subjunctive present, third-person singular	*Je veux qu'il mang**e**.* I want him to eat.

L'Exception

The stem of some regular French verbs alters in certain forms to accurately represent the pronunciation. A soft *c*, as in the English word *cell*, takes a cedilla, *ç*, before *a, o,* or *u*. In order to represent a soft *g* sound, as opposed to a hard *g* sound, *g* will change to *ge* in front of *a* or *o*.

avan**c**er (to go forward) | man**g**er (to eat)
*J'avan**ç**ai.* | *Je man**ge**ai.*
I went forward. | I ate.

Exercise 1

Translate the following verbs and place them in the appropriate verb group.

to be, to eat, to finish, to go forward, to have, to do

Group 1	Group 2	Group 3	Other Irregular Verbs

Exercise 2

Correct any spelling mistakes in the following sentences. Note: Not all sentences include mistakes.

1. Il commence.

_____

_____

2. Nous avancons.

_____

_____

3. Vous avançez.

_____

_____

4. Elle mangea.

_____

_____

5. Je bougai.

_____

_____

Exercise 3

Complete the crossword puzzle below by providing the French translation of each infinitive.

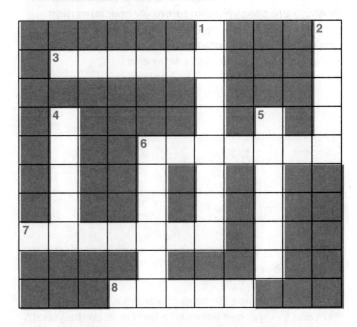

Across
3. to eat
6. to be able to
7. to take
8. to come

Down
1. to translate
2. to go
4. to finish
5. to fall down
6. to lose

34

35 Verbs *Present Tense Regular -er Verbs*

Most French verbs belong to the first (-*er*) group.

To conjugate an -*er* verb in the present tense, the infinitive ending is removed, and the present tense endings are attached to the stem. Almost all verbs of the first group are regular and do not deviate from the standard tense endings: *e, es,* and *e* for singular subjects, and *ons, ez,* and *ent* for plural.

	Singular	Plural
	*j'aim**e*** I **like**	*nous aim**ons*** we **like**
*aim**er*** to like, to love	*tu aim**es*** you **like**	*vous aim**ez*** you **like** (formal or plural)
	*il/elle/on aim**e*** he/she/it/one **likes**	*ils/elles aim**ent*** they **like**

*Est-ce que tu **aimes** skier?*
Do you **like** skiing?

Y usually becomes *i* in front of a silent *e*. However, verbs that end in -*ayer* can either take the *i* or keep the *y*. Both spellings are correct.

payer (to pay)
*Je **paie/paye** 600 euros pour mon logement.*
I **pay** 600 euros for my apartment.

*Nous **payons** 600 euros pour notre logement.*
We **pay** 600 euros for our apartment.

L doubles to *ll* and *t* doubles to *tt* in front of a silent *e*.

appeler (to call)
*Il m'appe**ll**e ce soir, nous vous appelons demain.*
He will call me tonight, we will call you tomorrow.

jeter (to throw)
*Je lui je**tt**e la boule. Nous lui jetons la boule.*
I throw him the ball. We throw him the ball.

When the second-to-last syllable of a verb ends with an accented *é* and the following consonant is followed by a silent *e*, *é* becomes *è*. When the second-to-last or third-to-last syllable ends with *e* and the following consonant is followed by a silent *e*, *e* becomes *è*.

préférer (to prefer)
*Je préf**è**re venir avec toi.*
I prefer coming with you.

se lever (to get up)
*Je me l**è**ve à huit heures.*
I get up at eight.

Attention!

It is possible to form a question in French by inverting the order of the subject and the verb. If the verb is in the first singular person, the final -*e* becomes either -*é* or -*è*. Both spellings are correct.

*Aim**é**-je étudier?/Aim**è**-je étudier?*
Do I like to study?

However, the interrogative construction *est-ce que* is more common for French questions, notably for those involving *je*.

Est-ce que j'aime étudier?
Do I like to study?

The first verb group also includes most so-called new verbs: verbs derived relatively recently, often from foreign words.

informatiser (to computerize)
médiatiser (to promote/expose through the media)
e-mailer (to send an e-mail)

*Ce système **informatisé** permet l'identification de toutes les merchandises envoyées.*
This **computerized** system allows the identification of all received products.

La Langue Vivante

In France, the English noun *e-mail* was originally translated to the French noun *mèl*, then later *courriel*. However, now most French speakers prefer to use the English noun *e-mail* or *mail*. The verb form, *e-mailer* (to send an e-mail), is not as commonly used as the noun form.

Attention!

French does not have progressive tenses (*to be* + the -*ing* form of another verb). As a rule, the progressive present in English is translated as the present tense in French.

*Cette année, **j'étudie** le français.*
This year, I **am studying** French.

The expression *en train de* (literally: *by way of*) is used to emphasize that someone is in the middle of an action.

*Il est **en train d'étudier**.*
He **is (in the middle of) studying**.

Exercise 1

Monique is a student at Chambéry University. Use the correct present-tense conjugation of the verb in parentheses to complete the following passage about her.

(**1.**) Je m' _____(appeler) Monique et j' _____

(étudier) à l'Université de Chambéry. (**2.**) Vivre ici n'est pas trop

cher: le département _____(payer) pour mon logement

et ma famille m' _____(aider) avec mes dépenses

quotidiennes. (**3.**) Chaque jour je me _____(lever) à

sept heures du matin et je prends une douche avant de sortir.

(**4.**) Puis mes copines et moi, nous _____(manger)

un croissant à la cafétéria et nous _____(étudier)

à la bibliothèque avant de commencer les cours.

(**5.**) J' _____(aimer) bien étudier ici parce qu'il est très

facile de se connaître. (**6.**) En fait, je _____(préférer)

vivre dans une communauté où les gens _____

(communiquer) aisément, plûtot que me sentir perdue dans

une grande ville. (**7.**) Il est vrai que parfois on s' _____

(ennuyer) à Chambéry, mais nous _____(apprécier) la

possibilité d'étudier et vivre dans un petit village.

Exercise 2

Translate the following sentences using the correct present-tense verbs.

1. The restaurants downtown usually open at 7:30 p.m. and close at midnight.

   _____

   _____

2. The professor speaks very fast, and I often ask him to repeat.

   _____

   _____

3. Look at (you, plural) the fixed menu, but I suggest ordering four different dishes so we can share them all.

   _____

   _____

4. Every day my brother buys his favorite newspaper.

   _____

   _____

Exercise 3

Combine the following elements to form complete sentences, conjugating verbs in the present tense when necessary.

1. Vendredi / nettoyer / maison / acheter / pain

   _____

   _____

2. Didier / regarder / photo / penser / belle

   _____

   _____

3. Voyager / jamais / amis / cet été / décider / partir ensemble

   _____

   _____

4. Joséphine / appeler / mère / chaque jour

   _____

   _____

5. Aimer / copine / envoyer / cadeau / anniversaire

   _____

   _____

35

To conjugate an *-ir* verb in the present tense, the infinitive ending is removed and the present tense endings are attached to the stem: *is* and *it* for singular subjects and *issons*, *issez*, and *issent* for plural.

	Singular	Plural
finir (to finish)	*je finis* I finish	*nous finissons* we finish
	tu finis you finish	*vous finissez* you finish (formal or plural)
	il/elle/on finit he/she/it/one finishes	*ils/elles finissent* they finish

Quand je finis, nous pouvons y aller.
When I **finish,** we can go.

L'Exception

A number of *-ir* verbs are irregular and do not follow the regular *-ir* conjugation pattern. Instead, these verbs follow the conjugation pattern of regular Group 1 (*-er*) verbs. These irregular *-ir* verbs include *ouvrir* (to open), *couvrir* (to cover), *découvrir* (to discover), *offrir* (to offer), and *souffrir* (to suffer).

	Singular	Plural
ouvrir (to open)	*j'ouvre* I open	*nous ouvrons* we open
	tu ouvres you open	*vous ouvrez* you open (formal or plural)
	il/elle/on ouvre he/she/it/one opens	*ils/elles ouvrent* they open

*Ils **ouvrent** toutes les portes de la maison.*
They **open** every door in the house.

L'Exception

Three other common *-ir* verbs follow an irregular conjugation pattern: *partir* (to leave), *sortir* (to go out), and *dormir* (to sleep).

	Singular	Plural
partir (to leave)	*je pars* I leave	*nous partons* we leave
	tu pars you leave	*vous partez* you leave (formal or plural)
	il/elle/on part he/she/it/one leaves	*ils/elles partent* they leave
sortir (to go out)	*je sors* I go out	*nous sortons* we go out
	tu sors you go out	*vous sortez* you go out (formal or plural)
	il/elle/on sort he/she/it/one goes out	*ils/elles sortent* they go out
dormir (to sleep)	*je dors* I sleep	*nous dormons* we sleep
	tu dors you sleep	*vous dormez* you sleep (formal or plural)
	il/elle/on dort he/she/it/one sleeps	*ils/elles dorment* they sleep

*Chaque jour Michèle **dort** jusqu'à onze heures. Quand elle **sort** de la maison, je **pars** du bureau.*
Every day Michèle **sleeps** until eleven. When she **goes out of** the house, I **am leaving** the office.

Exercise 1

Form complete sentences by conjugating the *-ir* verbs below according to the subject indicated.

1. Marie/dormir

_____

_____

2. mes parents/partir

_____

_____

3. tu/haïr

_____

_____

4. nous/choisir

_____

_____

5. les enfants/ouvrir

_____

_____

Exercise 2

Correct the following verbs with the correctly conjugated form. Note: Not all verbs are incorrect.

1. Mon frère dormit beaucoup.

_____

_____

2. Il finit ses devoirs très tard le soir.

_____

_____

3. Quand il se couche, il ouvrit la fenêtre.

_____

_____

4. Je haïs quand il fait ça!

_____

_____

Exercise 3

Compose a short passage describing a relative, such as a parent or grandparent, using the following *-ir* verbs, conjugated in the present tense.

réussir (to succeed), finir (to finish), obéir (to obey), partir (to leave), se souvenir (to remember)

_____

_____

_____

_____

_____

_____

_____

_____

_____

_____

_____

_____

_____

_____

36

Most verbs ending in *-re* are actually irregular, but many follow a set pattern of irregularity. It is possible to identify the kind of *-re* verb based on its stem and conjugate it according to one of the following categories.

To conjugate a regular *-re* verb in the present tense, the infinitive ending is removed and the present tense endings are attached to the stem: *s* or no ending for singular subjects, and *ons, ez,* and *ent* for plural.

	Singular	Plural
attend**re** (to wait)	*j'attend**s*** I wait	*nous attend**ons*** we wait
	*tu attend**s*** you wait	*vous attend**ez*** you wait (formal or plural)
	il/elle/on attend (**no ending**) he/she/it/one waits	*ils/elles attend**ent*** they wait

*Nous **attendons** le métro.*
We **are waiting** for the subway.

Some common regular *-re* verbs include:

attendre	to wait (for)
défendre	to defend
descendre	to descend, to exit (a mode of transportation)
entendre	to hear
perdre	to lose
prétendre	to claim
rendre	to give back, to return (an item)
répondre	to answer
vendre	to sell

*Et nous **descendons** à Montmartre.*
And we **are getting off** at Montmartre.

The first category of irregular *-re* verbs drops the *d* in the stem in the first- and second-plural person (*nous* and *vous*), and doubles the *n* in the third-plural person (*ils* and *elles*).

	Singular	Plural
prend**re** (to take)	*je prend**s*** I take	*nous pren**ons*** we take
	*tu prend**s*** you take	*vous pren**ez*** you take (formal or plural)
	il/elle/on prend he/she/it/one takes	*ils/elles pren**nent*** they take

*Que **prenez**-vous? Je **prends** un café.*
What are you **having**? I am **having** a cup of coffee.

The second category includes a double *t* in the stem. These verbs drop one *t* in all singular forms (*je, tu, il, elle,* and *on*).

	Singular	Plural
batt**re** (to beat)	*je bat**s*** I beat	*nous batt**ons*** we beat
	*tu bat**s*** you beat	*vous batt**ez*** you beat (formal or plural)
	Il/elle/on bat he/she/it/one beats	*ils/elles batt**ent*** they beat

*Ils sont méchants: Ils **battent** toujours leur pauvre chien.*
They are mean: They always **beat** their poor dog.

The third category also includes words with double-*t* stems. They are conjugated the same as the second group in the present tense, but have different past participles and different forms in the *passé simple*.

	Singular	Plural
mett**re** (to put)	*je met**s*** I put	*nous mett**ons*** we put
	*tu met**s*** you put	*vous mett**ez*** you put (formal or plural)
	il/elle/on met he/she/it/one puts	*ils/elles mett**ent*** they put

***Mets**-toi à la gauche du placard.*
Move to the left of the closet.

The fourth category is conjugated like regular *-re* verbs, with the exception of the third-singular person (*il, elle,* and *on*). In the present tense, these verbs adds a *t* after the stem.

	Singular	Plural
romp**re** (to break)	*je romp**s*** I break	*nous romp**ons*** we break
	*tu romp**s*** you break	*vous romp**ez*** you break (formal or plural)
	il/elle/on rompt he/she/it/one breaks	*ils/elles romp**ent*** they break

*Chaque fois qu'ils viennent, ils **rompent** quelque chose.*
Every time they come, they **break** something.

The fifth category drops the *d* in the stem in all forms and adds a *g* in front of the first *n* of the plural endings (*nous, vous, ils* and *elles*).

	Singular	Plural
peindre (to paint)	*je pein**s*** I paint	*nous pei**gnons*** we paint
	*tu pein**s*** you paint	*vous pei**gnez*** you paint (formal or plural)
	*il/elle/on pein**t*** he/she/it/one paints	*ils/elles pei**gnent*** they paint

*Cet artiste **peint** avec passion.*
This artist **paints** with passion.

Attention!

A sixth group of irregular -*re* verbs have completely unique conjugations. These conjugations follow no set pattern and need to be memorized. The most common verbs among these are *suivre* (to follow), *rire* (to laugh), *connaître* (to know), *boire* (to drink), *plaire* (to like), *aller* (to go), *faire* (to do/to make), *dire* (to say).

*Je **bois** de la bière et vous **buvez** un verre d'eau.*
I **drink** beer and you **drink** a glass of water.

*Est-ce que tu **vas** au Canada cet été?*
Are you **going to** Canada this summer?

Exercise 1

Choose the appropriate -*re* verb to complete each of the following sentences. Conjugate the verbs correctly according to their subject.

abattre (to bring down), corrompre (to corrupt), reprendre (to resume), joindre (to join), remettre (to put back), craindre (to fear)

1. Beaucoup de politiciens _____ les électeurs pour avoir leurs votes.

2. Elle _____ sa vie en main et change de ville.

3. Je _____ ordre dans ma chambre.

4. Vous _____ toutes les barrières culturelles qui vous séparent de nous.

5. Tu _____ le livre à sa place et en prends un autre.

Exercise 2

Find and correct the mistakes in the following sentences.

1. Chaque jour tu m'attend au café.

_____

2. Il prendt le train à six heures.

_____

3. Nous vous entendions parler.

_____

4. Ces artistes peindrent de tableaux magnifiques.

_____

Exercise 3

Your cousin is visiting next week. Write him an e-mail, giving him directions to meet you downtown. Use the following -*re* verbs, conjugating them in the present tense.

prendre (to take), rejoindre (to join), attendre (to wait), descendre (to get off), perdre (to lose), répondre (to answer), vendre (to sell)

_____

_____

_____

_____

_____

_____

37

Many *-er* verbs take regular endings but have two different stems. These verbs, also known as *boot* or *shoe* verbs, are grouped in six categories. Their irregular stems occur in all singular forms (*je, tu, il/elle*) and the third plural person (*ils/elles*) form.

Stem-changing verbs ending in *-ayer* have an optional stem-ending change: *y* may change to *i* in all forms except for *nous* and *vous.*

	Singular	Plural
pa**yer** (to pay)	je pay**e**/pa**ie** I pay	nous pay**ons** we pay
	tu pay**es**/pa**ies** you pay	vous pay**ez** you pay (formal or plural)
	il/elle/on pay**e**/ pa**ie** he/she/it/one pays	ils/elles pay**ent**/pa**ient** they pay

Tu **payes/paies** *ton addition.*
You **pay** your bill.

Verbs ending in *-oyer* or *-uyer* change their stem ending from *-oy* or *-uy* to *-oi* or *-ui* in all forms except for *nous* and *vous.*

	Singular	Plural
nett**oyer** (to clean)	je netto**ie** I clean	nous nettoy**ons** we clean
	tu netto**ies** you clean	vous nettoy**ez** you clean (formal or plural)
	il/elle/on netto**ie** he/she/it/one cleans	ils/elles netto**ient** they clean

Ils ne **nettoient** *jamais leur chambre.*
They never **clean** their room.

Verbs ending in *-eler* change their stem ending from *-l* to *-ll* in all forms except for *nous* and *vous.*

	Singular	Plural
app**eler** (to call)	j'appe**lle** I call	nous appel**ons** we call
	tu appe**lles** you call	vous appel**ez** you call (formal or plural)
	il/elle/on appe**lle** he/she/it/one calls	ils/elles appe**llent** they call

*Il s'***appelle** *Jean.*
His **name** is Jean.

Verbs ending in *-eter* change their stem from *-t* to *-tt* in all forms except for *nous* and *vous.*

	Singular	Plural
j**eter** (to throw)	je je**tte** I throw	nous jet**ons** we throw
	tu je**ttes** you throw	vous jet**ez** you throw (formal or plural)
	il/elle/on je**tte** he/she/it/one throws	ils/elles je**ttent** they throw

Il **jette** *la poubelle.*
He's **throwing** out the garbage.

Stem-changing verbs containing *e* in the second-to-last syllable, except for the *-eler* and *-eter* verbs, take a grave accent on this *e* (*è*) in all forms except for *nous* and *vous.*

	Singular	Plural
cr**ever** (to die, to burst)	je cr**è**ve I die	nous crev**ons** we die
	tu cr**è**ves you die	vous crev**ez** you die (formal or plural)
	il/elle/on cr**è**ve he/she/it/one dies	ils/elles cr**è**vent they die

Ils **crèvent** *de faim.*
They are **starving**.
(Literally: They are **dying** of hunger.)

L'Exception

Though their stems are similar to the other stem-changing verbs described, *geler* (to freeze), *peler* (to peel), and *acheter* (to buy) all take a grave accent on the first *e* (*è*) in all forms except for *nous* and *vous*.

Tu **pèles** *les pommes de terre.*
You **peel** the potatoes.

Il **achète** *une nouvelle voiture.*
He **buys** a new car.

Verbs with an accented *é* in the second-to-last syllable shift the accent to *è* in all forms except for *nous* and *vous.*

	Singular	Plural
	*je consid**è**re* I consider	*nous considér**ons*** we consider
considérer (to consider)	*tu consid**è**res* you consider	*vous considér**ez*** you consider (formal or plural)
	*Il/elle/on consid**è**re* he/she/it/one considers	*ils/elles consid**è**rent* they consider

*Il ne **considère** pas ma situation.*
He doesn't **consider** my situation.

Attention!

Verbs with more than one accented *é* can be tricky. Only the final *é*, the *é* preceding the infinitive ending, changes accent.

*Je préf**è**re manger à huit heures.*
I prefer to eat at eight.

Exercise 1

Complete the crossword puzzle by conjugating the following verbs according to the subject in parentheses.

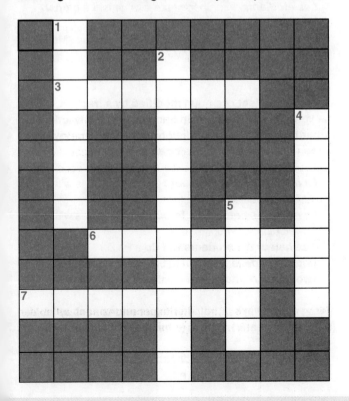

Across
3. to pay (nous)
6. to prefer (je)
7. to clean (je)

Down
1. to call (elle)
2. to consider (nous)
4. to throw (ils)
5. to peel (tu)

Exercise 2

Lucie and Claudine have different points of view on how to spend money. Complete their dialogue by using the correctly conjugated forms of the following verbs.

payer (to pay), préférer (to prefer), appeler (to call), acheter (to buy), jeter (to throw)

Lucie: Mais c'est pas vrai!
Claudine: Mais si! Il m'a laissée là, toute seule.
Lucie: Et qu'est-ce que tu vas faire maintenant?
Claudine: J'_____ mon analyste!
Lucie: Il est où, ton analyste?
Claudine: Rue des Moulins. C'est pas mal du tout.
Lucie: Et combien tu le _____?
Claudine: 100 euros la séance.
Lucie: Tu sais, parfois j'ai l'impression que tu _____ _____ ton argent par les fenêtres.
Claudine: Pourquoi?
Lucie: Je ne sais pas, pourquoi tu ne t'_____ _____ pas quelque chose de joli?
Claudine: Parce que je ne m'_____
pas Paris Hilton et je _____
dépenser mon argent pour quelque chose d'utile!

Exercise 3

Match the verbs in column A with the corresponding English translations in column B.

A	B
_____ **1.** vous considérez	a. I pay
_____ **2.** tu gèles	b. they prefer
_____ **3.** je paie	c. you freeze
_____ **4.** nous jetons	d. we throw
_____ **5.** ils préfèrent	e. you consider

38

As a general rule, French verbs agree in person and number with their subjects. If there are multiple subjects, the verb is plural.

> *Elle travaille avec mon cousin.*
> **She works** with my cousin.

> *Arnaud et Pauline ont acheté une belle maison.*
> **Arnaud and Pauline bought** a beautiful house.

A collective noun is a singular noun that refers to a collection; the collection may be stated (for example, *a packet of letters*) or unstated (for example, *the team*). When a collective noun is followed by a noun (such as *letters*), the verb may be either singular or plural, depending on the emphasis. If the emphasis is put on the collective noun, the verb is singular; if the emphasis is on the individuals making up the collective group, the verb is plural.

> *La multitude* (singular) *des gens marchait* (singular) *dans les rues de la ville.*
> **The group** of people **was walking** in the streets of the city.

> *Une foule de questions* (plural) *lui venaient* (plural) *à l'esprit.*
> A bunch **of questions came** to his mind.

La Langue Vivante

The emphasis placed on a collective noun depends on the intentions of the writer or the intonation of the speaker's voice. Emphasis is hard to detect in the written form and the singular or plural conjugations are mostly interchangeable.

Attention!

Certain collective nouns generally emphasize the individuals composing the group rather than the group collectively and therefore take a plural verb. These include nouns ending in -*aine,* which is a suffix added to numbers to express an approximation, such as *dizaine* (about ten). Others in this category include: *tas* (a lot), *multitude* (multitude), *majorité* (majority), *foule* (crowd, bunch), *infinité* (infinity), *poignée* (handful). However, as in English, the choice of singular or plural is often left to the speaker.

> *Un tas de livres ont* (plural) *été achetés par cet homme.*
> *Un tas de livres a* (singular) *été acheté par cet homme.*
> **A lot of books were** bought by this man.

Agreement is required when the collective noun is intended figuratively or is used without a determinant.

> *Un tas d'idées intéressantes ont surgi lors de la réunion.*
> **A lot** (literally: **an accumulation**) of interesting ideas came up at the meeting.

> *Nombre de questions ont trouvé réponse au cours de la réunion.*
> A **number** (exact number not specified) of questions found an answer during the meeting.

When a noun is modified by an indefinite expression, the verb must agree in number with the noun. Such quantifying expressions would include *la plupart* (most), *beaucoup de* (much of, a lot of), *bien des* (many), *peu de* (little of), *assez de* (enough of), *trop de* (too much of), *tant de* (so much/many), or *combien de* (how much/many). Any adjectives that follow must still agree in gender and number with the noun in quantity.

> *Beaucoup de patience* (singular noun) *sera* (singular verb) *demandée* (singular adjective) *de vous.*
> **Much patience will be required** of you.

Attention!

Some of the indefinite expressions above may replace the noun they refer to, if the noun is understood. In these cases, the verb is conjugated to agree with the noun replaced.

> *Les étudiants se préparent aux examens. La plupart souhaitent* (plural) *faire un doctorat.*
> **The students** are getting ready for their exams. **Most of them want** to do a Ph.D.

When the subject is a noun modified by a fraction, the verb generally agrees in number with the fraction rather than the noun modified by that fraction. However, agreement with the noun is often acceptable.

> *La moitié des étudiants fera* (singular, agrees with *la moitié*) *un doctorat.*
> *La moitié des étudiants feront* (plural, agrees with *des étudiants*) *un doctorat.*
> **One half of the students will do** a Ph.D.
> *Deux tiers de la tarte ont* (plural) *été mangés.*
> **Two thirds of the pie** were eaten.

The verb is always plural after expressions such as *millier* (about a thousand), *million* (a million), *milliard* (a billion).

> *Un million de visiteurs sont arrivés.*
> **One million** tourists **arrived.**

The verb is always singular when the subject is introduced by the phrase *plus d'un* (more than one). The verb is plural when the subject is introduced by the phrase *moins de deux* (less than two).

Plus d'un sera heureux de le savoir.
More than one will be happy to know it.

Moins de deux semaines me *séparent* du voyage.
I am leaving on my trip in **less than two weeks.**
(Literally: **Less than two weeks separate** me from the trip.)

Attention!

When *de* is preceded by a quantifier (*beaucoup, un tas, nombre, une infinité*, etc.), it is always invariable. *De* agrees with the noun that follows only when it is a partitive, and means *some.*

J'ai gagné un million de dollars.
I won a million dollars.

Des enfants jouent dans le parc.
Some children are playing in the park.

Exercise 1

Read the following sentences and conjugate the verb in the tense indicated.

1. Une multitude d'insectes _____ (envahir, passé composé) la prairie.

2. Beaucoup de persévérance _____ (être, future) nécessaire pour terminer ce projet.

3. La plupart de ses collègues _____ (participer, passé composé) à ce type de réunion.

4. La plupart des concurrents, je dirais plutôt tous, _____ (souhaiter, present) entrer dans l'administration.

5. Moins de deux heures _____ (suffire, future) pour terminer cette relation.

Exercise 2

Choose among the following expressions and verbs to compose complete sentences in the present tense that describe each of the pictured scenes.

Expressions:
beaucoup de (much, a lot of), un tas de (a lot of), milliers de (thousands of), quelques (some), une multitude de (a multitude of), la plupart de (most of)

Verbs:
visiter (to visit), admirer (to admire), prendre des photos (to take pictures)

1. _____

2. _____

3. _____

The infinitive is the basic form of a verb, which changes form when conjugated. In English, the infinitive is the *to* form, as in *to eat* or *to sleep*.

The French infinitive is a single word ending in *-er, -i,* or *-re.*

dormir	to sleep
jeter	to throw
manger	to eat
perdre	to lose

The infinitive can be used in the unconjugated form as a noun, either as the subject or as the object of a sentence. In English, this use is usually expressed by a gerund.

> ***Parler*** *avec lui n'est pas facile.*
> **Talking** to him is not easy.

The infinitive can also follow a conjugated verb, with or without a preposition in between, depending on the context.

> *C'est* *facile à* ***croire.***
> It **is** easy **to believe.**

> *Je* ***veux danser*** *avec lui.*
> I **want to dance** with him.

The infinitive can replace an imperative in written commands, instructions, or warnings.

> ***Ajouter*** *du sel et* ***mélanger.***
> **Add** salt and **mix.**

When a main clause has the same subject as the subordinate clause, the infinitive can be used instead of a subjunctive or non-subjunctive verb.

> *Je suis heureux d'y* ***participer.***
> I am happy **to participate** in it.

The infinitive can also be used when a main clause includes an impersonal subject.

> *Il faut le* ***dire.***
> It's necessary **to say** it.

Exercise 1

Complete the following sentences using the appropriate infinitive from the options provided.

reprocher (blame), appeler (to call), pleurer (to cry), tourner (to turn), partir (to leave)

1. _____, c'est mourir un peu.

2. Est-ce que tu peux m'_____ demain?

3. _____ à droite et puis à gauche.

4. Je n'ai rien à me _____.

5. _____ maintenant est inutile.

Exercise 2

Translate the following sentences into English.

1. Manger, boire, et dormir sont des plaisirs simples mais essentiels.

_____

_____

2. Il faut admettre que lire Proust n'est pas facile.

_____

_____

3. Si tu as quelque chose à dire, il faut le faire maintenant.

_____

_____

4. Je n'aime pas jouer au tennis, mais j'adore le regarder.

_____

_____

5. Danser? Non, merci, je préfère rester assis.

_____

_____

Exercise 3

Transform the following imperatives to impersonal commands using the infinitive.

1. Éteignez vos portables!

_____

_____

2. Mets toujours la ceinture de sécurité!

_____

_____

3. Coupe l'oignon très fin!

_____

_____

4. Remettons les livres à ses places!

_____

_____

5. Ne parlez pas au conducteur!

_____

_____

40

Verbs Être

Être (*to be*) is one of the most common French verbs. It is used in many common idiomatic expressions and as an auxiliary verb for compound tenses and the passive voice.

Être is an irregular verb with a completely unique present-tense conjugation, which is not based on the infinitive stem.

	Singular	Plural
être (to be)	je **suis** I am	nous **sommes** we are
	tu **es** you are	vous **êtes** you are (formal or plural)
	il/elle/on **est** he/she/it/one is	ils/elles **sont** they are

*Je **suis** américaine, et vous?*
I **am** American, and you?

Être is used with adjectives, nouns, and adverbs to describe a temporary or permanent state of being.

*Il **est** sympathique.*
He **is** nice.

*Je **suis** à Lyon.*
I'm **in** Lyon.

*Nous **sommes** français.*
We **are** French.

*Il **est** au café.*
He **is** at the cafe.

Être is used to describe someone's profession.

*Je **suis** professeur.*
I **am** a professor.

Attention!

The indefinite article is not used to describe someone's profession with *être*.

*Ma mère **est médecin.***
My mother **is a doctor.**

Être is the auxiliary for many verbs in compound tenses. It is also used to form the passive form.

Passé composé: *Je **suis allé** chez lui.*
I **went to** his place.

Passive form: *Il **est aimé** de tout le monde.*
He **is loved** by everybody.

Être is also used in several common idiomatic expressions, such as c'est or il est.

c'est, il est	it is, that is
ça y est	that's it, it's done
c'est ça	that's it, that's right
c'est/on est/nous sommes (jeudi, le trente mai)	it is (Thursday, May 30)
en être	to take part in
est-ce (que)	it is what? (used to ask questions)
être de	to be at/in (figuratively)
être en train de + infinitive	to be (in the process of) + present participle
il est possible que	it is possible that
N'est-ce pas?	Right? Isn't that so?

C'est difficile à dire.
It's hard to say.

*Il **est possible** qu'il reste avec nous.*
It's possible that he will stay with us.

Attention!

When discussing the weather in French, the verb *faire* is used, rather than *être*.

*Il **fait** beau.*
It's nice out.

*Il **fait** du vent.*
It's windy.

Être can also be used with the preposition à followed by a stressed pronoun to indicate possession.

*Ce chien **est à moi.***
This **is my dog.**

Exercise 1

Translate the following sentences using *être*.

1. That's it, I am going home.

_____

_____

2. It's April 30.

_____

_____

3. Do you study French at the university?

_____

_____

4. I think I know you, right?

_____

_____

Exercise 2

Fill in the blanks using the appropriate form of *être*.

1. Il _____ deux heures de l'après-midi.

2. Mon frère et moi _____ allés au stade hier.

3. Tu _____ journaliste.

4. Vous _____ partis à neuf heures.

5. Je _____ Canadien.

Exercise 3

Juliette just made a new friend. She's putting together an e-mail to describe herself. Translate Juliette's message.

I am a student at the Sorbonne university. I am twenty years old. I am French, but my parents are Russian. They are two very interesting people: my father is a sculptor, my mother is a lawyer. They are both fond of opera, but me, I am more interested in film. I am a fan of Carax, do you know him? He's a real genius, right? What else ... I am fairly good-looking. I am thin but not starved. My hair is blond and my eyes are green. And you? What do you look like? I am curious too ...

_____

_____

_____

_____

_____

_____

_____

_____

_____

_____

_____

_____

Verbs *Avoir*

Avoir (*to have*) is one of the most common French verbs. It is used in many idiomatic expressions and as an auxiliary verb.

Avoir, like *être,* has an irregular present-tense conjugation not based on its infinitive stem.

	Singular	Plural
avoir (to have)	*j'ai* I **have**	*nous* **avons** we **have**
	tu **as** you **have**	*vous* **avez** you **have** (formal or plural)
	il/elle/on **a** he/she/it/one **has**	*ils/elles* **ont** they **have**

Nous **avons** *un enfant.*
We **have** a child.

Avoir means *to have* in most contexts, particularly when expressing possession.

J'ai deux livres.
I **have** two books.

J'ai une idée.
I **have** an idea.

Attention!

The construction *avoir à* can mean *to have to,* though this English expression is more commonly translated by *devoir.*

J'ai à finir mes devoirs.
Je dois finir mes devoirs.
I **have to finish** my homework.

Avoir is used in several idiomatic expressions, many of which are expressed in English with a form of the verb *to be.*

avoir chaud	to be hot
avoir froid	to be cold
avoir faim	to be hungry
avoir soif	to be thirsty
avoir peur de	to be afraid of
avoir raison	to be right
avoir tort	to be wrong
Avoir ... ans	to be ... years old
avoir besoin de	to need
avoir envie de	to feel like
avoir honte	to be ashamed
avoir l'air + adjective	to look + adjective

avoir l'air de + noun	to look like a + noun
avoir mal à la tête, *aux yeux,* *à l'estomac*	to have a headache, an eye ache, a stomachache
avoir mal au coeur	to be sick to one's stomach
avoir sommeil	to be sleepy
en avoir	to have guts/nerve
n'avoir qu'à	to just/only have to
avoir de la chance	to be lucky
avoir l'intention de	to intend to

J'ai de la chance de te connaître.
I **am lucky** to know you.

Tu as froid?
Are you **cold**?

The expression *il y a,* meaning *there is* or *there are,* is very common. It is made up of a subject (*il*), a pronoun (*y*), and *avoir* in the third singular person (*a*). This expression is often followed by an indefinite article or a number plus a noun. The verb is the same for singular or plural quantities, but changes form to reflect tense.

Il y a un chien dans votre jardin.
There is a dog in your garden.

Il y a trois chandelles sur la table.
There are three candles on the table.

Attention!

When followed by a period of time, *il y a* means *ago.*

Je lui ai parlé il y a deux jours.
I talked to him **two days ago.**

Attention!

When *il y a* is used in a negative construction, *n'* is placed in front of *y* and *pas* after *a*. Because this is a negative construction expressing quantity, an indefinite article that follows changes to *de.*

Il n'y a pas d'enfants ici.
There aren't any children here.

Avoir is the auxiliary verb taken by most French verbs in compound tenses.

Passé composé: *J'ai mangé.*
I **ate.**

Exercise 1

Use the proper *avoir* expression to describe the action in the following illustrations.

1. _____

2. _____

3. _____

4. _____

Exercise 2

Translate the following sentences using *avoir* in the proper form.

1. Marie is always cold and her little brother is always hot.

   _____

   _____

2. "Are you hungry?" "No, I am just a bit thirsty."

   _____

   _____

3. "How old are you?" "I am thirty years old."

   _____

   _____

Exercise 3

Read the following sentences and decide whether *être* or *avoir* is used correctly. If the usage is wrong, rewrite the sentence using the correct verb.

1. Charles est onze ans.

   _____

   _____

2. Nous sommes envie de jouer au tennis.

   _____

   _____

3. Je besoinne d'acheter de la viande.

   _____

   _____

42

The *passé composé* is the most common past tense in French. It is a compound verb tense that translates both the preterite (*I finished*) and present perfect (*I have finished*) in English. For most verbs, the auxiliary verb *avoir* (to have) is used, but for some, *être* is used.

The *passé composé* is formed with the present tense of the auxiliary verb *avoir* plus the past participle of the verb being expressed.

	Singular	Plural
parler (to talk)	*j'ai parlé* I (have) talked	*nous avons parlé* we (have) talked
	tu as parlé you (have) talked	*vous avez parlé* you (have) talked (formal or plural)
	Il/elle/on a parlé he/she/it/one (has) talked	*ils/elles ont parlé* they (have) talked

Ils ont parlé tout le soir.
They **talked** the whole night.

Attention!

Verbs (other than *être*) are either transitive or intransitive. The action of a transitive verb is transferred to an object or person. Transitive verbs answer the questions *who?* or *what?* The action of an intransitive verb is not transferred to an object or person. Intransitive verbs, which often describe motion, don't directly answer the questions *who?* or *what?*

All transitive verbs and most intransitive verbs use *avoir* as their auxiliary. However, some intransitive verbs use the auxiliary verb *être*.

Il a couru. (intransitive with *avoir*)
He **ran.**

Il est allé en France. (intransitive with *être*)
He **went** to France.

Nous sommes nés le 15 mai. (intransitive with *être*)
We **were born** on May 15.

The *passé composé* is used to express an action or state of being completed in the past.

As-tu vu Marie ce weekend?
Did you **see** Marie this weekend?

The *passé composé* also describes an action repeated a specific number of times in the past.

Nous avons mangé dans ce restaurant deux fois.
We **ate** in this restaurant twice.

The *passé composé* can be used to express a series of actions completed in the past.

Lundi, il a vu sa copine, a parlé à l'avocat, et a acheté un livre.
On Monday he **saw** his girlfriend, **talked** to his lawyer, and **bought** a book.

The *passé composé* also describes the beginning of an event or action, or a transition from one state to another.

Il a commencé à courir.
He **started** to run.

Attention!

The intransitive verb *naître* (to be born) is active and takes the auxiliary verb *être*.

Je suis né en France. (active voice)
I **was born** in France. (passive voice)

Exercise 1

Trasform the following sentences from the present tense to the *passé composé* using the auxiliary verb *avoir*.

1. Aujourd'hui je lis ton livre.

   _____

   _____

2. Puis je fais mes devoirs.

   _____

   _____

3. Vers midi je vois David.

   _____

   _____

4. Il veut manger à un nouveau café près de l'université.

_____

_____

5. À trois heures, j'appelle Carole pour étudier ensemble.

_____

_____

écrire

3. _____

_____

Exercise 2

The following pictures show what Sabine did while on vacation. Compose sentences using the verb indicated in the _passé composé_ to describe her trip.

prendre

1. _____

_____

manger

2. _____

_____

Exercise 3

What did you do on _your_ vacation? Use the verbs below in the _passé composé_ to describe your last trip.

prendre (to take), arriver (to arrive), explorer (to explore), connaître (to know), inviter (to invite), accompagner (to accompany)

_____

_____

_____

_____

_____

_____

_____

_____

_____

_____

_____

43

Some intransitive verbs form the *passé composé* with the auxiliary verb *être*. This past tense is formed with the present tense of the auxiliary *être* plus the past participle of the verb being expressed.

	Singular	Plural
arriver (to arrive)	*je* **suis arrivé(e)** I **(have) arrived**	*nous* **sommes arrivé(e)s** we **(have) arrived**
	tu **es arrivé(e)** you **(have) arrived**	*vous* **êtes arrivé(e)(s)** you **(have) arrived** (formal or plural)
	il/elle/on **est arrivé(e)** he/she/it/one **(has) arrived**	*ils/elles* **sont arrivé(e)s** they **(have) arrived**

*Il **est arrivé** à Marseille.*
He **arrived** in Marseille.

When conjugating verbs that take *être* in the *passé composé,* or other compound verb form, the past participle must agree in gender and number with the subject. This is not true for verbs that take the auxiliary verb *avoir*.

*Nous étions **arrivés.***
We had arrived.

*Elles sont **venues.***
They came.

All verbs that use *être* as the auxiliary for compound tenses are intransitive. While most intransitive verbs take *avoir*, some, primarily verbs describing motion, require *être*. The following are some of the most common *être* verbs.

aller	to go
arriver	to arrive
descendre (*redescendre*)	to descend, to go downstairs (to descend again, to go downstairs again)
entrer (*rentrer*)	to enter (to enter again)
monter (*remonter*)	to climb (to climb again)
mourir	to die
naître (*renaître*)	to be born (to be born again)
partir (*repartir*)	to leave (to leave again)
passer	to pass, to spend time
rester	to stay
retourner	to return
sortir (*ressortir*)	to go out (to go out again)
tomber (*retomber*)	to fall (to fall again)
venir (*devenir, parvenir, revenir*)	to come (to become, to get to, to come again)

*Elle **est partie.***
She **left.**

*Ils **sont restés.***
They **stayed.**

L'Exception

Not all intransitive verbs of motion take *être* as an auxiliary. Some common verbs of motion that take *avoir* include:

courir (to run)
*Il **a couru.***
He **ran.**

marcher (to walk)
*Il **a marché.***
He **walked.**

quitter (to leave)
*Il **a quitté** la ville.*
He **left** town.

Some verbs have both a transitive and intransitive meaning, depending on the subject. The auxiliary of some of these verbs will change accordingly.

Intransitive:	*Il **s'est promené.*** He **walked.**
Transitive:	*Il **a promené** le chien.* He **walked** the dog.
Intransitive:	*Il **est passé** nous voir.* He **came by** to see us.
Transitive:	*Il **a passé** un examen.* He **took** an exam.

Pronominal verbs, or those introduced by a reflexive or reciprocal pronoun, always take the auxiliary verb *être* in the *passé composé.*

*Il **s'est tué.***
He **killed himself.**

Exercise 1

Change the sentences below from the present to the
passé composé.

1. Aujourd'hui j'arrive chez moi à quatre heures.

_____

_____.

2. Je me prépare un toast et je vais dormir un peu.

_____

_____.

3. Quand je me lève, je me souviens d'appeler Annie.

_____

_____.

4. Vers six heures, je me promène au centre-ville.

_____

_____.

5. Quand je rentre, je me mets une jolie robe et je sors encore avec ma copine.

_____

_____.

Exercise 2

Translate the following passage using the *passé compose* **where appropriate. Note: The auxiliary verb is not always** *être.*

Last week I had fun reading a very interesting article about romantic relationships, and I learned that in order to be happy, you have to keep a certain distance from your partner. I immediately went to see my boyfriend/girlfriend at a cafe because I found this topic quite interesting, but he/she told me: "If you want to keep a distance, let me help: this morning I moved out." I went back to the office and threw the article away.

_____

_____

_____

_____

_____

_____

Exercise 3

The paragraph below describes a family visit to the zoo. Complete the sentences by choosing the appropriate auxiliary verb to form the *passé compose.*

(**1.**) Dimanche dernier mes enfants et moi _____ (aller) au zoo. (**2.**) Nous _____ (voir) beaucoup d'animaux et nous _____ (s'amuser). (**3.**) Philippe, mon petit garçon, _____ (s'approcher) de la cage des lions, mais quand le lion _____ (sortir), il a _____ (courir) vers moi terrorisé et _____ (commencer) à pleurer. (**4.**) Alors je lui _____ (acheter) une glace et tout _____ (redevenir) normal. (**5.**) Martine, elle, ne _____ (avoir peur) quand un singe plus gros qu'elle _____ (poser) une patte sur son épaule. (**6.**) Elle _____ (rire) et _____ (mettre) sa petite main sur l'épaule du singe. (**7.**) Ma femme _____ (prendre) une photo que nous voulons accrocher dans sa chambre. (**8.**) Les parents des autres enfants _____ (venir) nous dire que notre petite Martine est une fillette très courageuse, et moi, je _____ (se sentir) orgueilleux comme un lion!

44

45 Verbs *Plus-Que-Parfait*

The *plus-que-parfait,* or pluperfect, describes an action already completed in the past. In French, it is a compound verb tense formed by combining the imperfect form of an auxiliary verb (*avoir* or *être*) with the past participle. The *plus-que-parfait* corresponds to the English *had* + a past participle, such as *had done something.*

	Singular	Plural
parler (to talk)	*j'avais parlé* I **had talked**	*nous avions parlé* we **had talked**
	tu avais parlé you **had talked**	*vous aviez parlé* you **had talked** (formal or plural)
	il/elle/on avait parlé he/she/it/one **had talked**	*ils/elles avaient parlé* they **had talked**

J'avais parlé de ce que l'on a vu hier.
I **talked** about what we saw yesterday.

The *plus-que-parfait* is used primarily in narration to report events that occurred before another past event took place. The second past event may be either mentioned in the same sentence or implied.

Il n'avait pas mangé (avant de faire ses devoirs).
He **had**n't **eaten** (before doing his homework).

Attention!

The *plus-que-parfait* is sometimes expressed in English in the preterite. However, when it is clear that an action *had* been completed before another one in the same time period, it must be expressed by the *plus-que-parfait* in French.

J'ai acheté le chocolat que vous m'aviez recommandé.
I bought the chocolate that you **had recommended.**
I bought the chocolate that you **recommended.**

The *plus-que-parfait* is also used in *if* clauses to express a hypothetical situation in the past that is contrary to what actually happened. In this sense, the *plus-que-parfait* expresses a wish or a regret about past events. The verb modified by the *si* clause takes the past conditional tense.

Nous y serions allés si nous avions su.
We would have gone if we **had known.**

Exercise 1

Translate the following sentences using the *plus-que-parfait.*

1. I had just returned from my vacation when I received your call.

_____

_____.

2. She bought several art books that she had studied in college.

_____

_____.

3. The hotel had lost our reservation.

_____

_____.

4. You and Marthe had already cleaned the entire house before I came back.

_____

_____.

5. Baby Paul was already born when his father got to the hospital.

_____

_____.

Exercise 2

You just got back from a recent trip and are talking with a friend about what you did. Answer his questions by using the *plus-que-parfait* in complete sentences.

1. Quels préparatifs avais-tu déjà faits une semaine avant le départ?

_____

_____.

2. Est-ce que tu avais déjà visité cet endroit? Quels pays avais-tu déjà visité?

_____

_____.

3. Est-ce tu avais déjà fait un voyage comme celui-ci? Quel type de logement avais-tu préféré en passé?

_____

_____.

4. Avant de partir, qu'est-ce que tu avais projété de faire pendant le séjour?

_____

_____.

5. Avais-tu jamais pensé d'aimer le pays que tu as visité au point de vouloir y vivre? Est-ce que ça t'était jamais arrivé avant cette expérience?

_____

_____.

Exercise 3

Compose sentences in the _plus-que-parfait_ to describe what Jean-Louis had already done by lunchtime yesterday.

Il n'était même pas midi et ...

1. _____

_____.

2. _____

_____.

3. _____

_____.

4. _____

_____.

5. _____

_____.

45

46 Verbs *The Passé Simple*

The *passé simple* is a unique literary form expressing the past in a narrative context. It is only used in formal writing and, in extremely rare cases, in very formal speech.

The *passé simple* for verbs in Group 1 (*-er* verbs) is formed by removing the infinitive ending and adding the *passé simple* endings.

	Singular	Plural
parler (to talk)	je parl**ai** I talked	nous parl**âmes** we talked
	tu parl**as** you talked	vous parl**âtes** you talked (formal or plural)
	Il/elle/on parl**a** he/she/it/one talked	ils/elles parl**èrent** they talked

Ils **parlèrent** de Madame Le Blanc.
They **talked** about Madame Le Blanc.

Regular verbs in Groups 2 and 3 remove the infinitive endings and add the appropriate endings.

	Singular	Plural
finir (to finish)	je fin**is** I finished	nous fin**îmes** we finished
	tu fin**is** you finished	vous fin**îtes** you finished (formal or plural)
	il/elle/on fin**it** he/she/it/one finished	ils/elles fin**irent** they finished
rendre (to return)	je rend**is** I returned	nous rend**îmes** we returned
	tu rend**is** you returned	vous rend**îtes** you returned (formal or plural)
	il/elle/on rend**it** he/she/it/one returned	ils/elles rend**irent** they returned

Le petit Nicolas **finis** l'école au mois de juin.
Little Nicolas **finished** school in June.

Some *-ir* and *-re* verbs have an irregular stem in the *passé simple*. Common examples include:

Infinitive	*Passé Simple* Stem
s'asseoir (to sit down)	s'ass-
conduire (to drive)	conduis-
dire (to say)	d-
écrire (to write)	écriv-
faire (to do, to make)	f-
joindre (to join)	joign-
mettre (to put)	m-
naître (to be born)	naqu-
peindre (to paint)	peign-
prendre (to take)	pr-
rire (to laugh)	r-
voir (to see)	v-

Most irregular *-ir* and *-re* verbs whose past participle ends in *-u* use the past participle as their *passé simple* stem. The *passé simple* endings for these verbs are *-s, -s, -t, -^mes, -^tes,* and *-rent*.

Infinitive	Past Participle Stem
avoir (to have)	eu-
boire (to drink)	bu-
connaître (to know)	connu-
courir (to run)	couru-
croire (to believe)	cru-
devoir (to have to)	du-
falloir (to be necessary)	fallu-
lire (to read)	lu-
pleuvoir (to rain)	plu-
pouvoir (to be able to)	pu-
recevoir (to receive)	reçu-
savoir (to know)	su-
valoir (to be worth)	valu-
vivre (to live)	vécu-
vouloir (to want)	voulu-

L'Exception

Être (to be), *mourir* (to die), and *venir* (to come) take the following irregular forms in the *passé simple*.

	être	mourir	venir
je	fus	mourus	vins
tu	fus	mourus	vins
il	fut	mourut	vint
nous	fûmes	mourûmes	vînmes
vous	fûtes	mourûtes	vîntes
ils	furent	moururent	vinrent

Exercise 1

Change the following sentences from the present to the *passé simple* tense.

1. Tu ne crois jamais à ce que te dis.

_____

_____.

2. Tu penses que ton point de vue est le seul qui compte.

_____

_____.

3. Et puis tu finis toutes nos conversations en haussant les paules.

_____

_____.

4. Mais j'en ai ras le bol, et je pars demain.

_____

_____.

5. Tu n'y crois pas, mais c'est ce que je vais faire.

_____

_____.

Exercise 2

You're putting together a biography of your grandfather (*pépé*) Pierre. Use the *passé simple* to describe the events of his youth in the following illustrations.

1. _____

2. _____

3. _____

46

The future tense is used to discuss events that will happen at a future point. The future has only one set of endings for all verb groups. Most verbs, even many irregular verbs, use their infinitive as the stem for the future tense.

To form the future tense of verbs whose infinitive ends in -er or -ir, the future endings are added to the infinitive.

	Singular	Plural
parler (to talk)	je parler**ai** I will talk	nous parler**ons** we will talk
	tu parler**as** you will talk	vous parler**ez** you will talk (formal or plural)
	il/elle/on parler**a** he/she/it/one will talk	ils/elles parler**ont** they will talk
finir (to finish)	je finir**ai** I will finish	nous finir**ons** we will finish
	tu finir**as** you will finish	vous finir**ez** you will finish (formal or plural)
	il/elle/on finir**a** he/she/it/one will finish	ils/elles finir**ont** they will finish

*Je ne **parlerai** plus jamais avec lui.*
I **will** not **talk** to him anymore.

*Ils **finiront** ce projet l'année prochaine.*
They **will finish** this project next year.

For verbs whose infinitive ends in -re, the final e of the infinitive is dropped before adding the future endings.

	Singular	Plural
rendre (to return)	je rendr**ai** I will return	nous rendr**ons** we will return
	tu rendr**as** you will return	vous rendr**ez** you will (formal or plural) return
	il/elle/on rendr**a** he/she/it/one will return	ils/elles rendr**ont** they will return

*Vous nous **rendrez** l'argent dans deux mois.*
You **will return** our money in two months.

Many verbs have irregular stems in the future tense but still take the regular future endings. Some common verbs of this type are listed below.

Infinitive	Future stem
acheter (to buy)	*achèter-*
appeler (to call)	*appeller-*
aller (to go)	*ir-*
avoir (to have)	*aur-*
devoir (to have to)	*devr-*
envoyer (to send)	*enverr-*
essayer (to try)	*essaier-/essayer-*
être (to be)	*ser-*
faire (to do, to make)	*fer-*
pleuvoir (to rain)	*pleuvr-*
pouvoir (to be able to)	*pourr-*
savoir (to know)	*saur-*
venir (to come)	*viendr-*
voir (to see)	*verr-*
vouloir (to want)	*voudr-*

*Quand tu **auras** ton enfant, nous **irons** à la plage tous ensemble.*
When you **have** your baby, we **will** all **go** to the beach together.

*On se **verra** quand elle le **voudra**.*
We **will see** each other when she **wants**.

Exercise 1

You're enjoying a lazy Friday afternoon. Your friend is asking if you did the following things, but you are not doing much today. Say no, and then use the future tense to say that you will do these things in the future.

Example: Tu as envoyé le courier?
<u>Non, je l'enverrai demain/la semaine prochaine/mardi matin, etc.</u>

1. Tu viens ce soir?

_____

_____

2. Tu es allé voir le dentiste?

_____

_____

3. Tu as appelé tes parents?

_____

_____

4. Tu as fini ton projet?

_____

_____

5. Tu as fait la vaisselle?

_____

_____

Exercise 2

Combine the elements and conjugate the verb below to form complete sentences using the future tense.

Example: Je/aller dans le parc/pleuvoir.
                 <u>J'irai dans le parc s'il ne pleuvra pas.</u>

1. Tu/lire un bon livre/retourner du bureau

_____

_____

2. Sophie/finir un e-mail/Berthe dormir

_____

_____

3. Joseph et Marie/regarder un film/arriver à la maison

_____

_____

4. Nous/être/chez nous/tout le soir

_____

_____

5. Vous/prendre l'avion/partir pour l'Allemagne

_____

_____

Exercise 3

A fortune-teller recently told you about some unexpected things that will happen to you. Use the following verbs to explain what she said about your future.

attendre (to wait for), arriver (to arrive), faire démarrer (to start something), comprendre (to understand), demander (to ask), commencer (to start), connaître (to know), devenir (to become), faire (to do, to make), fréquenter (to attend, to see), rencontrer (to meet), partir (to leave), permettre (to allow)

_____

_____

_____

_____

_____

_____

_____

_____

_____

_____

_____

_____

The imperfect tense describes actions that repeated or continued in the past. It is often translated into English as *used to do, was doing*, or *would do*. Most commonly the English imperfect uses *was* or *were* plus the gerund, or *-ing*, form of the verb, such as in *she was running*.

Verbs in all groups form the imperfect by removing the *-ons* ending from the present-tense *nous* form and adding the imperfect endings.

	Singular	Plural
	*je parl**ais*** I talked	*nous parl**ions*** we talked
parler (to talk)	*tu parl**ais*** you talked	*vous parl**iez*** you talked (formal or plural)
	*il/elle/on parl**ait*** he/she/it/one talked	*ils/elles parl**aient*** they talked

***Être* is the only irregular verb in the imperfect tense. *Être* has an irregular stem (*ét-*) but uses the same imperfect endings as regular verbs.**

	Singular	Plural
	j'étais I was	*nous étions* we were
être (to be)	*tu étais* you were	*vous étiez* you were (formal or plural)
	il/elle/on était he/she/it/one was	*ils/elles étaient* they were

The imperfect is used to describe an ongoing state of being or a repeated or incomplete action in the past. The beginning and end of the state or action are not indicated.

> *Elle ne me **rendait** jamais mes poupées.*
> She never **used to return** my dolls.

The imperfect tense expresses habitual and repetitive past actions, or actions continuous over a certain period of time in the past.

> *Chaque dimanche il **venait** me voir.*
> Every Sunday he **visited/would visit** me.

The imperfect tense is used to describe qualities, such as physical, mental, or emotional states, of people and things in the past.

> *Il **était** toujours fatigué.*
> He **was** always tired.

The imperfect tense is used to describe weather, time, and age in the past.

> *Quand j'**avais** sept ans, je **jouais** avec mes copains.*
> When I **was** seven, I **used to play** with my friends.

The imperfect is often used to describe past actions in progress while another event was taking place. The other event may be in the *passé composé* tense or imperfect tense.

> *J'**étais** au marché et j'**ai acheté** (passé composé) des pommes.*
> I **was** at the market and **I bought** some apples.

> *Je **dormais** pendant que tu **lisais** (imperfect).*
> I **was sleeping** while you **were reading.**

Attention!

The imperfect tense of the expression *être en train de* can be used to emphasize that someone was in the middle of doing something.

> *Il **était en train d'étudier** quand je suis arrivé.*
> He **was in the middle of studying** when I arrived.

Attention!

In order to keep the soft sound, verbs ending in *-cer* and *-ger* take a minor spelling change in the imperfect. The *c* in *-cer* verbs changes to *ç* before the endings beginning with *a*, and the *g* in *-ger* verbs changes to *ge* before the endings beginning with *a*.

> *Quand il était petit, Max **mangeait** peu, **lançait** son assiette par les fenêtres, et **étudiait** la nuit.*
> When Max was young, he **used to eat** little, **would throw** his plate out the window, and **studied** at night.

The imperfect is used to describe wishes or suggestions, as well as conditions in *if* clauses. When an *if* clause modifies another, the verb in the main (result) clause takes the conditional.

> *Si j'**avais** le temps, j'**irais** au Canada.*
> If I **had** time, I **would go** to Canada.

Exercise 1

Change the following sentences from the present tense to the imperfect tense.

1. Aujourd'hui je me lève à neuf heures et je vais au bureau.

_____

_____

2. Je viens chez toi pour un café et j'achète un croissant pour Pierre.

_____

_____

3. Quand j'arrive, il y a toujours beaucoup de travail qui m'attend.

_____

_____

4. Avant de commencer, je passe un coup de fil à ma mère et je bavarde avec mes collègues.

_____

_____

Exercise 2

Complete the following passage describing Julie by inserting the correct imperfect form of *avoir* or *être* based on the subject.

(**1.**) Quand elle _____ trois ans, Julie

_____ une petite fille belle et sympathique.

(**2.**) Elle _____ brune et _____ les

yeux bleus. (**3.**) À douze ans Julie _____ les

cheveux noirs et elle n' _____ plus très heureuse:

elle _____ toujours amoureuse et triste parce

que ses amours n' _____ jamais capables

de retourner son amour. (**4.**) Julie _____

beaucoup de problèmes avec les garçons de son âge, elle

_____ une adolescente comme les autres. (**5.**)

A vingts ans Julie _____ les cheveux rasés et

elle _____ un tas d'amis qui l'aimaient bien. (**6.**)

Elle n'_____ plus seule et elle _____

toujours satisfaite des choses qu'elle _____.

Exercise 3

Translate the following sentences using the imperfect tense.

1. Yesterday the weather was really cold.

_____

_____

2. When I was younger, I didn't like it.

_____

_____

3. Every winter my family went to the country.

_____

_____

4. We took many walks and slept a lot.

_____

_____

48

As a general rule, the imperfect describes past actions or conditions that were continuous in the past. The *passé composé* describes events that occurred at a specific time and were completed in the past or that maintain a link to the present.

Imperfect:	*Enfant, j'**étais** rarement malade.* As a child, I **was** seldom ill.
Passé composé:	*Enfant, j'**ai été** malade cinq fois.* As a child, I **was** sick five times.

More specifically, the imperfect is used to describe habits or patterns. The *passé composé* is used to describe a succession of completed actions that took place during a precise period of time or for a definite number of times in the past.

Imperfect:	*Il **étudiait** souvent le soir.* He often **studied** in the evening.
Passé composé:	*Il **a étudié** pendant trois mois.* He **studied/has studied** for three months.

The imperfect is usually translated in English as a progressive past form when describing an ongoing event in the past (such as *was walking*). The imperfect is often used in a sentence with the *passé composé* to express an ongoing action interrupted by a sudden event.

*Il **pleuvait** (imperfect) et j'**écoutais** (imperfect) la pluie.*
It **was raining** and I **was listening** to the rain.

*J'**écoutais** (imperfect) la pluie quand il **est arrivé** (passé composé).*
I **was listening** to the rain when he **arrived.**

Exercise 1

Change the following sentences from the *passé composé* to the imperfect. Add expressions of time to indicate habit or repetition.

1. Ce matin j'ai dormi jusqu'à dix heures.

_____

_____

2. L'été dernier nous sommes allés à la mer.

_____

_____

3. Quand j'ai terminé l'école, j'ai fait un voyage merveilleux.

_____

_____

4. Cet après-midi j'ai pris un café avec Sylvain.

_____

_____

5. Je n'ai jamais menti.

_____

_____

Exercise 2

Julien recently went to Paris. Complete the following paragraph describing his trip by filling in the correct tense (imperfect or *passé composé*) of the verbs in parentheses.

(**1.**) Quand il _____ (habiter) à Paris, Julien

_____ (être) toujours triste. (**2.**) Il _____

(faire) un froid de loup, il _____ (pleuvoir)

toujours, et Julien ne _____ (savoir) pas quoi

faire pour passer le temps. (**3.**) Un jour il _____

(rencontrer) un étudiant qui, comme lui, _____

(étudier) à la Sorbonne. (**4.**) Ils _____ (devenir)

amis et ils _____ (commencer) à se fréquenter

chaque jour. (**5.**) Ils _____ (aller) manger au

restaurant, _____ (se promener) sur la Seine,

_____ (aimer) la même musique et les mêmes

livres. (**6.**) Leur amitié _____ (grandir) et ils

_____ (continuer) à se voir même quand ils

_____ (quitter) Paris et _____

(retourner) chez eux.

Exercise 3

Last Wednesday was such a beautiful spring day that you decided to take a walk in the park. While you were there, something extraordinary happened. Complete the following story using either the imperfect or the *passé composé*, depending on the context.

1. Mercredi il faisait très beau, par conséquent je _____

   _____

   _____

2. J'étais en train de marcher dans le parc quand _____

   _____

   _____

3. C'était la première fois que _____

   _____

   _____

4. Après avoir échangé quelques mots _____

   _____

   _____

5. Et enfin _____

   _____

49

The future anterior is a compound future tense form that describes an action to be completed in the future. It corresponds to the English *will have done*.

The future anterior is a compound verb formed by the future form of the auxiliary verb (*avoir* or *être*) plus the past participle.

	Singular	Plural
parler (to talk)	*j'***aurai parlé** I **will have talked**	*nous* **aurons parlé** we **will have talked**
	tu **auras parlé** you **will have talked**	*vous* **aurez parlé** you **will have talked** (formal or plural)
	il/elle/on **aura parlé** he/she/it/one **will have talked**	*ils/elles* **auront parlé** they **will have talked**
aller (to go)	*je* **serai allé(e)** I **will have gone**	*nous* **serons allé(e)s** we **will have gone**
	tu **seras allé(e)** you **will have gone**	*vous* **serez allé(e)s** you **will have gone** (formal or plural)
	il/elle/on **sera allé(e)** he/she/it/one **will have gone**	*ils/elles* **seront allé(e)s** they **will have gone**

*Quand j'***aurai terminé** *mon discours, vous pourrez poser vos questions.*
When I **have finished** my speech, you will be able to ask your questions.

The future anterior is used to describe an action that will have happened or will be finished by a specific point in the future.

Je **serai parti** *à midi.*
I will **have left** at noon.

Quand tu arriveras, ils **auront** *déjà* **mangé.**
When you arrive, they **will have** already **eaten.**

In subordinate clauses introduced by the conjunctions *aussitôt que* (as soon as), *dès que* (as soon as), *lorsque* (when), *quand* (when), *une fois que* (once), and *après que* (after), the future anterior expresses a future action which will be completed before the action in the main clause. These actions are usually expressed in the present tense or past tense in English.

Ils le feront aussitôt qu'elle **sera partie.**
They will do it as soon as she **has left.**

La Langue Vivante

The future anterior is often used to make simple assumptions regarding past events.

Mon frère n'est pas ici; il **aura oublié.**
My brother isn't here; he **must have forgotten.**

Exercise 1

Compose complete sentences using the future anterior form of each verb below.

1. venir (to come)

_____

_____

2. perdre (to lose)

_____

_____

3. appeler (to call)

_____

_____

Exercise 2

Marc has a problem and has written you a letter asking for your advice. Choose between the verbs in parentheses and complete the letter by conjugating them in the future anterior.

Cher ...

Je t'écris parce que tu es mon meilleur ami et je suis sûr que

tu pourras comprendre ma situation. (**1.**) Tu sais que dans

une semaine je _____ (être marier/se

promener) avec Mireille. (**2.**) Dès que nous _____

(terminer/commencer) les travaux dans la maison, nous

_____ (aller/quitter) à Londres.

(**3.**) Nous y _____ (passer/visiter) deux

mois. (**4.**) Lorsque nous _____ (enseigner/

perfectionner) notre anglais, nous _____

(partir/aller) pour New York chercher un boulot. (**5.**) Après que

nous _____ (devenir/avoir) riches, nous

_____ (partir/retourner) ici. Tout le monde

dit que ce que nous voulons faire est complètement fou. Et toi,

qu'est-ce que tu en penses?

Marc

Exercise 3

What will you have done by this time tomorrow? Complete the following statements using the verbs provided below.

travailler (to work), manger (to eat), aller (to go), boire (to drink), rêver (to dream)

Example: À six heures demain matin ... j'aurai déjà mangé.

1. À dix heures demain matin ...

_____

2. À trois heures demain ...

_____

3. À cinq heures demain ...

_____

4. À huit heures demain soir ...

_____

5. À minuit demain ...

_____

Exercise 4

Choose the correct form of the future anterior from among the options provided.

1. Après qu'elle _____ ses courses, elle rentrera.
 a. aura fait
 b. aura faite
 c. sera fait
 d. sera faite

2. Elles _____ vers sept heures.
 a. auront finies
 b. seront finies
 c. auront fini
 d. seront fini

3. Ce soir il_____ ces deux projets.
 a. aura terminés
 b. sera terminé
 c. aura terminé
 d. sera terminés

4. Marie partira après que tu lui_____ au revoir.
 a. sera dite
 b. sera dit
 c. aura dite
 d. aura dit

5. Est-ce que vous _____ avant moi?
 a. serez arrivés
 b. serez arrivé
 c. aurez arrivés
 d. aurez arrivé

50

In French, as in English, verbs have three different characteristics that can determine their form: tense (the time the action takes place), voice (active or passive), and mood (the attitude of the subject). The most common mood is the indicative, which describes facts and indicates certainty or objectivity. The conditional mood generally expresses possibility, often dependent on certain conditions. In English, the conditional mood is usually expressed with *would*.

To form the present conditional of -*er* verbs and most -*ir* verbs, the conditional ending is added to the infinitive. For most -*re* verbs, the final *e* is dropped from the infinitive before the conditional ending is added.

	Singular	Plural
parler (to talk)	je parler**ais** I would talk	nous parler**ions** we would talk
	tu parler**ais** you would talk	vous parler**iez** you would talk (formal or plural)
	il/elle/on parler**ait** he/she/it/one would talk	ils/elles parler**aient** they would talk
rendre (to return)	je rendr**ais** I would return	nous rendr**ions** we would return
	tu rendr**ais** you would return	vous rendr**iez** you would return (formal or plural)
	il/elle/on rendr**ait** he/she/it/one would return	ils/elles rendr**aient** they would return

*M'**appellerais-tu** à deux heures, s'il te plaît?*
Would you **call** me at two, please?

*J'**aimerais** partir pour l'Inde.*
I **would like** to leave for India.

Attention!

The endings in the conditional are the same as the endings in the imperfect tense.

*Je finir**ais** ce travail, mais je n'en ai pas le temps.*
I **would finish** this job, but I don't have time.

Verbs that have irregular stems in the future tense use the same irregular stems in the conditional. These verbs take the standard conditional endings.

Infinitive	Conditional stem
acheter (to buy)	*achèter-*
appeler (to call)	*appeller-*
aller (to go)	*ir-*
avoir (to have)	*aur-*
devoir (to have to)	*devr-*
envoyer (to send)	*enverr-*
essayer (to try)	*essaier-*
être (to be)	*ser-*
faire (to do, to make)	*fer-*
pleuvoir (to rain)	*pleuvr-*
pouvoir (to be able to)	*pourr-*
savoir (to know)	*saur-*
venir (to come)	*viendr-*
voir (to see)	*verr-*
vouloir (to want)	*voudr-*

The conditional mood is primarily used to express a hypothetical situation in the main clause of an *if* statement. It is often paired with a verb in the imperfect tense.

*Je **mangerais** (conditional) si j'**avais** (imperfect) faim.*
I **would eat** if I **were** hungry.

The conditional mood is used to express modality (desires, wants, needs, requests, suggestions) in French. In English, modality is usually expressed with auxiliaries such as *would*, *could*, *may*, *might*, or *must*. When used in the conditional, *vouloir* (to want) expresses a polite request or desire, *devoir* (to have to) expresses a modest necessity, and *pouvoir* (to be able to) expresses possibility or a very polite request.

*Il **devrait venir**, je pense.*
He **should be coming**, I think.

*****Pourrais**-tu me **passer** le sel?*
Could you **pass** salt?

Attention!

The conditional mood can be used to make certain indicative expressions more polite.

Indicative Expression
*il se **peut*** (it **may** be)

puis-je (**may** I?)

pouvons-nous (**may** we?)

Conditional Expression
*il se **pourrait*** (it **might** be; expresses a lesser possibility)

pourrais-je (**might** I?; more polite)

pourrions-nous (**might** we?; more polite)

*Il se **pourrait** qu'il vienne.*
He **might** come.

Pourrais-je emprunter ce livre ?
Might I borrow this book?

As in English, the conditional present also serves to express something that would occur later in time than a previously expressed action.

| Future indicative: | *Il dit qu'il **viendra.*** |
| | He says he **will come.** |

| Conditional: | *Il a dit qu'il **viendrait.*** |
| | He said he **would come.** |

Attention!

The verb *aimer* (to love) used in the conditional mood is used to express a polite desire, sometimes one that cannot be fulfilled.

J'aimerais bien te voir, mais je dois travailler.
I would love to see you, but I have to work.

Exercise 1

So many things, so little time! Use the present conditional to say that each person would do the first action provided but can't because of the second action.

1. Anne/préparer un bon dîner/faire les courses

_____

_____

2. Laure/aller au cinéma/être seule

_____

_____

3. Robert/promener son chien/être malade

_____

_____

Exercise 2

What would you do with the items listed below? Form complete sentences using the present conditional of the verbs provided.

1. Un aéronef/faire

_____

2. Un kilo de diamants/vendre/donner

_____

3. Un petit tigre/amener

_____

Exercise 3

You are at a restaurant in the village of Saint Paul de Vence, and you have a few requests for the waiter. Express your requests politely by rewriting the following sentences in the present conditional.

1. Apportez-moi le menu!

_____

2. Quel est le meilleur vin?

_____

3. Je préfère du blanc.

_____

51

The French past conditional is used to express actions that would have occurred in the past under different circumstances or events that are not guaranteed to occur in the future.

The past conditional is formed with the auxiliary verb (*avoir* or *être*) conjugated in the conditional present plus the past participle.

	Singular	Plural
parler (to talk)	*j'aurais parlé* I would have talked	*nous aurions parlé* we **would have talked**
	tu aurais parlé you **would have talked**	*vous auriez parlé* you **would have talked** (formal or plural)
	il/elle/on aurait parlé he/she/it/one **would have talked**	*ils/elles auraient parlé* they **would have talked**
aller (to go)	*je serais allé(e)* I **would have gone**	*nous serions allé(e)s* we **would have gone**
	tu serais allé(e) you **would have gone**	*vous seriez allé(e)s* you **would have gone** (formal or plural)
	il/elle/on serait allé(e) he/she/it/one **would have gone**	*ils/elles seriont allé(e)s* they **would have gone**

Tu aurais parlé pendants des heures!
You **would have talked** for hours!

Tu serais venu à huit heures.
You **would have come** at eight.

The past conditional is often used in the main (or result) clause of *if* statements to express what would have happened if another event had taken place. The unmet condition in the subordinate clause is expressed in the *plus-que-parfait*.

Il serait passé s'il l'avait su.
He **would have** come by if he had known.

Attention!

The past conditional can also be used in a sentence when an unmet condition is implied.

J'y serais allé à ta place.
I **would have gone** in your place.

The past conditional is used to express an unrealized desire in the past.

Elles auraient aimé te voir, mais c'était trop tard.
They **would have loved** to see you, but it was too late.

The past conditional can also describe an uncertain or unverified fact. This specific use is often seen in news reports.

La bombe aurait fait six victimes.
The bomb **would have caused** six casualties.

Exercise 1

Read each of the following scenarios. What would you have done if in these situations? Express your answer using the past conditional.

1. André voulait devenir peintre, mais un jour il a vu une exposition de Nicolas-Henri Jardin et il a changé d'avis et il est devenu architecte. Comment aurais-tu réagi?

   _____

   _____

2. L'été dernier Monique est tombée en skiant et s'est rompue une jambe. À partir de ce moment, elle n'a plus skié. Qu'aurais-tu fait?

   _____

   _____

3. Daniel travaillait dans une agence immobilière et avait une passion pour le piano. Il faisait beaucoup de concerts et venait de commencer une carrière prometteuse comme pianiste. Un jour, son chef lui a dit qu'il aurait dû partir au Japon et Daniel a démissionné. Aurais-tu fait la même chose?

_____

_____

Exercise 2

Combine the elements to say what you would, could, or should have done, using the past conditional.

Example: Lundi dernier/aller chez le médecin/dormir/rater le rendez-vous
Lundi dernier j'aurais dû aller chez le médecin, mais j'ai dormi jusqu'à midi et j'ai raté mon rendez-vous.

1. Hier soir/pouvoir aller dormir/voir un film

_____

_____

2. Ce matin/vouloir prendre l'autobus/se réveiller tard

_____

_____

3. Enfant/devoir comprendre/être facile

_____

_____

4. L'été dernier/vouloir partir/avoir un accident

_____

_____

5. Il y a une minute/vouloir donner un bisou/être à la maison

_____

_____

Exercise 3

You are telling a friend what the following people said they would have done at your party. Form complete sentences as shown in the example.

Example: César arrivera tard.
César a dit qu'il serait arrivé tard.

1. Sonia portera du vin.

_____

_____

2. David pensera à la musique.

_____

_____

3. Marc achètera de la bouffe.

_____

_____

4. Sylvie retournera de la mer à temps.

_____

_____

5. Sabine dansera comme une folle.

_____

_____

52

In French, as in English, verbs have three different characteristics: tense (the time the action takes place), voice (active or passive), and mood (the attitude of the subject). The most common mood is the indicative, which describes facts and indicates certainty or objectivity. The subjunctive mood expresses doubt, uncertainty, possibility, or personal opinion on the part of the subject. The subjunctive mood can also be used to express emotion or desire, or to offer suggestions.

The subjunctive is generally used in a subordinate clause introduced by the conjunction *que* (that) or *qui* (who). The main clause preceding it is usually in the indicative mood.

| main clause (indicative) | + | *que/qui* | + | subordinate clause (subjunctive) |

*Je crains **que ma mère soit fatiguée.***
I am afraid **that my mother is tired.**

The subjunctive is formed by adding the appropriate subjunctive endings to the plural third person (*ils/elles*) present tense stem of the verb.

	Singular	Plural
*aim**er*** (to love)	*(que) j'aim**e*** I love	*(que) nous aim**ions*** we love
	*(que) tu aim**es*** you love	*(que) vous aim**iez*** you love (formal or plural)
	*(que) il/elle/on aim**e*** he/she/it/one love(s)	*(que) ils/elles aim**ent*** they love
*fin**ir*** (to finish)	*(que) je fin**isse*** I finish	*(que) nous fin**issions*** we finish
	*(que) tu fin**isses*** you finish	*(que) vous fin**issiez*** you finish (formal or plural)
	*(que) il/elle/on fin**isse*** he/she/it finish(es)	*(que) ils/elles fin**issent*** they finish

Attention!
The subjunctive forms of many Group 3 verbs are composed from irregular stems and need to be memorized.

When a verb expressing emotion or desire, offering a suggestion, or giving an order is present in the main clause, the subjunctive is often used in the subordinate clause.

*Je **préfère** que tu **viennes** à huit heures.*
I **prefer** that you **come** at eight.

The subjunctive is used to express doubt, uncertainty, possibility, and eventuality.

*Il n'est pas sûr qu'ils **puissent** participer.*
It's not certain that they **can** participate.

*Je l'invite à condition que son frère **vienne** aussi.*
I am inviting her on the condition that her brother **comes** too.

Attention!
Some of the more common expressions requiring a subordiante clause in the subjunctive include:

à condition que	provided that
à moins que	unless
afin que	so that
avant que	before
bien que	even though
jusqu'à ce que	until
pour que	so that
quoi que	no matter what
quoique	even though
sans que	without

Bien que *tu sois malade, tu dois travailler.*
Even though you are ill, you have to work.

Attention!
The verbs *penser* (to think), *espérer* (to hope), and *croire* (to believe) do not take the subjunctive.

*Je **pense** que tu es jolie.*
I **think** you are cute.

The subjunctive is often used after a main clause in which a superlative is present, or after the words *premier* (first), *dernier* (last), or *seul* (only).

*C'est le **meilleur** livre que je **connaisse**.*
It is the **best** book (that) I **know.**

*Tu es la **seule** personne qui **lise** ces livres.*
You are the **only** person who **reads/to read** these books.

Exercise 1

It's election time, and a few issues are up for debate. Indicate your opinion on each of the following issues by choosing between the affirmative and negative expressions and then completing each sentence with the subjunctive.

1. les citoyens / aller voter aux élections politiques.

Il faut que _____

_____ .

2. aujourd'hui les femmes / être plus protégées qu'autrefois.

Je pense que _____

_____ .

3. les travailleurs / vouloir protester pour leurs droits.

Je crois que _____

_____ .

4. tu / s'informer avant de voter.

Je suis sûr(e) que _____

_____ .

5. les politiciens / faire face aux problèmes de leur électorat.

Il est important que _____

_____ .

Exercise 2

You want your friend Luc to get more involved in the community. Conjugate the following infinitive verbs using the subjunctive to suggest what he could do.

Tu vois, je veux que tu

1. _____ (avoir) confiance en les jeunes.

2. _____ (faire) un effort pour ta communauté.

3. _____ (dire) ton opinion.

4. _____ (aller) aux débats politiques.

Exercise 3

Sophie has some problems with the people in her town. In the following paragraph, cross out the incorrect verbs and replace them with the correct subjunctive or indicative conjugation.

(**1.**) Sophie pense que nous ne respectons _____ pas notre ville. (**2.**) Elle regrette que nous n'avons _____ pas envie d'obéir aux règles civiques les plus fondamentales quand nous n'utilisons _____ pas la poubelle pour nos déchets et que nous abîmions _____ les forêts de notre pays. (**3.**) Sophie est convaincue que l'éducation civique et écologique est _____ essentielle pour que la mentalité des gens change, mais elle pense aussi qu'aucune structure éducative existante peut _____ faire ça d'une façon satisfaisante. (**4.**) Mais elle n'est pas complètement découragée: il faut que les gens redécouvrissent _____ la valeur de la nature et des villes dans lesquelles ils habitent, et elle croit qu'une bonne politique communautaire modifisse _____ l'état des choses.

53

A verb participle is a verb form that is used as an adjective.

As in English, each verb in French has both a present and a past participle.

*L'étudiant **lisant** ce livre est intelligent.* (present)
The student **reading** this book is smart.

*Le livre **lu** par mon ami est* Bonjour Tristesse. (past)
The book **read** by my friend is *Bonjour Tristesse.*

As a general rule, present participles are formed by replacing the first-person plural (*nous*) ending of the indicative present (*-ons*) with the ending *-ant.*

	Present-tense *Nous* Form	Present Participle
aimer (to like)	**aim**ons (we like)	aim**ant** (liking)
finir (to end)	**finiss**ons (we end)	finiss**ant** (ending)
attendre (to wait)	**attend**ons (we wait)	attend**ant** (waiting)

L'Exception

Être and *avoir* are commonly used verbs that have irregular present-participle forms and are not based on the first-person plural form of the verb.

	Present-tense "We" Form	Present Participle
être (to be)	sommes	ét**ant** (being)
avoir (to have)	avons	ay**ant** (having)

Present participles are often used as subordinate conjunctions to describe an action that occurs simultaneous to another action. In these cases, the present participles are invariable and do not change form to agree with the subject.

*La fille **courant** vers nous **est** ma nièce.*
The girl **running** towards us **is** my niece.

Attention!

Present participles are used more extensively in English than in French. In French, it is more common to use conjunctions, such as *que, qui, lequel, dont,* or *où,* plus the conjugated verb, or to use noun forms not based on the verb. In some cases, as in English, it is also possible to use an infinitive, rather than the present participle.

*Je l'ai vu **qui lisait** ce livre.*
*Je l'ai vu **lire** ce livre.*
I saw him **read** this book.

When present participles are used as normal adjectives and not as subordinating conjunctions, they agree in gender and number with the subject.

aimant (present participle)
*La soeur de Luc est une femme très **aimante*** (adjective).
Luc's sister is a very **loving** woman.

Attention!

When used verbally and not as simple adjectives to describe nouns, present participles can be directly followed by a direct or indirect object, an adverb, or an adverbial group.

*des femmes **aimant cet** homme*
women **loving this** man

*des femmes **aimant passionnément***
women **loving passionately**

The present participle of the auxiliaries *avoir* and *être* can be combined with the past participles of other verbs. In this case, it has a past tense meaning and can also express the passive voice.

*un ami **ayant lu** le livre* (past)
a friend **having read** the book

*un livre **étant lu*** (passive)
a book **being read**

Exercise 1

Rewrite the following sentences using the appropriate present participle: either verbally (as a subordinating conjunction) or as a simple adjective describing a noun.

1. Elle a appelé à l'avance et elle est arrivée à huit heures du matin.

_____

_____

2. Gérard était en retard et on n'a pas pu partir.

_____

_____

3. Elles sont des filles qui aiment beaucoup.

_____

_____

4. Ces filles ont du talent et donnent beaucoup de concerts.

_____

_____

5. Il les a vus pendant qu'ils arrangeaient leur rendez-vous.

_____

_____

Exercise 2

Give the corresponding present participles of the verbs provided below.

1. étudier (to study) _____

2. finir (to finish) _____

3. avoir (to have) _____

4. être (to be) _____

5. venir (to come) _____

Exercise 3

Use the present participles from Exercise 2 along with the elements below to form complete sentences.

rater un examen (to fail an exam)
discuter (to discuss)
louer un appartement (to rent an apartment)
retourner chez soi (to go back home)
aimer le froid (to like the cold weather)

1. _____

_____

2. _____

_____

3. _____

4. _____

_____

5. _____

_____

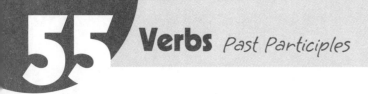

Verbs *Past Participles*

The past participle is generally equivalent to the past tense form of an English verb (as in, *spoke* or *finished*). The past participle has many uses in French.

The past participle is formed by removing the ending from the infinitive form, and adding the appropriate past participle ending. For most regular -*er* and -*ir* verbs, the ending is simple: -*é* for -*er* verbs and -*i* for most -*ir* verbs.

manger (to eat)	*mang**é*** (eaten)
finir (to finish)	*fin**i*** (finished)

Verbs in Group 3 generally form their past participles by adding -*i*, -*is*, -*t*, or -*u* to their infinitive stem, depending on the verb. Because of the irregular nature of the verbs of this group, each past participle has to be memorized individually.

Infinitive	Past participle
aller (to go)	*allé* (gone)
dire (to say)	*dit* (said)
devoir (to have to)	*dû* (had to)
dormir (to sleep)	*dormi* (slept)
entendre (to hear)	*entendu* (heard)
faire (to do)	*fait* (done)
mettre (to put)	*mis* (put)
pouvoir (to be able to)	*pu* (been able to)
voir (to see)	*vu* (seen)
vouloir (to want)	*voulu* (wanted)
prendre (to take)	*pris* (taken)
venir (to come)	*venu* (come)

Attention!

Avoir (to have to) and *être* (to be) also have irregular past participles: *eu* (had) and *été* (been).

Past participles can be used as adjectives to modify nouns, either alone or following the verb *être*. In this case, they act as normal adjectives and agree in gender and number with the subject.

*Monique est **fatiguée.***
Monique is **tired.**

The past participles can be used alone. In these cases, they agree in gender and number with the noun they refer to.

***Fatiguée** par une longue journée, Léa dort.*
Tired from a long day, Léa is sleeping.

Past participles can also be used to describe the cause specified in the main sentence.

*Sa journée **terminée,** Luc dort.*
His day **having ended,** Luc is sleeping.

Attention!

The past participle of *devoir* (*to have to*) is *dû* in the masculine. The feminine and plural forms of this participle (*due, dus, dues*) do not have an accent.

*Le projet est **dû** lundi.*
The project is **expected** on Monday.

*Tes excuses sont **dues.***
Your apologies are **expected.**

L'Exception

Used alone as a question, response, or interjection, the past participle is invariable, such as for *entendu* or *compris* (*understood*) or *terminé* (*ended*).

*Elle doit partir, **compris**?*
She must leave, **understood**?

When used in front of a noun or *que* (*that*) and not describing a specific noun, the following past participles are invariable: *attendu* (*waited*), *y compris* (*included*), *non inclus* (*not included*) *excepté* (*except for*), *ôté* (*subtracted*), *ouï* (*heard*), *passé* (*past*), *supposé* (*supposed*), and *vu* (*seen*).

*Ils dorment tous, **y compris** Léa.*
They are all sleeping, **including** Léa.

***Vu** ses problèmes, Léa a quitté la ville.*
In light of her problems, Léa left town.

The past participle is used after the infinitive of *avoir* to form a past-tense form of the participle.

*Après **t'avoir vu,** Hélène m'a appelé.*
After **seeing you/having seen you,** Hélène called me.

Attention!

When the direct-object pronouns *le, la,* and *les* precede the infinitive *avoir* in a participial construction, the past participle agrees in gender and number with the pronoun.

*Je t'avais remercié de les avoir **invités.***
I had thanked you for having **invited** them.

Exercise 1

Rewrite the sentences below using the past participle, as shown in the example.

Example: Tu bois tout le lait et puis tu peux sortir.
<u>Ayant bu tout le lait, tu peux sortir.</u>

1. Écoute cette chanson, puis chante avec moi.

_____

_____

2. J'écris ces questions, puis je réponds.

_____

_____

3. Quand je trouve les lettres, je m'en vais.

_____

_____

4. Je considère tes résultats et je dis que tu n'as pas étudié.

_____

_____

5. Si on mange tous les bonbons, on se sent mal.

_____

_____

Exercise 2

Use the correct past-participle forms of the following verbs to complete the sentences below.

vendre (to sell), aller (to go), arriver (to arrive), préférer (to prefer), avoir (to have), connaître (to know), monter (to go up)

1. Hier Francine a _____ une journée très intense.

2. À neuf heures elle est _____ faire les courses au marché.

3. Une heure plus tard, elle est _____ dans le bus pour aller au centre-ville.

4. Elle a toujours _____ l'autobus au métro; elle n'aime pas voyager dans les tunnels.

5. _____ dans le magasin, elle a_____ un galériste qui aime beaucoup son travail, et elle lui a _____ tous ses tableaux.

Exercise 3

Choose the correct option to complete each sentence.

1. _____ nous allons au parc.
   a. Après mangeant
   b. Après avoir mangé
   c. Après manger

2. _____ ça sera plus rapide.
   a. Ayant trouvée la solution,
   b. Ayant trouvé la solution,
   c. Ayant trouver la solution,

3. _____ je sors.
   a. Ayant envoyé les lettres,
   b. Ayant envoyés les lettres,
   c. Ayant envoyées les lettres,

4. _____ tu peux partir.
   a. Ayant photocopis les papiers,
   b. Ayant photocopier les papiers,
   c. Ayant photocopié les papiers,

55

The gerund is a form of the present participle of the verb and corresponds to the *-ing* verb form used as a noun in English. A gerund is used to describe an action related to and simultaneous with the action of the main verb. In English, it would often be used with *while* or *upon*.

The gerund has two tenses: the present tense, simple form, and the past tense, compound form. The present-tense gerund is formed with the construction *en* plus the present participle.

Present participle: *Je vois un homme **courant** dans la rue.*
I see a man **running** in the street.

Gerund: *Je lis un livre **en courant** dans la rue.*
I read a book **while running** in the street.

Attention!

While the present participle modifies a noun, the gerund describes something related to a verb.

*J'**ai vu** Muriel **sortant** (present participle) du bureau.*
I **saw** Muriel **leaving** the office. (I **saw** her **as** she **was leaving**.)

*J'**ai vu** Muriel **en sortant** (present-tense gerund) du bureau.*
I **saw** Muriel **upon leaving** the office. (I **saw** her **when** I **was leaving**.)

If two or more gerunds are used in a sentence, *en* is repeated before each one.

*Je mange **en lisant**, **en écoutant** la radio, et **en** te parlant.*
I eat while **reading**, **listening** to the radio, and **talking** to you.

The past-tense gerund is formed by combining the gerund of the auxiliary *être* or *avoir* plus the past participle of the verb.

*Elle a grossi en **n'ayant** jamais trop **mangé.***
She got fat **without eating (having eaten)** too much.

The gerund, particularly in the past tense, is also used to explain how or why something happens. Similar to the English construction *having* + past participle, the past tense gerund expresses an action that has caused another action.

*Il est très fatigué **ayant marché** toute la journée.*
He is very tired, **having walked** the whole day.

Attention!

In English, the gerund functions as a noun, either as a subject or object, and often describes an action in general. In French, however, the gerund is not used in these cases. Instead, either the infinitive or a noun not based on the verb form would be used.

***Lire** est un plaisir.*
Reading is a pleasure. (Literally, **To read** is a pleasure.)

***La lecture** de ce livre est un plaisir.*
Reading this book is a pleasure.
(Literally, **The reading** of this book is fun.)

Exercise 1

Translate the following sentences using the gerund.

1. Paul heard a child screaming while leaving the house.

_____

_____

2. He ran to him calling the police.

_____

_____

3. While talking to him, Paul understood the situation.

_____

_____

4. Paul started laughing while hanging up.

_____

_____

5. He patted the child on his head, promising to buy him a new balloon.

_____

_____

Exercise 2

You love multitasking, and this fast-paced society is moving just your way. What things, and how many, can you do simultaneously? Look at the following prompts and complete the sentences using the gerund.

1. Je parle au telephone avec mon ami en _____

_____.

2. Je fais la cuisine en _____

_____.

3. Je prends ma douche en _____

_____.

4. Je fais mes courses en _____

_____.

5. Je dîne en _____

_____.

Exercise 3

But you are not a superhero! Use the gerund to say what you do when *not* doing the following things.

1. Je ne bouge pas en _____

_____.

2. Je ne peux pas m'asseoir en _____

_____.

3. Je n'arrive pas à me concentrer en _____

_____.

4. Je ne bois jamais en _____

_____.

5. Je ne dîne pas au restaurant en _____

_____.

56

The action of a reflexive verb refers back to the subject performing it. The reflexive verb is formed by adding the reflexive pronoun *se* to the beginning of the verb. Some common reflexive verbs in French include:

s'approcher de	to approach
s'asseoir	to sit down
se baigner	to bathe, swim
se brosser	to brush
(les cheveux, les dents)	(one's hair, teeth)
se casser (la jambe)	to break (one's leg)
se coiffer	to fix one's hair
se coucher	to go to bed
se couper	to cut oneself
se déshabiller	to get undressed
se doucher	to take a shower
se fâcher	to get angry
s'habiller	to get dressed
se laver	to wash
(les mains, la figure)	(one's hands, face)
se lever	to get up
se maquiller	to put on makeup
se marier (avec)	to get married (to)
se moquer de	to make fun of
se moucher	to blow one's nose
se peigner	to comb one's hair
se raser	to shave
se regarder	to look at oneself
se reposer	to rest
se réveiller	to wake up
se souvenir de	to remember

The reflexive pronouns *me* (myself), *te* (yourself), *se* (himself/herself/themselves), *nous* (ourselves), and *vous* (yourselves), always precede a conjugated reflexive verb and agree with the subject.

	Singular	Plural
	je m'amuse	*nous nous amusons*
	I enjoy myself	we enjoy ourselves
s'amuser (to enjoy oneself)	*tu t'amuses*	*vous vous amusez*
	you enjoy yourself	you enjoy yourselves (formal and plural)
	il/elle/on s'amuse	*ils/elles s'amusent*
	he/she/it/one enjoys himself/herself/itself/oneself	they enjoy themselves

*Je **me souviens** de toi.*
I **remember** you.

Attention!

Me, *te*, and *se* become *m'*, *t'*, and *s'* in front of a vowel or mute *h*.

*Le petit André **s'habille** tout seul.*
Little André **gets dressed** all by **himself**.

*Tu **t'amuses** beaucoup.*
You **have fun** a lot.

Reflexive verbs can also appear in the infinitive form.

*Je cherche à **me souvenir** de toi.*
I'm trying **to remember** you.

When using a reflexive verb to ask a question, the expression *est-ce que* is more often used than subject-verb inversion or intonation. When asking a question using inversion, the reflexive pronoun precedes the inverted construction.

*Est-ce que tu **te laves** les cheveux tous les jours?*
***Te laves**-tu les cheveux tous les jours?*
*Tu **te laves** les cheveux tous les jours?*
Do you **wash your** hair every day?

Attention!

Unlike in English, possessive adjectives are rarely used to refer to a part of the body in French. Instead, the reflexive pronoun is used to indicate possession and the definite article is used in front of the part of the body.

*Je **me lave** les mains.*
I'm **washing my** hands.

Exercise 1

Translate the following sentences. Note: Not all verbs are reflexive.

1. Every day Christine gets up at seven.

   _____

   _____

2. She takes a shower, gets dressed, and has breakfast.

   _____

   _____

3. Then she gets ready to leave, but only after a very strong coffee.

   _____

   _____

4. When she arrives at the office, she sits down at her desk and starts making phone calls.

   _____

   _____

5. At night, she returns home very tired and usually falls asleep at ten.

   _____

   _____

Exercise 2

Give the opposite reflexive verb of the following verbs.

Example: se lever: <u>s'asseoir</u>

1. être ambitieux: _____

2. se stresser: _____

3. s'ennuyer: _____

4. se réveiller: _____

5. se baigner: _____

Exercise 3

Use reflexive verbs to write a paragraph describing your typical daily routine.

_____

_____

_____

_____

_____

_____

_____

_____

_____

_____

_____

_____

57

Reflexive verbs always take the auxiliary verb *être* in the *passé composé*. The reflexive past participle and the reflexive pronoun agree in gender and number with the subject, except when the reflexive pronoun is an indirect object.

> *Simone et Charlotte **se sont levées** tôt.*
> Simone and Charlotte **got up** early.

> *Elles **se sont acheté** une belle voiture.*
> They **bought themselves** a nice car.

L'Exception

When a reflexive verb refers to an indirect object, the past participle does not change to agree with the reflexive pronoun.

> *Elle s'est **dit la vérité**.*
> She **told** herself **the truth**.

Attention!

The reflexive pronoun can be a direct object referring back to the subject, notably in some cases where a transitive verb is followed by a prepositional phrase.

> ***Elle s'**est occupée du chien.*
> **She** took care of the dog.
> (Literally, **She** occupied **herself** with the dog.)

When a reflexive verb is used in the infinitive, the reflexive pronoun agrees with the subject and precedes the infinitive.

> *Je vais **m'habiller**.*
> **I'm** going **to get dressed**.

When a reflexive verb is used in the imperative, a disjunctive, or emphatic, a pronoun is used. The pronoun is placed after the verb and linked to it with a hyphen. The reflexive pronouns *me* and *te* change to the stressed pronouns *moi* and *toi* in the imperative.

> *Réveille-**toi**!*
> Wake up!

Attention!

In the indicative mood, the reflexive pronoun always precedes the verb, regardless of verb tense.

> *Nous **nous moquions** de vous.*
> We **used to make fun** of you.

> *Ils **se reposeront** demain.*
> They **will rest** tomorrow.

> *Nicole **se marierait** immédiatement.*
> Nicole **would get married** right away.

Exercise 1

Yesterday, Martine had a very full day. Use reflexive verbs in the past tense to describe what she did in each of the following pictures.

1. _____

_____

2. _____

_____

2. Elle a téléphoné à sa copine et s'est _____ (se mettre) à pleurer.

3. Puis elle s'est _____ (se dire), "Mais pourquoi ne pas profiter de la situation?"

4. Martine s'est _____ (se regarder) dans la vitrine d'une boutique et s'est souri.

5. "Vas-y," a-t-elle pensé. "Tu t'es _____ (se tromper) de gare, mais tu peux quand même t'amuser!"

3. _____

_____

Exercise 3

Yesterday was a very important day for Lucie: She had her first job interview for an important company. Use the following reflexive expressions to describe her exciting adventure.

se laver les dents   se serrer la main
s'asseoir dans le métro   se dire au revoir
se présenter

Example: <u>Hier Lucie s'est lavé les dents avec un soin particulier.</u>

4. _____

_____

1. _____

_____

2. _____

_____

3. _____

_____

5. _____

_____

4. _____

_____

Exercise 2

Complete the following sentences by filling in the correct past participle of the reflexive verbs in parentheses.

1. Martine ne s'est pas _____ (se souvenir) de descendre à Paris.

58

Some verbs change meaning in reflexive expressions. Many of these verbs are not reflexive in English.

Non-reflexive verb	Reflexive verb
aller (to go)	*s'en aller* (to go away)
amuser (to amuse)	*s'amuser* (to have a good time)
appeler (to call)	*s'appeler* (to be named)
arrêter (to stop somebody or something)	*s'arrêter* (to stop oneself)
demander (to ask)	*se demander* (to wonder)
débrouiller (to disentangle)	*se débrouiller* (to manage, get by)
dépêcher (to send quickly)	*se dépêcher* (to hurry)
diriger (to be in charge of)	*se diriger vers* (to move toward)
éloigner (to move something away)	*s'éloigner* (to move oneself away)
endormir (to put to sleep)	*s'endormir* (to fall asleep)
ennuyer (to bother)	*s'ennuyer* (to be bored)
entendre (to hear)	*s'entendre* (to get along)
fâcher (to make angry)	*se fâcher* (to get angry)
habituer (to get in the habit of)	*s'habituer à* (to get used to)
inquiéter (to alarm)	*s'inquiéter* (to worry)
installer (to install)	*s'installer* (to settle in, to move in)
mettre (to place, to put)	*se mettre à* (to begin to)
perdre (to lose)	*se perdre* (to get lost)
promener (to take for a walk)	*se promener* (to take a walk)
rendre compte de (to account for)	*se rendre compte de* (to realize)
réunir (to gather, to collect)	*se réunir* (to meet, to get together)
tromper (to deceive)	*se tromper* (to be mistaken)
trouver (to find)	*se trouver* (to be located)

*Le taxi **se dirigeait** vers la campagne.*
The taxi was **heading toward** the country.

*Cette femme **trompe** son mari depuis cinq ans.*
This woman **has been cheating** on her husband for five years.

Exercise 1

Christine and Jeanne have just moved to a new house. Translate the following sentences describing their first day.

1. Elles viennent de s'installer dans leur nouvelle maison.

2. Elles ont installé une nouvelle télévision dans le séjour.

3. Jeanne a mis tous ses livres sur l'étagère de sa chambre.

4. Christine s'est mise à nettoyer la cuisine.

5. Christine et Jeanne se sont amusées à préparer leur premier dîner.

Exercise 2

Provide the correct French translation, conjugating the verb according to the subject indicated, for each of the following phrases. Note: Not all verbs are reflexive.

1. she headed toward _____

2. they went away _____

3. I lose _____

4. he stops _____

5. they (feminine) managed _____

6. I wonder _____

7. they (masculine) will get angry _____

8. you (familiar) began to _____

9. you (familiar) hear _____

10. she made a mistake _____

Exercise 3

Complete the following sentences by choosing among the reflexive verbs provided and conjugating them according to the context. Note: When using the *passé composé,* change the past participle when necessary.

se laver (to wash), s'habiller (to get dressed), se succéder (to follow), s'appeler (to be called), se lever (to get up), se promener (to take a walk), s'envoler (to fly away)

1. Cette fille _____ Justine.

2. Chaque jour Katie _____ à six heures,

_____, _____, et

_____ dans le parc.

3. Hier soir Luc est sorti avec Muriel. Les minutes

_____, les heures _____,

et il a complètement oublié de rentrer.

The voice of a sentence can be either active or passive, depending on whether the subject or the object of the verb is emphasized. French uses the active and passive voices in much the same way as English.

In an active-voice construction, the subject of the sentence performs the action, and the object receives it. In the passive voice, the subject is being acted upon by the object (also called the agent). The passive voice is often used when reporting facts and summarizing what happened in a certain situation.

Active: ***Mathieu lit*** *le journal.*
           Mathieu is reading the newspaper.

           Une jeune fille a écrit *ce livre.*
           A young girl wrote this book.

Passive: ***Le journal est lu*** *par Mathieu.*
           The newspaper is read by Mathieu.

           Ce livre a été écrit *par une jeune fille.*
           This book was written by a young girl.

The passive voice is formed with the verb *être* plus the past participle of the main verb. The agent is not always mentioned in a passive voice construction. When the agent is mentioned, it is introduced by a preposition: in general, *par* (by) when describing action and *de* (by) when describing a state of being.

Le pain **est fait par Ludivine.**
Bread **is made by Ludivine.**

Le pain de Ludivine ***est aimé de tout le monde.***
Ludivine's bread **is loved by everybody.**

Attention!

The past participle agrees in gender and number with the subject of *être*, not the agent.

Les courses *sont* ***faites*** *par Chantal.*
Shopping is **done** by Chantal.

Attention!

The following common verbs are followed by the preposition *de* in the passive voice:

aimer	to love
détester	to detest
haïr	to hate
respecter	to respect
admirer	to admire
craindre	to fear
couvrir	to cover

Attention!

Only transitive verbs can be put in the passive voice.

Active: *Je* ***mange un croissant.***
               I **eat a croissant.**

Passive: ***Le croissant est mangé***
               par moi.
               The croissant is eaten by me.

The passive voice can be used in all tenses and moods.

Les devoirs **sont faits** (present tense) *par Betty.*
Homework **is done** by Betty.

Il faut que les devoirs **soient faits** (subjunctive mood) *par Betty.*
It is necessary that homework **is done** by Betty.

Les devoirs **seront faits** (future tense) *par Betty.*
Homework **will be done** by Betty.

The passive voice has a formal tone in French and is used less frequently than in English. The expression *c'est* is often used as an alternative to the passive voice to emphasize either the performer or the recipient of the action.

Ce livre a été écrit par une jeune fille.
This book was written by a young girl.

C'est une jeune fille qui a écrit ce livre.
It was a young girl who wrote this book.

C'est le livre qu'**a écrit** la jeune fille?
Is this the book that the young girl **wrote**?

When the performer is not identified, the unspecified pronoun *on* can be used instead of the passive voice.

Passive: *Ce livre a **été écrit** en 2001.*
                      This book **was written** in 2001.

Indefinite pronoun: ***On a écrit** ce livre en 2001.*
                      This book **was written** in 2001.
                      (Literally, **One wrote** this book in 2001.)

Exercise 1

Change the following sentences from the active to the passive voice. Use context to decide between the prepositions *par* and *de*.

1. Les touristes aiment le sud de la France.

_____

_____

2. Ils ne vendent pas bien ce roman en ce moment.

_____

_____

3. Ta tante a vu son mari et sa maîtresse dans le parc.

_____

_____

Exercise 2

You are traveling across France and have just met an American tourist who looks lost. Your new friend tells you that he forgot his dictionary in his hotel room, and he is unable to communicate with anyone. Help him by translating the following sentences using the passive voice.

1. Is popcorn sold here?

_____

_____

2. Is the tip included in the bill?

_____

_____

3. Are Gitanes cigarettes still smoked by all French painters?

_____

_____

4. Will Americans always be considered loud cowboys?

_____

_____

Exercise 3

Passive or active? Read the following sentences and decide whether they are in the active (A) or passive (P) form.

1. _____Ce chanteur est connu dans plusieurs pays.

2. _____Je suis allée chez le docteur.

3. _____La femme avait été soupçonnée par la police.

4. _____Il n'est jamais parti de Paris.

60

Imperatives are used in persuasive speech and to give orders and advice.

The imperative is formed by adding the imperative ending to the infinitive stem of the verb. Imperatives have only first-person plural and second-person singular and plural forms.

	Singular	**Plural**
aimer (to love)		*(nous) aim**ons**!* let's love!
	*(tu) aim**e**!* (you) love!	*(vous) aim**ez**!* (you) love!
finir (to finish)		*(nous) fini**ssons**!* (we) finish!
	*(tu) fini**s**!* (you) finish!	*(vous) fini**ssez**!* (you) finish!

avoir to have	***être*** to be
(tu) aie (you) have (sing.)	*(tu) sois* (you) are (sing.)
(nous) ayons let us have	*(nous) soyons* let us be
(vous) ayez (you) have (pl.)	*(vous) soyez* (you) are (pl.)

With the exception of *avoir* and *être*, the present imperative of verbs in the third group is the same as their corresponding *tu*, *nous,* and *vous* forms of the present tense.

When an imperative is followed by one or more pronouns, all elements are linked by a hyphen.

*Donne-le-**moi**!*
Give it **to me**!

The *-s* is dropped in the *tu* imperative form of *-er* verbs, unless they come before *y* or *en*.

Va! Go!	*Va**s-y**!* Go **ahead**!
Mange! Eat!	*Mange**s-en**!* Eat **some**!

L'Exception

The *-s* is not needed if *en* or *y* is followed by an infinitive or if *en* is being used as a preposition.

*Va y **regarder** de plus près!*
Go **take** a closer look at it!

*Mange **en silence**!*
Eat **in silence**!

Attention!

The pronouns *moi* and *toi* become *m'* and *t'* when preceding the pronouns *y* and *en*.

*Parle-**moi**!* Talk **to me**!	*Parle-**m'en**!* Tell **me about it**!
*Va-**t'en**!* Go away!	*Mets-**t'y**!* Put **yourself there**!

La Langue Vivante

It is more common to hear *Parle-moi de ça!* (Literally: Speak to me of that!) and *Mets-toi là!* (Literally: Put yourself there!) than to hear *Parle-m'en!* or *Mets-t'y!* Both constructions are correct and essentially translate as the same thing.

Exercise 1

Paul never helps at home, and Cécile isn't happy about it. Today Cécile has finally decided to tell Paul what tasks he needs to complete before she returns from work. Use the following verbs in the imperative form to complete Cécile's half of the conversation.

se lever (to get up), nettoyer (to clean), garder (to keep), attendre (to wait for), travailler (to work), faire les courses (to shop), oublier (to forget), prendre (to take), faire la cuisine (to cook), commencer (to start), payer (to pay), aller (to go), se taire (to shut up)

1. Paul: —Mais Cécile ... j'ai oublié ...

Cécile: —_____

_____

2. Paul: —Oui, je t'entends ... je promets que la prochaine fois ...

Cécile:—_____

_____

3. Paul: —Quoi? Tu es sérieuse?

Cécile: —_____

_____

4. Paul: —Non, ce n'est pas vrai!

Cécile: —_____

_____

5. Paul: —Mais attends! ...

Cécile: —_____

_____

6. Paul: —Quoi?

Cécile: —_____

_____

7. Paul: —Mais c'est impossible!

Cécile: —_____

_____

8. Paul: —Mais attends ...

Cécile: —_____

_____

Exercise 2

Change the polite requests below to blunt orders using the imperative.

1. Est-ce que tu peux acheter du lait? _____

_____

2. Je vous conseille de dormir. _____

_____

3. On ne veut pas sortir? _____

_____

4. Je t'invite à faire tes devoirs. _____

_____

5. Je te demande d'avoir confiance. _____

_____

Exercise 3

You are managing a community meeting that is a bit undisciplined. Use the imperative form of the verbs below to give specific directions to each member.

écrire (to write), appeler (to call), mettre (to put), envoyer (to send), être (to be)

1. Justin, _____!

2. Albert, _____!

3. Monique et Lucien, _____!

4. Lola, _____!

5. Frank, _____!

61

Avoir means *to have* or *to own*. *Avoir* also appears in many idiomatic French expressions where the verb *to be* would be used in English. These expressions take *avoir* (*to have*), rather than *être* (*to be*), because the French verbs describe nouns rather than adjectives. For example, to express age, the French would say, *I have 30 **years*** (noun) rather than *I am 30 years **old*** (adjective).

Attention!

Avoir has an irregular present-tense conjugation.

Singular		Plural	
*j'**ai***	I **have**	*nous **avons***	we **have**
*tu **as***	you **have**	*vous **avez***	you **have** (formal or plural)
*il, elle, on **a***	he, she, one **has**	*ils, elles **ont***	they **have**

Avoir means to own.

*Ma famille **a** une maison à la campagne.*
My family **owns** a house in the country.

La Langue Vivante

Possession can also be indicated using the expression *être à* (to belong to).

À qui est ce chapeau?
Whose hat is this?

*Ce chapeau **est à moi**!*
This hat **is mine**!

Avoir is commonly used in descriptions of people and things. In many cases, French uses *avoir* + noun/ adjective where English uses noun + *to be* + adjective.

*Christophe **a** les yeux noirs; il **a** les cheveux courts et bruns; il **a** un long nez.*
Christophe's eyes **are** dark; his hair **is** short and black; his nose **is** long.

*Notre voisin **a l'air** triste.*
Our neighbor **looks** sad.

The expression *avoir* + number + *ans* (years) is used to express age.

*Ma grand-mère **a 95 ans**.*
My grandmother **is 95**.

À cinq ans, *on aime jouer.*
At 5 years old, one likes to play.

La Langue Vivante

Avoir is also used when asking someone's age.

*Quel **âge avez-vous**?* (formal)
*Quel **âge as-tu**?* (informal)
How **old are you**?

Avoir is used to express physical sensations and emotions.

*Marie **a froid**.*
Marie **is cold**.

*Elle **a faim**.*
She **is hungry**.

*Stephane **a chaud**.*
Stephane **is hot**.

*Il **a soif**.*
He **is thirsty**.

Avoir is also used to express needs and desires.

*Nous **avons besoin de** vacances.*
We **need** a vacation.

*Le chat **a envie de** sortir.*
The cat **feels like** going out.

Avoir is used to discuss rights or entitlement.

*Tu **as droit à** une explication.*
You **are entitled to** an explanation.

*On **n'a pas le droit de** stationner ici.*
You **don't have the right to** park here.

Avoir is also used when expressing the state of being right or wrong.

*J'**ai** toujours **raison**.*
I **am** always **right**.

*Ils **ont tort**.*
They **are wrong**.

Avoir is used in the idiomatic expression *il y a*, which, depending on context, can mean *there is, there are, ago,* or *is happening*.

*Qu'est-ce qu'**il y a**?*
What**'s happening**?

Il y a dix ans, *je suis allée en Bretagne.*
Ten years ago, I went to Brittany.

*Dans sa chambre, **il y a** un lit et une armoire.*
In her bedroom, **there is** a bed and a closet.

Exercise 1

Fill in the following blanks with the correctly conjugated form of _avoir_.

1. Normalement, toute personne _____ une nationalité.

2. Vous _____ l'air content!

3. Les petites filles _____ des fleurs dans les mains.

4. Nous _____ très faim.

5. On _____ trois minutes pour se préparer.

Exercise 2

Imagine you are describing yourself to a friend in an online chat room. Use complete sentences with the verb _avoir_ to describe yourself according to the following prompts.

1. your age:

   _____

2. what you look like:

   _____

3. your worst fear:

   _____

4. what is under your bed:

   _____

5. your desires:

   _____

Exercise 3

Translate the following sentences into French using the correct form of _avoir_.

1. Nadia's hair is very short; her feet are small; she seems happy.

   _____

   _____

2. At fifty, you need to have fun just like at twenty.

   _____

   _____

3. Whose dog is it? It is Magalie's.

   _____

   _____

4. They are afraid of regretting their decision.

   _____

   _____

5. The clouds seem to announce rain, and I don't have my umbrella with me.

   _____

   _____

6. Waiters are entitled to a meal in this restaurant.

   _____

   _____

62

Special Verbs Savoir and Connaître

In French, there are two verbs that can express the English phrase *to know*: *savoir* and *connaître*. Though their translation into English is the same, these words are not interchangeable. Context dictates which verb should be used.

Savoir means *to know* when referring to a piece of information.

> *Savez-vous où est la boulangerie?*
> **Do you know** where the bakery is?

> *Je ne sais pas qui a téléphoné.*
> **I don't know** who called.

When followed by a verb in the infinitive form, *savoir* means *to know how to do something*.

> *Je sais parler français.*
> I **know how to speak** French.

> *Tu sais conduire?*
> Do you **know how to drive**?

Connaître means *to know* or *to be familiar with* when discussing a person or place.

> *Je connais Marc. Je connais Nice.*
> I **know** Marc. I **know** Nice.

> *Elle connaît les coutumes de cette région.*
> She's **familiar with** the customs of this area.

Attention!

In the preterite tense, *connaître* means *met* (for the first time) or *began to know*.

> *J'ai connu un homme qui était jardinier.*
> **I met** a man who was a gardener.

Attention!

Both *savoir* and *connaître* have irregular present-tense conjugations.

	Singular		
	savoir	*connaître*	
je	*sais*	*connais*	I know
tu	*sais*	*connais*	you know
il	*sait*	*connaît*	he knows
elle			she knows
on			one knows

	Plural		
	savoir	*connaître*	
nous	*savons*	*connaissons*	we know
vous	*savez*	*connaissez*	you know (formal or plural)
ils elles	*savent*	*connaissent*	they know

Exercise 1

Conjugate *connaître* and *savoir* in the present tense according to the following subject pronouns.

1. connaître:

je _____

on _____

vous _____

elles _____

2. savoir:

tu _____

ils _____

nous _____

il _____

Exercise 2

Use context to determine whether *savoir* or *connaître* should be used in the following sentences.

1. Elle _____ pourquoi il pleure.

2. _____-vous Paris? C'est une ville charmante.

3. Tu _____ jouer du piano?

4. Je _____ bien la rue des Rosiers.

5. Ma tante _____ préparer le boeuf bourguignon.

Exercise 3

Combine elements from each of the following columns to form five logical sentences. Determine whether *savoir* or *connaître* is appropriate in each case.

Amélie	savoir	chanter
Christo et Jeanne-Claude	connaître	jouer la comédie
Daniel Auteuil	(ne pas)	ma grand-mere
tu		parler chinois
je		Central Park

1. _____

_____

2. _____

_____

3. _____

_____

4. _____

_____

5. _____

_____

Exercise 4

How do you know? Determine which option would best complete each of the following sentences and then circle your answer. Note: More than one answer may be possible for each question.

1. Isabelle ne sait pas
a. où je suis.
b. faire un gâteau.
c. Gérard Depardieu.

2. Nous connaissons
a. les peintures de Cézanne.
b. envoyer un fax.
c. la Provence.

3. Madame Martin ne sait pas
a. parler anglais.
b. New York.
c. qui inviter.

4. Veux-tu connaître
a. comment dessiner un boa?
b. mes parents?
c. la Bretagne?

Exercise 5

Translate the following sentences into French using the correct verb for *to know*.

1. She knows this music.

_____

_____

2. George met his wife when he was 20.

_____

_____

3. They don't know where to go.

_____

_____

4. I don't know how to choose pineapples.

_____

_____

63

Special Verbs *Faire*

In most contexts, *faire* means *to make* and *to do*. However, *faire* is also used in many idiomatic expressions.

Attention!

Faire has an irregular present-tense conjugation.

Singular		Plural	
je **fais**	I make/do	nous **faisons**	we make/do
tu **fais**	you make/do	vous **faites**	you make/do (formal or plural)
il, elle, on **fait**	he, she, one makes/does	ils, elles **font**	they make/do

When discussing an action, *faire* translates as *to do* or *to make* in English.

*Les Gauthier **font** leurs courses dans une boutique bio.*
The Gauthier family **do** their shopping in an organic store.

***Faisons** la lessive.*
Let's do the laundry.

*Personne n'aime **faire** le ménage.*
Nobody likes **to do** housework.

Faire translates as *to make* when referring to food preparation.

*Je **fais** une omelette tous les dimanches.*
I **make** an omelet every Sunday.

*Le boulanger **fait** un gâteau.*
The baker is **making** a cake.

***Fais**-moi un café bien fort.*
Make a strong coffee for me.

Attention!

Faire can also express the action of cooking itself, as in the expression *faire la cuisine*.

*Il aime **faire la cuisine**.*
He likes **to cook**. (Literally: He likes **to do the cooking**.)

Faire is commonly used in impersonal expressions describing the weather.

Quel temps fait-il?	*Il **fait** froid/chaud/beau/bon/gris/humide.*
What's the weather **like?**	It **is** cold/hot/sunny/pleasant/grey/humid.

*Il **fait** combien?*	*Il **fait 30 degrés** Celsius.*
What **is** the temperature?	It **is** 30 degrees Celsius.

Faire is also used in expressions referring to music and sports. In these cases, *faire* can translate as *to play* in English. Because sports and music are not quantifable nouns, *faire* is generally followed by the partitive article in these cases.

*Il **fait** du football et il **fait** de l'alpinisme/de la randonnée.*
He **plays** soccer and he **does** mountain climbing.

*Elle **fait** du piano et elle **fait** du chant.*
She **plays** the piano and she **sings.**

Attention!

In negative sentences, *faire du/de la/de l'/des* become *faire de/d'*.

*Vous **faites du** football le samedi?*	→	Do you **play** soccer on Saturdays?
*Non, nous **ne faisons pas de** football.*	→	No, we **don't play** soccer.

Faire or the reflexive form of *faire, se faire,* followed by an infinitive expresses an action that is performed on the subject. This construction is used for actions for actions that are delegated to another person and are often expressed with the passive voice in English.

*Je **fais livrer** une pizza.*
I**'m having** a pizza **delivered.**

*Tu **te fais couper les cheveux** régulièrement.*
You **get a haircut** regularly.

***Faites cuire** le gâteau à four chaud.*
Cook the cake in a warm oven.

*Le suspect **se fait interroger** par la police.*
The suspect **is being interrogated** by the police.

Exercise 1

Answer the following questions based on your personal experience.

1. Quel temps fait-il aujourd'hui?

_____

_____

2. Quelle température fait-il aujourd'hui?

_____

_____

3. Qui fait la cuisine chez vous?

_____

_____

4. Faites-vous du sport? Quel sport?

_____

_____

5. Faites-vous de la musique? Quel est votre instrument?

_____

_____

Exercise 2

Combine elements from each of the following columns to form three affirmative sentences and two negative sentences.

Les députés	faites	du volley
Vous	font	des exercices
Claude Débussy	fait	la cuisine
Thierry Henry	fais	du piano
Je	(ne pas)	des discours

1. _____

_____

2. _____

_____

3. _____

_____

4. _____

_____

5. _____

_____

Exercise 3

Translate the following passive sentences into French using _faire_.

1. I'm getting a massage today!

_____

_____

2. He was arrested by the police yesterday.

_____

_____

3. Have your car washed.

_____

_____

64

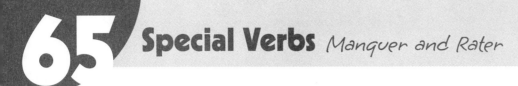

Although *manquer* can be regularly used when meaning *to miss*, its use in a French sentence differs from the English equivalent. *Rater* can also be used as a slang word in certain instances where *manquer* would be grammatically correct.

Manquer is a regular verb that can express a longing for a person, a place, or a thing.

*Paris me **manque**.*
I **miss** Paris.

*Ses parents lui **manquent**.*
She **misses** her parents.

*Je te **manque**?*
Do you **miss** me?

*Tu me **manques** beaucoup.*
I **miss** you very much.

Attention!

The subject of an English sentence using *to miss* is the object in an equivalent French sentence. *Manquer* would be literally translated as *is missing to me*.

Incorrect:	***Tu** (subject) manques à moi.* **You** are missing to me.
Correct:	***Tu** (object) me manques.* I miss **you.**
Incorrect:	***Vous** (subject) manquez à nous.* **You** are missing to us.
Correct:	***Vous** (object) nous manquez.* We miss **you.**

The expression *manquer de* means *to lack something*.

*La directrice **manque de** patience.*
The director **lacks** patience.

*Il **ne manque pas de** culot!*
He **doesn't lack** nerve!

Manquer and rater both mean to miss when referring to a mode of transportation.

*Nous allons **manquer** l'avion!*
We're going to **miss** the plane!

***Rate** pas ton train!*
Don't **miss** your train!

La Langue Vivante

In colloquial French, negative sentences often omit *ne* but retain *pas*. For example, *ne manque pas ton train* becomes *rate pas ton train* in everyday speech.

Manquer and *rater* can both be used in reference to an event that is missed.

*Malheureusement, Remi **a raté** le début du film.*
Unfortunately, Remi **missed** the beginning of the movie.

*Sa famille ne **manque** jamais La Roue de la fortune.*
His family never **misses** *Wheel of Fortune.*

Rater is often used as slang in cases where *manquer* means to fail. Ne pas réussir (to not be successful) or échouer (to fail) can also be used in these cases, when speaking formally.

*Nicolas ne veut pas **rater** son examen.*
Nicolas doesn't want to **fail** his exam.

*Elle n'**a pas réussi**.*
She **wasn't successful.**

*Ma mère n'**échoue** jamais à ce qu'elle entreprend.*
My mother never **fails** at what she undertakes.

Exercise 1

Match the following situations in column A with the correct verb in column B.

A	B
_____ **1.** you miss your grandparents	
_____ **2.** you missed your train	a. rater
_____ **3.** you fail an exam	b. manquer
_____ **4.** you missed class	

Exercise 2

Fill in the following blanks with the correct *to miss* verb.

1. Ma télévision ne fonctionne plus. C'est pour cette raison

   que _____ le match de foot.

2. Nous ne devons pas _____ de politesse.

3. Complétez les phrases avec les mots qui _____.

4. Mon frère me _____.

5. Les étudiants qui _____ leurs tests sont

   plus stressés que les autres.

Exercise 3

Translate the following sentences into French using the correct verb.

1. This apartment lacks light.

   _____

   _____

2. The two sisters never miss an occasion to sing.

   _____

   _____

3. She misses the beautiful apple trees of her garden.

   _____

   _____

4. Gérard never fails at anything.

   _____

   _____

5. They miss you every day.

   _____

   _____

Exercise 4

Transform the following informal sentences into formal sentences.

1. On a raté notre examen hier.

   _____

   _____

2. Rate pas ton train!

   _____

   _____

3. Je suis arrivé au ciné en retard et j'ai raté le début du film.

   _____

   _____

4. Elle rate ses gâteaux à chaque fois.

   _____

   _____

5. Oh, zut! Tu as encore raté la sortie d'autoroute!

   _____

   _____

Exercise 5

Imagine you are sent to space on a mission. Use complete sentences using *manquer* to describe the five things from Earth you would miss the most.

1. _____

   _____

2. _____

   _____

3. _____

   _____

65

66 Special Verbs Partir, Quitter, and Sortir

Partir (to leave), *quitter* (to leave), and *sortir* (to go out) have very similar meanings, but they all have specific uses in French.

Partir (to leave, to go away) is the opposite of *arriver* (to arrive). *Partir* can be used alone or followed by a preposition.

Ils **sont partis.**
They **left.**

Elle **part pour** Marseille.
She**'s leaving for** Marseille.

La Langue Vivante

The idiomatic expression *s'en aller* (to go away, to leave) is a reflexive construction often used to in place of *partir* in the present tense. It rarely appears in the past tense.

Je m'en vais.
I'm **leaving.**

Elles vont s'en aller.
They're going to **leave.**

Quitter means *to leave something* or *someone*. *Quitter* is usually followed by a direct object, the person or thing being left.

Claude **quitte son travail** à sept heures tous les soirs.
Claude **leaves his work** at seven every evening.

Julie va **quitter la France** pour la Réunion.
Julie is going to **leave France** for Réunion.

Elle **a quitté son ami.**
She **left her boyfriend.**

La Langue Vivante

On the phone, *ne quitte pas* (informal) and *ne quittez pas* (formal) mean *hold on*.

Bonjour! Je voudrais parler à Viviane.
Hi! I'd like to speak to Viviane.

Ne quitte pas; je vais la chercher.
Hold on, I'll get her.

Sortir (to come out, to go out) is the opposite of *entrer* (to come in, to enter). *Sortir* can be used alone or followed by a preposition.

Vous **sortez?**
Are you **going out?**

Sors de ta chambre.
Come out of your bedroom.

Sortir can also mean *to go out for the evening* or *to go out with someone*.

Tu veux **sortir** ce soir?
Do you want to **go out** tonight?

Léa et Miguel **sortent** ensemble.
Léa and Miguel **are going out** together.

Attention!

Quitter follows the regular conjugation pattern. *Partir* and *sortir* both have irregular present-tense conjugations.

		Singular	
	partir	**sortir**	
je	pars	sors	I leave / I go out
tu	pars	sors	you leave / you go out
il elle on	part	sort	he, she one leaves/goes out

		Plural	
	partir	**sortir**	
nous	partons	sortons	we leave / we go out
vous	partez	sortez	you leave / you go out (formal or plural)
ils elles	partent	sortent	they know

Partir and *sortir* take the auxiliary verb *être* in the past tense. *Quitter* takes the auxiliary verb *avoir*.

		Singular	
	partir	**sortir**	**quitter**
je	suis parti(e)	suis sorti(e)	ai quitté
tu	es parti(e)	es sorti(e)	as quitté
il elle on	est parti(e)	est sorti(e)	a quitté

		Plural	
	partir	**sortir**	**quitter**
nous	sommes parti(e)s	sommes sorti(e)s	avons quitté
vous	êtes parti(e)(s)	êtes sorti(e)(s)	avez quitté
ils elles	sont parti(e)s	sont sorti(e)s	ont quitté

L'Exception

When followed by a direct object, *sortir* becomes a transitive verb meaning *to take something out.* In the past tense, the auxiliary *avoir* is used.

*J'**ai sorti** le chien.*
I **took** the dog **out.**

Exercise 1

Fill in the following blanks with the correct verb: *partir, sortir,* or *quitter.*

1. Luc aimerait bien _____ avec Elise.

2. Ils _____ Paris pour toujours!

3. Si les cambrioleurs ne _____ pas de la

maison, la police va tirer.

4. Quand son amie _____ avec lui, elle ne

le _____ pas des yeux.

5. Ne _____ pas! Tu n'as pas mangé ton

dessert!

Exercise 2

Change the verbs in the following sentences from present tense to past tense.

1. Valentin sort la table dans le jardin.

_____

2. Vous partez quand?

_____

3. Pour quelle raison quittez-vous votre travail?

_____

4. Ils partent en Italie.

_____

5. Vraiment?! Tu sors avec Louis?

_____

Exercise 3

Translate the following sentences into French using the correct verb.

1. If that crocodile doesn't go away, I'm not coming out of this cabin.

_____

_____

2. Armelle left her work; she left her house; and she left the country.

_____

_____

3. If you go out after me, don't forget to close the door.

_____

_____

4. Hello Mr. Sabatier. Please hold on. (on the phone)

_____

_____

5. Since when have my two colleagues been going out together?

_____

_____

66

Special Verbs *Rentrer, Revenir, and Retourner*

Rentrer, revenir, and *retourner* all express meaning of the English phrase *to go back* or *to return*. However, these French verbs are not interchangeable, and their usage depends on context.

Rentrer means *to go home* or *to come back to* (a previous location).

> *Je **rentre** chez moi.*
> I'm **going home.**

> *Ils **rentrent** en France en octobre.*
> They**'re coming back** to France in October.

Revenir expresses the repeated action of *venir* (to come). In English it would translate as *to return, to come back, to come again.*

> *Revenez bientôt.*
> **Come again** soon.

> *Elle va **revenir** dans cinq minutes.*
> She's going to **come back** in five minutes.

Attention!

Revenir has an irregular present-tense conjugation that is based on the conjugation of *venir* but adds the prefix *re-*.

Singular		Plural	
*je **reviens***	I **return**	*nous* **revenons**	we **return**
*tu **reviens***	you **return**	*vous **revenez***	you **return** (formal or plural)
il, elle, on **revient**	he, she, one **returns**	*ils, elles* **reviennent**	they **return**

Retourner (to go back, to go again) expresses the repeated action of *aller* (to go). A location must always be specified when using *retourner*, even if the location is expressed with the object pronoun *y* (there).

> *Retournons à Montréal.*
> **Let's go** to Montreal **again.**

> *Je **retourne** chez le docteur demain.*
> I'm **going back** to the doctor's tomorrow.

> *Retournez-y.*
> **Go back** there.

Attention!

The reflexive expression *se retourner* means *to turn around.*

> *Retourne-toi; dis-lui au revoir.*
> **Turn around**; say good-bye to her.

Rentrer, revenir, and retourner all take the auxiliary verb *être* in the past tense. Their past participles are *rentré, revenu,* and *retourné,* respectively.

Singular		
	Auxiliary	**Past Participle**
je	*suis*	*rentré(e)*
tu	*es*	*revenu(e)*
il/ elle/ on	*est*	*retourné(e)*

Plural		
	Auxiliary	**Past Participle**
nous	*sommes*	*rentré(e)s*
vous	*êtes*	*revenu(e)(s)*
ils/ elles	*sont*	*retourné(e)s*

L'Exception

When followed by a direct object, *rentrer* and *retourner* mean *to put inside* and *to turn inside out/to turn over,* respectively. They both take the auxiliary verb *avoir* in the past tense in these cases.

> *J'ai rentré le chat.*
> I **took** the cat **back inside.**

> *Retourne ta veste pour l'aérer.*
> **Turn** your jacket **inside out** to air it.

Exercise 1

Fill in the blanks below with the correct verb: *rentrer, revenir,* or *retourner.*

1. Je suis fatiguée. Je _____ à la maison!

2. Je suis allée à la poste hier et j'y _____ aujourd'hui.

134

3. Monique est venue nous voir jeudi. Elle va _____ dimanche.

4. Le Frisbee _____ rapidement.

5. Nous _____ au village de notre enfance.

2. _____

_____

3. _____

_____

4. _____

_____

Exercise 2

Change the following sentences from present tense to past tense.

1. Chantal rentre à midi le samedi.

_____

_____

2. Les ouvriers ne retournent pas au travail.

_____

_____

3. Les enfants reviennent de vacances en août.

_____

_____

4. Valentin rentre les chaises.

_____

_____

Exercise 4

Translate the following sentences using the correct verb.

1. If you are sick, don't go back to work.

_____

_____

2. When are you coming home tonight?

_____

_____

3. They turned their T-shirts inside out.

_____

_____

4. It's too windy. Let's take the plants back in.

_____

_____

Exercise 3

Use elements from each column below to form four logical sentences.

Mon oncle et ma tante	retournent	en Alsace
tante	rentrent	de voyage
tante	reviennent	de vacances
tu		dans trois jours
Merlin		
mon chien et moi		

1. _____

_____

67

Both *habiter* and *vivre* can be used to mean *to live, to dwell,* or *to reside in.*

Tu **habites/vis** *à Paris.*
You **live** in Paris.

Ils **habitent/vivent** *ici depuis trois ans.*
They **have been living** here for three years.

La Langue Vivante

Habiter may or may not be followed by a preposition preceding the name of the place. The decision is up to the speaker.

Elle **habite** *(à) New York.*
She **lives** in New York.

When used alone, followed by an adjective of manner, or followed by a period of time, *vivre* means *to be alive, to exist,* or *to dwell.*

Il **vit**!   *Je* **vis** *seule.*
He **is alive**!   I **live** alone.

Vivre can also mean *to experience* or *to go through,* in the figurative sense of experiencing something.

Nathalie **vit** *un drame.*
Nathalie **is going through** a difficult time.

*J'*ai *beaucoup* **vécu.**
I **experienced** a lot.

Attention!

Habiter is a regular *-er* verb, but *vivre* has an irregular present-tense conjugation. The past participle for *vivre* is the irregular *vécu.*

Singular		Plural	
je **vis**	I live	*nous* **vivons**	we live
tu **vis**	you live	*vous* **vivez**	you live (formal or plural)
il, elle, on **vit**	he, she, one lives	*ils, elles* **vivent**	they live

Exercise 1

Conjugate *vivre* in the present or past tense, according to the context of each of the following sentences.

1. Vous _____ seule, madame?

2. Louis XVI et Marie-Antoinette _____ à

Versailles.

3. Les hommes _____ jusqu'à 77 ans, les

femmes _____ jusqu'à 84 ans.

4. Nous _____ une catastrophe naturelle

l'année dernière.

5. Où _____-tu en ce moment?

Exercise 2

How do you live? Determine which of the options would best complete each of the following sentences and then circle your answers. Note: There may be more than one correct answer for each item.

1. Dimitri habite ...
   a. rue Mouffetard.
   b. avec sa soeur.
   c. en 2007.

2. Nous habitons ...
   a. aujourd'hui.
   b. ensemble.
   c. et c'est ce qui compte.

3. Edith Piaf a vécu ...
   a. en France.
   b. avec des hommes.
   c. des situations difficiles.

Exercise 3

Translate the following sentences into English.

1. Où te vois-tu vivre dans dix ans?

   _____

   _____

2. C'est un poisson qui vit en eau douce.

   _____

   _____

3. Vous habitez boulevard Raspail, à Paris, n'est-ce pas?

   _____

   _____

4. Elle vit; c'est merveilleux.

   _____

   _____

5. Tu as mal vécu cette transition.

   _____

   _____

Exercise 4

Translate the following sentences into French using the correct form of *to live*.

1. Let me live!

   _____

   _____

2. She lives in a small apartment with her brother.

   _____

   _____

3. Tell me, where in Paris do you live?

   _____

   _____

4. We're alive today.

   _____

   _____

5. He lived in the Middle Ages.

   _____

   _____

68

Faire la connaissance de, *rencontrer*, and *retrouver* can all mean *to meet*. Each verb has specific uses depending on the information being conveyed.

The phrase *faire la connaissance de* means *to meet for the first time* or *to get acquainted*. The form of this expression can vary and can be used with possessive adjectives. Because *connaissance* is a feminine noun, possessive adjectives *ma, ta, sa, notre, votre, leur* are used. In some cases, no article or possessive adjective accompanies the expression.

J'**ai fait la connaissance de** la fiancée de mon frère.
I **met** my brother's fiancée.

Sophie? Vous **ferez sa connaissance** ce soir.
Sophie? You **will meet her** tonight.

Faisons connaissance, d'accord?
Let's get acquainted, OK?

Rencontrer and its reciprocal form, *se rencontrer*, can also mean *to meet for the first time* or *to get acquainted*.

Lucas **a rencontré** sa femme en 1968.
Lucas **met** his wife in 1968.

Vous **vous êtes** déjà **rencontrés**?
Have you already **met (each other)**?

Rencontrer can also mean *to run into someone*.

J'**ai rencontré** ton père au supermarché!
I **ran into** your father at the supermarket!

La loi **a rencontré** de nombreux opposants.
The law **ran into** many opponents.

La Langue Vivante

Tomber sur quelqu'un can be used when to mean *to meet someone by chance* or *to bump into someone*.

Devine sur qui Marc **est tombé.**
Guess who **Marc bumped into.**

Retrouver and its reflexive form, *se retrouver*, mean *to meet up with*, when referring to a friend or someone you already know.

Nous allons **retrouver** un ami au café.
We'**re meeting up** with a friend at the café.

Ils **se retrouvent** après les cours.
They **meet up** after classes.

Retrouver also means *to find* or *to regain* when referring to someone or something previously lost.

Il **a retrouvé** un ami d'enfance.
He **found** a childhood friend.

Retrouvez votre calme.
Regain your calm.

The reflexive verb *se retrouver* can mean *to find yourself in a situation*, similar to the idiomatic English phrase *to wind up in*.

Elle **se retrouve** orpheline.
She **is now** an orphan.

Tintin **s'est retrouvé** dans un monastère tibétain.
Tintin **wound up** in a Tibetan monastery.

Exercise 1

Match the French sentences in column A with the correct English translation in column B.

	A	B
_____	**1.** Je te retrouve dans le métro.	a. Here I am, alone.
_____	**2.** J'ai fait sa connaissance hier.	b. I regained my solitude.
_____	**3.** Je me retrouve seule.	c. See you in the subway.
_____	**4.** J'ai rencontré Paul dans le métro.	d. I met him yesterday.
_____	**5.** J'ai retrouvé ma solitude.	e. I met Paul in the subway.

Exercise 2

Fill in the following blanks with the correct *to meet* verb.

1. Il va vous présenter. Vous allez _____.

2. Après les vacances, les enfants _____ l'école.

3. Le monsieur ne _____ pas ses clés de voiture.

4. Oh! Je _____ Joëlle au café!

5. Ce film _____ de vives critiques.

Exercise 3

Translate the following sentences into French.

1. He is going to wind up without his car.

_____

_____

2. Regain your smile, my dear.

_____

_____

3. Did you find your watch?

_____

_____

4. I would like to meet them.

_____

_____

5. They ran into their accountant at the party.

_____

_____

Exercise 4

You are writing in your diary. Write five sentences describing events in your recent past related to the following prompts.

1. You met someone for the first time:

_____

_____

2. You found something that was previously lost:

_____

_____

3. You met up with someone:

_____

_____

4. You unexpectedly bumped into someone:

_____

_____

5. You suddenly found yourself in a situation:

_____

_____

69

Prendre means *to take*. It has a variety of possible meanings depending on the context of the sentence.

Prendre is specifically used in reference to things, and cannot be used when referring to people. (*Emmener* means *to take* in reference to people.)

Prends les clés.
Take the keys.

Le bébé a pris la tétine.
The baby **took** the pacifier.

Attention!

Prendre has an irregular present-tense conjugation. The past participle of *prendre* is *pris*.

Singular		Plural	
je **prends**	I take	nous **prenons**	we take
tu **prends**	you take	vous **prenez**	you take (formal or plural)
il, elle, on **prend**	he, she, one takes	ils, elles **prennent**	they take

Prendre means *to take* when referring to a means of transportation.

Je vais prendre l'avion.
I'm going to **take** the plane.

Mes cousins prennent le bus.
My cousins **take** the bus.

When followed by an expression of time, *prendre* means *to take an amount of time*. *Prendre* is interchangeable with *mettre* when used in this sense.

Ça prend une heure en bus.
It **takes** an hour by bus.

Elles ont pris leur temps.
They **took** their time.

Prendre is always used when discussing food. It means *to order* or *to have* in this case.

Qu'est-ce que vous allez prendre, madame?
What are you going to **order**, ma'am?

Je prends un jus d'orange.
I'm **having** an orange juice.

Prendre can also replace *emmener* (to take along people) or *venir/aller chercher* (to pick up).

Je vous prendrai à sept heures.
I'll **pick** you **up** at seven.

Je te prends avec moi.
I'm **taking** you with me.

Emmène-moi avec toi!
Take me with you!

La Langue Vivante

Suivre un cours is the formal French expression meaning *to take a class*. Recently, however, *prendre* has taken on this same meaning in colloquial French.

Elle suit un cours de physique.
She's **taking** a physics class.

Je veux prendre un cours d'informatique.
I want to **take** a computer science class.

Exercise 1

Combine elements from each of the following columns to form five affirmative sentences and two negative sentences.

Tu	prend	des vacances
Les sportifs	prennent	de l'alcool
Juliette Binoche	prends	le taxi
Vous	prenez	du piano
Je		une douche froide

1. _____

2. _____

3. _____

4. _____

5. _____

_____

6. _____

_____

7. _____

_____

Exercise 2

Answer the following questions with complete sentences based on your experience.

1. D'habitude, que prenez-vous quand vous allez au café?

_____

_____

2. Quel(s) moyen(s) de transport prenez-vous?

_____

_____

3. Combien de jours de vacances prenez-vous par an?

_____

_____

4. Quel cours aimeriez-vous prendre?

_____

_____

5. Combien de temps prenez-vous pour vous préparer le matin?

_____

_____

Exercise 3

Translate the following sentences into French.

1. Take the books with you.

_____

_____

2. Let's get a cheese sandwich.

_____

_____

3. They took two months off.

_____

_____

4. Will you take your bike or your car?

_____

_____

5. My uncle will pick us up tonight.

_____

_____

70

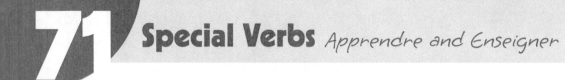

71 Special Verbs *Apprendre and Enseigner*

Enseigner means *to teach*; *apprendre* can mean either *to learn* or *to teach* according to the context.

When describing the learning process, *enseigner* means *to teach,* and *apprendre* means *to learn.*

> *Le professeur **enseigne** et les élèves **apprennent**.*
> The teacher **teaches** and the students **learn.**

> ***Apprenez** bien vos leçons.*
> **Learn** your lessons well.

Enseigner always means *to teach,* and may or may not be followed by an object.

> *Vous **enseignez**?*
> Do you **teach**?

> *Jean-Claude **enseigne** la littérature francophone.*
> Jean-Claude **teaches** francophone literature.

Apprendre can mean *to teach something to someone,* when the action is transferred to another person.

> *Valérie **apprend** la grammaire **à** Sam.*
> Valérie **is teaching** grammar **to** Sam.

> *Mon grand-père m'**a appris à** nager.*
> My grandfather **taught** me **how to** swim.

Attention!

When no direct or indirect object is present, *apprendre* can only mean *to learn.*

*J'**apprends**.*
I **am learning.**

Apprendre also means *to give the news* or *to hear about.*

> *Il m'**a appris** que Jacques était au Mali.*
> He **gave me the news** that Jacques was in Mali.

> *Nous **avons appris** la naissance de ton enfant.*
> We **heard about** the birth of your child.

Attention!

Apprendre has an irregular present-tense conjugation, based on the root word *prendre* (*to take*). The past participle of *apprendre* is *appris.*

Singular		Plural	
*j'**apprends***	I learn	*nous* **apprenons**	we learn
tu **apprends**	you learn	*vous* **apprenez**	you learn (formal or plural)
il, elle, on **apprend**	he, she, one learns	*ils, elles* **apprennent**	they learn

Exercise 1

Match the situations in column A with appropriate verb in column B.

A   B

_____ **1.** you always learn

_____ **2.** you learned a piece of news

_____ **3.** you're learning French

_____ **4.** you teach

a. enseigner
b. apprendre

Exercise 2

Fill in the blanks with the correct verb: *enseigner* or *apprendre*.

1. Hier, nous _____ le résultat de l'élection.

2. Quand on _____ ce qu'on aime, on

_____ bien.

3. Si tu _____ à cuisiner, tu me feras de

bons petits plats.

4. Mon rôle est de vous _____ la

grammaire française.

5. Observez et _____.

Exercise 3

Translate the following sentences into French.

1. They taught me how to dance the tango.

_____

_____

2. He used to teach math at a high school.

_____

_____

3. I heard about the news. Congratulations!

_____

_____

4. You are going to hear about how he survived.

_____

_____

5. Teaching is a difficult profession.

_____

_____

Exercise 4

List three important lessons you have learned in your life and three things you have taught other people.

1. _____

_____

2. _____

_____

3. _____

_____

4. _____

_____

5. _____

_____

6. _____

_____

71

In French, several different verbs are used to express *to take* or *to bring*, depending on what is being taken or brought.

Amener means *to bring along.* **Emmener means** *to take along.* **Both verbs are only used to refer to people, animals or vehicles.**

> **Amène** *ta grand-mère.*
> **Bring** your grandmother.

> *Ils* **ont emmené** *Max chez le vétérinaire.*
> They **took** Max to the veterinarian.

Both *prendre* **and** *emmener* **can be used with people.** **Prendre specifically means** *to pick someone up,* **as can** *aller chercher* **or** *venir chercher* **(depending on the point of view) and** *passer prendre.* **Emmener specifically means** *to take someone somewhere.*

> *Je* **prends** *Max avec moi.*
> I'm **taking** Marc with me.

> *Je vous* **prends** *à 8 heures.*
> I'm **picking** you **up** at 8.

> **Passe** *me* **prendre** *à huit heures.*
> **Pick** me **up** at eight.

> *Ton papa* **vient** *te* **chercher***?*
> Is your dad **picking** you **up**?

> **Emmenons** *Julie au concert.*
> **Let's take** Julie to the concert.

Apporter means *to bring along.* **Emporter means** *to take along/away.* **Both** *apporter* **and** *emporter* **refer only to things you can carry. (The root word** *-porter* **means** *to carry.***)**

> *Vous* **apportez** *le champagne?*
> **Are** you **bringing** the champagne?

> **Emporte** *un pull.*
> **Take** a sweater.

La Langue Vivante

In colloquial conversation, French speakers often forget the subtle differences of meanings between *amener*, *emmener*, *apporter*, and *emporter*, and instead use these verbs interchangeably. The recent influence of the Arabic population in France has also introduced the word *raboul*, which is often used in the imperative, in a similar manner as *apporter*.

> **Amène** *le gâteau.*
> **Bring** the cake.

> **Raboule** *le livre.*
> **Bring** the book.

Exercise 1

Fill in the following blanks with the correct verb: *amener*, *emmener*, *apporter*, or *emporter*.

1. Est-ce que tu peux m'_____ à l'aeroport?

2. Un joueur de foot_____ toujours son ballon avec lui.

3. C'est la fête du printemps: _____ des fleurs.

4. Nous allons en vacances et nous _____ notre chat avec nous.

5. N'_____ pas ta voiture si tu veux marcher.

Exercise 2

Combine elements from each of the following columns to form five logical sentences.

Les fourmis	amène	sa vieille voiture
Monsieur Hulot	emportent	de vacances
Tu	apportons	du gâteau
Xavier et moi	emmènes	mon poisson rouge

1. _____

_____

2. _____

_____

3. _____

_____

4. _____

_____

5. _____

_____

Exercise 3

You're planning a trip. Describe who and what you are taking along when you travel to the following places.

1. en Martinique:

_____

_____

2. dans les Alpes:

_____

_____

3. à Paris:

_____

_____

Exercise 4

Translate the following sentences into French.

1. I'm not taking my umbrella.

_____

_____

2. Bring the table.

_____

_____

3. Laure didn't come to pick you up?

_____

_____

4. We're taking my parents to the concert.

_____

_____

5. Bring your husbands along.

_____

_____

Mettre and *poser* can both mean *to put*, though each verb has specific uses depending on the information being conveyed.

Mettre means *to put* or *to place* a thing somewhere.

> *Elle **met** les fleurs dans le vase.*
> She **is putting** the flowers in the vase.

> *Ne **mets** pas tes doigts dans le nez.*
> Don't **put** your fingers **up** your nose.

Attention!

Mettre has an irregular present-tense conjugation. The past participle of *mettre* is *mis*.

Singular		Plural	
*je **mets***	I put	*nous **mettons***	we put
*tu **mets***	you put	*vous **mettez***	you put (formal or plural)
*il, elle, on **met***	he, she, one puts	*ils, elles **mettent***	they put

Mettre can be used to describe the act of putting on clothing or accessories.

> *Louis **a mis** sa cravate verte.*
> Louis **put on** his green tie.

Mettre also means *to turn/switch on* (a device).

> ***Mets** la radio, s'il te plaît.*
> **Switch on** the radio, please.

When followed by an expression of time, *mettre* means *to take* (a duration of time).

> *Jules et Jim **mettent** dix minutes en métro.*
> Jules and Jim **take** ten minutes by subway.

> *Tu **as mis** longtemps à arriver.*
> You **took** a long time to arrive.

La Langue Vivante

There are several common idiomatic expressions using *mettre*.

mettre la table	to set the table
mettre le feu	to set a fire
mettre en miettes	to make crumbs out of something
se mettre debout	to stand
se mettre à + infinitive	to start doing something
se mettre en colère	to get mad

Poser means *to put down* or *to put away*. It is the opposite of *to hold*.

> ***Pose** ton verre ici.*
> **Put** your glass here.

> *Je **pose** mon manteau et j'arrive.*
> I'm **putting away my** coat, and I'm coming.

Poser can also mean *to install*.

> *Selma **pose** un rideau jaune.*
> Selma **is installing** a yellow curtain.

> *On **pose** l'antenne.*
> We**'re installing** the antenna.

Poser can mean *to formulate*, when discussing an idea or asking a question.

> *Le professeur **a posé** le problème.*
> The teacher **formulated** the problem.

> *Puis-je **poser** une question?*
> May I **ask** a question?

Poser can mean *to pose*, as in sitting for a photographer, a painter, or a sculptor.

> *Voudriez-vous **poser** pour moi?*
> Would you want to **pose** for me?

> *Camille Claudel **a posé** pour Rodin.*
> Camille Claudel **posed** for Rodin.

Exercise 1

Conjugate *mettre* in the present tense according to the subject of each sentence below.

1. Vous _____ des gants en hiver?

2. Quand son fils _____ la musique, elle a mal à la tête.

3. _____ ton pantalon bleu.

4. Nous_____ nos lunettes au cinéma.

5. Les femmes _____ de jolis colliers.

Exercise 2

Answer the following questions with a complete sentence based on your experience.

1. Mettez-vous souvent la radio?

   _____

   _____

2. Qui met la table chez vous?

   _____

   _____

3. Aimeriez-vous poser pour un artiste?

   _____

   _____

4. Où posez-vous votre manteau quand vous arrivez chez vous?

   _____

   _____

5. Combien de temps mettez-vous pour arriver au travail?

   _____

   _____

Exercise 3

Determine which option would best complete each of the following sentences and then circle your answers. Note: There may be more than one correct answer for each item.

1. Voltaire a mis ...
   a. son inspiration à son service.
   b. des questions importantes.
   c. des vêtements élégants.

2. Tu poses toujours ...
   a. trop de questions!
   b. pour les photos!
   c. la télévision!

3. Je n'ai pas mis ...
   a. ta cravate.
   b. mon sac.
   c. la table.

73

A yes/no question can be formed by simply inserting *est-ce que* before the subject of an affirmative sentence. Though *est-ce que* literally means *is it that,* in context, it does not have an exact literal translation in English. However, it usually is used where English would use auxiliaries such as *are, is,* or *do* plus the main verb.

Est-ce que *tu viens?*
Are you coming? (Literally: **Is it that** you come?)

Est-ce que *tu aimes le thé vert?*
Do you like green tea? (Literally: **Is it that** you like green tea?)

Yes/no questions can also be formed through inversion, in which the order of the subject and the verb is switched. When using inversion, a hyphen is placed between the verb and the subject.

Tu viens.
You are coming.

Viens-tu?
Are you coming? (Literally: Come you?)

Tu aimes le thé vert.
You like green tea.

Aimes-tu le thé vert?
Do you like green tea? (Literally: Like you green tea?)

Attention!

When the subject of an inverted question is a third-person pronoun (*il, elle, on*) and the verb ends in a vowel, the hyphenated -*t*- is added between the verb and subject pronoun.

Est-ce qu'elle aime faire du jogging?
*Aime-**t**-elle faire du jogging?*
Does she like jogging?

Attention!

When using a compound verb tense requiring an auxiliary verb, such as in the *passé composé,* the subject pronoun is connected by a hyphen to the auxiliary verb.

Es-tu *venu(e)?*
Did you come?

As-tu aimé *le thé vert?*
Did you like green tea?

Questions can also be formed by adding the tag *n'est-ce pas* to the end of a sentence. This construction is similar to adding *right?* to the end of an English sentence. *N'est-ce pas* can also translate as *aren't you?* or *don't you?* or as *isn't he/she?* or *doesn't he/she?*

Tu viens, **n'est-ce pas***?*
You're coming, **right**? You're coming, **aren't you**?

Tu aimes le thé vert, **n'est-ce pas***?*
You like green tea, **right**? You like green tea, **don't you**?

La Langue Vivante

Just as in English, a question can be formed in spoken French by simply changing the intonation of an affirmative sentence. This method is quite common.

Tu viens?
Are you coming?

Tu aimes le thé vert?
Do you like green tea?

Exercise 1

Translate the following questions into French using *est-ce que*.

1. Does he like asparagus?

_____

_____

2. Is he from Lyon?

_____

_____

3. Did she finish her homework?

_____

_____

4. Did you study World War II?

_____

_____

5. Do you travel a lot?

_____

_____

6. Did you eat a ham sandwich?

_____

_____

Exercise 2

Translate the following questions into French using inversion.

1. Did you (plural) see the football game?

_____

_____

2. Does he like asparagus?

_____

_____

3. Does she have a favorite teacher?

_____

_____

4. Do you travel a lot?

_____

_____

5. Did you eat a ham sandwich?

_____

_____

6. Are you studying World War II?

_____

_____

Exercise 3

Translate the following questions into French using _n'est-ce pas._

1. Do you travel a lot?

_____

_____

2. Does he like asparagus?

_____

_____

3. Did he finish his homework?

_____

_____

4. Are you studying World War II?

_____

_____

5. Does Jack speak Spanish?

_____

_____

6. Is he from Lyon?

_____

_____

74

Questions that seek information, as opposed to those asking for a yes or no response, generally answer the questions *who, what, where, when, why,* and *how.*

Qui (who) is used to ask questions about people. Qui can be either the subject or direct object of the question.

Qui est ta mère?
Who is your mother?

Qui trouves-tu beau?
Who do you think is handsome?

Qui can also take a long form: qui est-ce qui when the subject, and qui est-ce que when the direct object. The meaning is the same as in the short form.

Qui est-ce qui est ta mère?
Who is your mother?

Qui est-ce que tu trouves beau?
Who do you think is handsome?

Three different question forms can be used when asking about things, events, thoughts, feelings, or abstract concepts: Que est-ce qui is used with the subject, que or qu'est-ce que is used with the direct object, and quoi is used with the object of a preposition. All of these would translate to what in English.

Que est-ce qui se passe?
What is happening?

Que faites-vous ce soir? Qu'est-ce que faites-vous ce soir?
What are you doing tonight?

À quoi pense-t-il?
What is he thinking **about**?

La Langue Vivante

Just as in English, a question can be formed in spoken French by simply stressing an affirmative sentence.

On va faire quoi?
What are we going to do? (Literally: We will do **what**?)

Quel can be used to ask what or which and usually precedes the verb être or the noun. If it refers to a specific noun, quel agrees in gender and number with that noun.

	Singular	Plural
Masculine	*quel*	*quels*
Feminine	*quelle*	*quelles*

Quel bâtiment préfères-tu?
Which building do you prefer?

Quel est ton bâtiment préféré?
Which is your favorite building?

Lequel (which one) is a combination of the definite article and quel. Like quel, lequel agrees with the noun it is replacing in gender and number. Lequel also forms contractions with the à and de.

	Singular	Plural
Masculine	*lequel* (which one) *auquel* (to which) *duquel* (of which)	*lesquels* (which ones) *auxquels* (to which) *desquels* (of which)
Feminine	*laquelle* (which one) *à laquelle* (to which) *de laquelle* (of which)	*lesquelles* (which ones) *auxquelles* (to which) *desquelles* (of which)

Laquelle est ta maison?
Which one is your house?

Veux-tu prêter mes verres? **Lesquels**?
You want to borrow my glasses? **Which ones**?

The question words comment (how), quand (when), combien (how many, how much), où (where) and pourquoi (why) can precede est-ce que or an inverted subject-verb question.

Comment marchent-ils?
How do they work?

Quand est-ce qu'elle revient après les vacances?
When does she come back after vacation?

Combien est-ce que tu as payé pour les boissons?
How much did you pay for the drinks?

Où est-ce que tu fais tes courses?
Where do you do your errands?

Pourquoi as-tu pleuré?
Why did you cry?

Exercise 1

Match the question words in column A to the appropriate questions in the column B.

A	B
_____ **1.** Quelle	a. vient chez toi ce soir?
_____ **2.** Avec qui	b. tu as mangé?
_____ **3.** Qu'est-ce que	c. est la date aujourd'hui?
_____ **4.** Qui	d. est-ce que tu aimes jouer? Tous sont des jouers talentueux.
_____ **5.** Laquelle	e. est ta fête préférée?

Exercise 2

Circle the correct question word in parentheses for each of the following questions.

1. (Quand / Pourquoi) est-ce que tu as choisi cette école? Pour la qualité de l'éducation ou la proximité de chez toi?

2. (Où / Combien) vas-tu?

3. (Combien / Quand) est-ce que tu as appris à jouer de la guitare?

4. (Quand / Comment) préférez-vous le café?

5. (Pourquoi / Qui) est le champion du monde de natation?

Exercise 3

Translate the following questions into French.

1. "My brother is studying abroad." "Which one? You have many brothers."

_____

_____

2. How much does this cost?

_____

_____

3. Which pencil is yours?

_____

_____

4. Why are you leaving?

_____

_____

5. Which exit is for the airport?

_____

_____

6. When is the store going to be open?

_____

_____

7. Who ate the last piece of pie?

_____

_____

75

76 Interrogatives *Other Uses of Interrogatives*

Non-verbal constructions are used when people address each other in a spontaneous and quick way.

Question words can be used on their own to obtain quick and pointed answers.

Qui?	Who?
Où?	Where?
Quand?	When?
Pourquoi?	Why?
Combien?	How much?
Comment?	How?
Quoi?	What?

Question words can also be combined with prepositions to form certain quick questions.

D'où?	From where?
Avec qui?	For whom?
Pour qui?	With whom?
Chez qui?	At whose home?
Depuis quand?	Since when?
Pour combien?	For how much?

N'est-ce pas **means** *isn't it?, don't I/we/you/they?,* **or** *doesn't he/she/it?* **This expression can be added to the end of an affirmative statement to ask for confirmation. The informal equivalent of** *n'est-ce pas?* **is** *hein?* **(right?).**

> *Vous êtes avocat, **n'est-ce pas**?*
> You are a lawyer, **right**? (Literally: You are a lawyer, **isn't it**?)

> *On y va, **hein**?*
> We're going, **right**?

Comment? **means** *pardon me?* **and is the polite way to ask people to repeat what they've said.**

> ***Comment***? *Je n'ai pas compris.*
> **Pardon me**? I didn't understand.

Quoi **(what?) is used informally to ask someone to clarify or repeat what they've said.** ***Quoi*** **is also used to express (negative) surprise.**

> ***Quoi***? *Tu peux répéter?*
> **What**? Can you repeat that?

> *J'ai perdu ma valise? **Quoi**?*
> I lost my suitcase? **What**?

Exercise 1

For each of the following scenarios, provide an appropriate interrogative response.

1._____

2._____

3._____

Exercise 2

For each of the situations in column A, choose the appropriate interrogative in column B.

	A	B
_____	**1.** Your cup of tea is exquisite.	a. Quoi?!
_____	**2.** Someone stole your book.	b. Hein?
_____	**3.** Your friend went to Mexico.	c. N'est-ce pas?
_____	**4.** You can't hear your mom on the phone.	d. Avec qui?

Exercise 3

Find the appropriate interrogative for each of the following statements.

1. Octave travaille pour une compagnie pharmaceutique.

   _____

2. Ce parfum coûte cher.

   _____

3. Nous rentrons en voiture.

   _____

4. Allons chez notre ami Rémi.

   _____

5. Votre frère est malade.

   _____

76

77 Negatives *Negative Sentence Structure*

The construction *ne ... pas* added to a verb is the standard way of forming a negative statement from an affirmative one.

*J'**aime** la biologie.*
I **like** biology.

*Je **n'aime pas** la biologie.*
I **don't like** biology.

Several other common negative expressions can be used with *ne* plus a verb to make a negative statement.

aucun(e)	none, not one
aucunement	in no way, not in the least
guère	hardly
jamais	never
ni	nor
ni ... ni	neither ... nor
nul(le)	no, none, nobody
nullement	in no way
nulle part	nowhere
plus	no longer, no more
personne	nobody
rien	nothing

*Il **ne** mange **ni** boit.*
He **neither** eats **nor** drinks.

*Il **n'**aime **nullement** Léa.*
He doesn't like Léa **in any way at all.**

*Il **n'**a parlé à **personne.***
He has **not** spoken to **anyone.**

*Il **n'**a **jamais** parlé.*
He has **never** spoken.

*Je ne vais **nulle part.***
I go **nowhere.**

La Langue Vivante

The negative constructions using *aucunement*, *guère*, and *nullement* are literary forms not commonly used in everyday speech.

Attention!

Ne ... que means *only*, similar to *seulement*. Its use is similar to the other negative constructions, though it is not technically considered a negative.

*Il **n'**aime **que** Léa.*
He **only** likes Léa. (Literally, He does **not** like **anyone but** Léa.)

Attention!

Negatives can be combined to form a negative statement. While in English this would form a double negative, in French there is only one negation. However, anytime *pas* is used, any combination with other negatives would form a double negative.

*Il **ne** parle **plus jamais** à **personne.***
He **doesn't** speak to **anyone anymore.**

*Il **ne** parle **pas** à **personne.***
He **doesn't** speak to **no one.**

Attention!

Aucun and *nul* can act as either adjectives or pronouns. In either case, they agree in gender with the nouns they modify or replace.

*Je n'ai **aucun** ami.*
*Je n'ai **aucune** amie.*
I **don't** have **any** friends. (Literally: I have **no** friend.)

*Des cousins? Je n'en ai **aucun.***
*Des cousins? Je n'en ai **aucune.***
Cousins? I have **none.** / I don't have any.

Exercise 1

Match the negative French words in column A with their English equivalents in column B.

	A		B
_____	**1.** aucune		a. hardly, few, little
_____	**2.** jamais		b. nothing
_____	**3.** guère		c. no one, nobody
_____	**4.** rien		d. neither, nor
_____	**5.** que		e. none
_____	**6.** personne		f. never
_____	**7.** ni		g. only

Exercise 2

Make each affirmative sentence below negative using the negative words in parentheses.

1. Je mange le boeuf. (jamais)

_____

_____

2. J'ai envie de faire grandes choses. (rien)

_____

_____

3. Il a une soeur. (que)

_____

_____

4. J'ai vu beaucoup de monde cet après-midi. (personne)

_____

_____

5. Elle aime bien son cousin et sa cousine. (ne ... ni)

_____

_____

Exercise 3

Translate the following sentences into French using the appropriate negative words.

1. I only eat chicken.

_____

_____

2. Nobody came to the theater tonight.

_____

_____

3. On the weekends, we don't go anywhere.

_____

_____

4. I don't have any (clean dishes).

_____

_____

5. He doesn't travel anymore.

_____

_____

77

Negative words can serve as a variety of parts of speech in French grammar.

Non (no), ***jamais*** (never), ***rien*** (nothing), and ***personne*** (no one) are often used as one-word negative responses to questions.

> *Qu'étudie-t-il?* ***Rien.***
> What does he study? **Nothing.**

Non plus (neither), the negative equivalent of *aussi* (too), can be used with the personal subject pronoun or following the verb.

> *Moi* ***aussi.***
> Me **too.**

> *Moi* ***non plus.***
> Me **neither.**

> *Il lit* ***aussi.***
> He reads **too.**

> *Il ne lit pas* ***non plus.***
> He does not read **either.**

The adjectives *aucun* and *nul* can modify a noun acting as a direct object or introducing an indirect object.

> *Je n'ai* ***aucune envie*** (direct object).
> I have **no desire.**

> *Je n'ai* ***nulle/aucune envie*** *d'elle* (indirect object).
> I have **no desire** for her.

> *Je n'en ai* ***nulle/aucune envie.***
> I have **no desire** for it (indirect object).

The pronoun *aucun* can modify a direct or indirect object or be an indirect object.

> *Il n'aime* ***aucune*** *d'elles.*
> He likes **none** of them (female).

> *Il ne parle* ***d'aucune*** *(d'elles).*
> He speaks **of none** (of them, female).

The pronouns *personne* and *rien* can function as direct or indirect objects.

> *Il ne donne* ***rien*** *à* ***personne.***
> He gives **nothing** to **nobody.** He doesn't give **anything** to **anybody.**

The pronouns *personne, rien, aucun,* and *nul* can also function as subjects.

> ***Personne*** *ne travaille.*
> **Nobody** works.

> ***Rien*** *ne marche.*
> **Nothing** works.

> ***Aucun*** *ne marche.*
> **None** work.

The adverbs *guère, jamais, nullement, plus,* and *rien* can follow the preposition *sans* (without) to modify an infinitive.

sans parler	without speaking
sans ***jamais*** *parler*	without **ever** speaking
sans ***rien*** *dire*	without saying **anything**
sans ***jamais rien*** *dire*	without **ever** saying **anything**

Guère, jamais, and *plus de* can also follow *sans* to modify a noun.

> *J'irai* ***sans plus de*** *doute.*
> I will go **without** doubting **anymore.**

The adjectives *aucun* and *nul* can follow *sans* to express *without any.*

> *J'irai* ***sans nul/aucun*** *doute.*
> I will go **definitely** go. (Literally: I will go **without any** doubt.)

Exercise 1

Answer the following questions using the one-word negatives.

1. Est-ce que tu aimes manger des cuisses de grenouilles (frogs' legs)?

   _____

2. Quand est-ce que tu es allé(e) à la lune?

   _____

3. Qui peut vivre pendant deux cents ans?

   _____

4. Qui peut être le président américain pendant vingt ans?

   _____

5. Qu'est on peut porter avec nous dans les poches pendant les examens finals au lycée?

   _____

6. Quand est-ce que tu vas à Saturne?

   _____

Exercise 2

Indicate the part of speech that the bolded negative words are acting as in the following sentences.

1. **Aucun** n'explique. _____

2. Il le sais **sans** rien dire. _____

3. **Personne** ne mange. _____

4. Il n'en mange **aucune**. _____

5. Je ne parle **d'aucun**. _____

Exercise 3

Translate the following sentences from English into French using the appropriate negative word.

1. "What are you doing?" "Nothing."

   _____

   _____

2. The candies I tasted? I didn't like any of them.

   _____

   _____

3. "Who did you invite to dinner at your house tonight?" "Nobody."

   _____

   _____

4. He wasn't on time either.

   _____

   _____

5. Spring is coming without doubt.

   _____

   _____

78

79 Conjunctions *Coordinating Conjunctions*

Coordinating conjunctions link two equal elements together. These elements may be single words, phrases, or entire clauses. The coordinating conjunctions in French are *mais, ou, et, donc, or, ni,* and *car.*

Et is used to convey simulaneity or union, similar to *and* in English.

> *J'aime le sucré, et j'aime le salé.*
> I like sweet things, **and** I like salty things.

> *Michel et Lisa vont au parc.*
> Michel **and** Lisa are going to the park.

Mais is used to convey opposition or contrast, similar to *but* in English.

> *Cette voiture pratique mais laide faisait beaucoup de bruit.*
> This convenient **but** ugly car made a lot of noise.

La Langue Vivante

Mais is used at the beginning of a sentence to emphasize the statement that follows.

> *Mais qui est là?*
> Who **(on earth)** is here?

Or is a formal, rhetorical way of expressing a contrast in thought or action, similar to *and yet* in English.

> *Vous l'aimez, or vous ne l'avez jamais rencontré.*
> You love him, **and yet** you've never met him.

Ou is used to express an alternative, similar to *or* in English. *Ou* may be repeated at the beginning of each element, similar to the expression *either ... or.*

> *C'est maintenant ou jamais.*
> It's now **or** never.

> *Ou tu dis oui, ou tu dis non.*
> **Either** say yes, **or** say no.

Ni (nor) conveys the idea of exclusion, usually when a list of things or persons is presented. The negative word *ne* is usually present in sentences with *ni,* appearing in front of the verb (or auxiliary verb in the past). *Ni* is repeated in front of each exluded thing or person.

> *Luc ne joue ni au basket ni au volley.*
> Luc plays **neither** basketball **nor** volleyball.

> *Ni Paul ni Pierre ne connaissent la vérité.*
> **Neither** Paul **nor** Pierre knows the truth.

Donc conveys the idea of a consequence, similar to *therefore* in English. The structure reason-*donc*-consequence is typically used.

> *Je suis adulte, donc je vote.*
> I am an adult; **therefore** I vote.

Attention!

Donc can also appear in the beginning or end of a sentence to emphasize an effect without stating the cause, introduce another topic in conversation, or punctuate speech without specific meaning (similar to *so* in English).

> *C'est l'heure, donc.*
> **So,** it's time.

Car expresses an obvious reason, similar to *because* or *since* in English. *Car* is similar to *donc* in that they are both used when expressing cause and effect; however, *car* follows the structure: consequence-*car*-reason, rather than reason-*donc*-consequence.

> *Je vote car je suis adulte.*
> I vote **since** I am an adult.

Exercise 1

Fill in the following sentences with the correct coordinating conjunction: *et, ni, ou, car,* or *mais.*

1. Elles vont prendre un fromage _____ un dessert aussi.

2. Tu veux une glace à la vanille _____ au chocolat?

3. Sébastien ne va pas skier _____ il est malade!

4. On va manger _____ on ira dormir.

5. Il ne fait _____ froid _____ chaud.

Exercise 2

Use coordinating conjunctions to form reactions to the following statements.

1. Il pleut _____

   _____

2. J'ai oublié mes clés _____

   _____

3. Nous avons faim _____

   _____

4. Elle est en retard _____

   _____

5. Ils ont des examens _____

   _____

Exercise 3

Translate the following sentences into French using the correct coordinating conjunction.

1. Muriel hates the cold, and yet she lives in the mountains.

   _____

   _____

2. I won't say no since I would like to try.

   _____

   _____

3. And I thought I was alone!

   _____

   _____

4. Neither you nor she did convince me.

   _____

   _____

5. Why on earth did Jeanne go out?

   _____

   _____

79

The two elements joined by a subordinating conjunction are not equal. Subordinating conjunctions link a main clause to a subordinate clause, which provides more information or context. The subordinating conjunctions in French are *que* (that), *comme* (as, because, like, since), *quand* (when), *lorsque* (when, formally), *puisque* (since, because), and *si* (if).

Que is a subordinating conjunction used after certain verbs to specify the content of the first action. Que is similar to *that* in English.

> *Je pense **que** tu es fort.*
> I think **(that)** you are strong.

> *Il t'a dit **que** c'était important.*
> He told you **(that)** it was important.

Comme introduces elements of cause, time, or manner. It translates as *as, because, like,* or *since* in English.

> ***Comme** il était tard, je suis allée dormir.*
> **Since** it was late, I went to sleep.

> ***Comme** il nous vit, il devient pâle.*
> **As** he saw us, he became pale.

> *J'ai rangé les livres **comme** tu le voulais.*
> I put the books away **like** you wanted.

Quand (when) and lorsque (when, formally) introduce a condition dependent on time. Lorsque becomes *lorsqu'* when followed by a vowel.

> ***Quand** tu seras vieux, tu comprendras.*
> **When** you are old, you will understand.

> *Ils ont fait connaissance **lorsqu'**il était soldat.*
> They met **when** he was a soldier.

Puisque means *since* or *because* and introduces an element of obvious cause.

> ***Puisque** je te le dis, crois-moi.*
> **Since** I'm telling you, believe me.

Si introduces a conditional element dependent on the main clause, similar to *if* in English. Si becomes *s'* when followed by *il*.

> *Nous pouvons danser **si** tu veux.*
> We can dance **if** you want.

> ***S'**il fait beau, nous irons à la campagne.*
> **If** the weather is nice, we'll go to the country.

Exercise 1

Fill in the following sentences with the correct subordinating conjunction: *comme, lorsque, que, si,* or *puisque.*

1. _____Cendrillon était jeune, elle travaillait dur.

2. Je ne veux pas _____tu sois malade.

3. _____c'est très important pour toi, je suis d'accord.

4. Je suis _____toi: idéaliste.

5. _____tu trouves des billets, allons au théâtre.

Exercise 2

Match each statement in column A with the appropriate concept describing it in column B.

A	B
_____ **1.** Lorsque c'est l'hiver, il neige.	a. content
_____ **2.** Si on y va, viens avec nous.	b. manner
_____ **3.** Je n'aime pas que tu t'inquiètes.	c. time
_____ **4.** Il est comme elle.	d. cause
_____ **5.** Puisque ça ne va pas, rentre.	e. condition

Exercise 3

Finish the following sentences by completing the clause introduced by each conjunction.

1. Je pense que _____

_____

2. J'ai froid donc _____

3. Je vais au supermarché car _____

_____

4. Je sors le soir si _____

_____

5. Je suis satisfaîte quand _____

_____

Exercise 4

Translate the following sentences into French using the correct subordinating conjunction.

1. Since you bought this bike, you don't need to walk.

_____

_____

2. Write to him that you accept.

_____

_____

3. As you wish!

_____

_____

4. If you are worried, talk to him.

_____

_____

5. As I arrived, I had an incredible idea.

_____

_____

80

81 Comparisons *Inequality and Equality*

Comparisons of inequality and equality are used to compare two or more people, things, or ideas.

The adjective *plus* (more) is commonly used when making a comparison of superiority. To compare two or more qualities, superiority is expressed with *plus* + the adjective + *que.* Two compare quantities, superiority is expressed with *plus de* + the noun + *que.* While the adjectives agree in gender and number as usual, the word *plus* is always invariable.

> *Il est **plus grand qu'**elle.*
> He is **taller than** she.
> (Literally: He is **more tall than** she.)

> *Il fait **plus froid qu'**hier.*
> It's **colder than** yesterday.
> (Literally: It is **more cold than** yesterday.)

> *J'ai eu **plus de cadeaux que** lui.*
> I got **more presents than** him.

L'Exception

Plus bon is not used to express *better than*. Instead, the adjective *bon* (good) is replaced by *meilleur(e)* to express a comparison. *Meilleur* agrees in gender and number with the noun it is referring to.

> *Il est **bon** mais elle est **meilleure** (que lui).*
> He is **good** but she is **better** (than he).

> *Stacy est un **meilleur** jouer de basketball que Franck.*
> Stacy is a **better** basketball player than Franck.

Similarly, the adjective *pire* (worse) replaces *plus mauvais*. *Pire* agrees in number, but not in gender, with the noun it modifies. Though *plus mauvais* is often heard in speech, it is grammatically incorrect.

> *Elle est **mauvaise** mais il est **pire** (qu'elle).*
> She is **bad** but he is **worse** (than she).

Plus petit is used to compare size and agrees in gender and number with the noun it modifies. To compare quantity or quality, rather than size, *moindre* replaces *plus petit*. *Moindre* agrees in number but not in gender with the noun it modifies.

> *Il est **petit** mais elle est **plus petite** (que lui).*
> He is **small** but she is **smaller** (than he).

> *Un **moindre risque** serait de prendra la route gauche.*
> It would be **less risky** to take the road on the left.

The adjective *moins* (less) is used when making a comparison of inferiority. When comparing qualities, inferiority is expressed with *moins* + the adjective + *que.* When comparing quantities, inferiority is expressed with *moins de* + the noun + *que.* While the adjectives agree in gender and number as usual, the word *moins* is always invariable.

> *Il est **moins grand qu'**elle.*
> He is **less tall than** she.

> *J'ai **moins de** bonbons **qu'**elle.*
> I have **less** candy **than** she **(does).**

If *que* introduces a subordinate clause, the particle *ne* sometimes precedes the verb in that clause. This is optional, and it does not express a negation.

> *Il a **moins d'**amis **qu'**il **ne** veut.*
> He has **fewer** friends **than** he wants.

> *Il a **plus d'**amis **qu'**il **ne** veut.*
> He has **more** friends **than** he wants.

Equality in quality is expressed with *aussi* + the adjective/adverb + *que.* Equality in quantity is expressed with *autant de* + the noun/verb + *que.* In English, this is expressed as *as much as, as many as,* or *as adjective as.*

> *Il mange **aussi** vite **qu'**elle.*
> He eats **as** fast **as** she does.

> *Il mange **autant de** pommes **qu'**elle.*
> He eats **as many** apples **as** she does.

Exercise 1

Circle the correct comparison word in parentheses to complete the following sentences.

1. Pour la personne qui achète, un prix de 250 euros est (pire / meilleur) qu'un prix de 100 euros.

2. Recevoir cinq cadeaux d'anniversaire est (pire / meilleur) que recevoir trois cadeaux.

3. Les orchidées sont (plus / moins) belles que les roses selon ma mère, qui adore les orchidées.

4. Même les tulipes sont (plus / moins) belles par rapport aux orchidées, dit-elle.

Exercise 2

Complete each sentence below comparing Anne-Laure and Justin's report cards.

1. Anne-Laure est _____ forte que Justin en maths.

2. La note de Justin en biologie est _____ que la note d'Anne-Laure.

3. La note d'Anne-Laure en biologie est _____ que la note de Justin.

4. Anne-Laure a _____ de difficulté en anglais que Justin.

5. La note d'Anne-Laure en français est _____ que l a note de Justin.

Exercise 3

Translate the following sentences into French.

1. I ate as much pizza as she did.

_____

_____

2. She speaks Spanish as well as she speaks Italian.

_____

_____

3. Jessica has as many brothers as sisters.

_____

_____

4. I eat as much meat as fish.

_____

_____

Exercise 4

Use adjectives to make comparisons between the pictures below.

Fabien   Caroline

1. _____

2. _____

3. _____

81

89 Comparisons *Superlatives*

There are two kinds of superlatives: relative superlatives and absolute superlatives.

Relative superlatives express the highest or lowest, or the most or least, in relation to a group or category. A relative superlative is expressed by placing a definite article or a possessive adjective before a comparative.

*C'est elle qui a **le plus d'**amis.*
She the one who has **the most** friends.

*Luc est **le meilleur** élève de son école.*
Luc is **the best** pupil in his school.

Attention!

As with simple comparisons, in superlative form the adjective *bon* becomes *meilleur*, the adjective *mauvais* becomes *pire*, and the comparative *plus petit* becomes *moindre*.

*Luc et Léa sont **mes meilleurs** étudiants.*
Luc and Léa are **my best** students.

*J'ai **le plus petit** chien du monde.*
I have **the smallest** dog in the world.

*Je n'en ai pas **la moindre** idée.*
I don't have **the slightest** idea.

There are two relative superlative constructions:

1) *le/la/les + moin/plus* + adjective + (*de/des*) + noun
2) *le/la/les* + noun + *le/las/les + moins/plus* + adjective

Though they vary slightly, both constructions have the same general meaning.

*Je préfère **la plus directe** des routes.*
I prefer **the most direct** route.

*Je préfère la route **la plus directe**.*
I prefer the route that is **most direct**.
(Literally: I prefer the route **the most direct**.)

The absolute superlative expresses the highest or lowest quality of a noun without relation to other nouns. *Très* (very) is the most commonly used adverb for absolute superlatives. It is used to stress the adjective.

*Il est **très gentil** et **extrêmement poli**.*
He is **very kind** and **extremely polite**.

*Il fait **très chaud** aujourd'hui.*
It is **very hot** today.

Certain adjectives cannot be used in the absolute superlative because their degree cannot be stressed. Common examples include *excellent*, *formidable*, and *exceptionnel*.

*Le film était **excellent**.*
    And not: *Le film était **très excellent**.*
The film was very **excellent**.

Exercise 1

Fill in the blanks with the correct superlatives to complete the following sentences.

1. L'Alaska est _____ grand état.

2. Le Rhode Island est _____ petit état.

3. Paris est _____ grande ville de France.

4. Je n'ai pas aimé *Spider-Man 3*. Entre les trois films *Spider-Man* c'était _____.

5. 104 degrés est _____ haute température qu'il a fait à Seattle.

6. Le mont Everest est _____ grande montagne du monde.

Exercise 2

Rewrite each sentence below to express the superlative.

1. David Beckham est un footballeur talentueux.

   _____

   _____

2. L'Amazone est une fleuve très longue.

   _____

   _____

3. Sarah est une élève très studieuse dans cette classe.

_____

_____

4. La Chine devient une économie importante.

_____

_____

5. L'Auvergne est une jolie région en France.

_____

_____

2. _____

3. _____

_____

Exercise 3

Write two sentences using superlatives to compare the items in the following illustrations. Begin each sentence with _Entre les trois_ (_Between the three_).

Fabien   Robert   Caroline

1. _____

_____

Exercise 4

Translate the following into French using absolute superlatives.

1. She is very smart.

_____

_____

2. The math exam was very difficult.

_____

_____

3. I'm very tricky.

_____

_____

4. Frankly, I think that he is very arrogant.

_____

_____

82

Numbers *Cardinal Numbers*

Cardinal numbers are the numbers used for counting (*one, two, three,* and so on).

un	one	*onze*	eleven
deux	two	*douze*	twelve
trois	three	*treize*	thirteen
quatre	four	*quatorze*	fourteen
cinq	five	*quinze*	fifteen
six	six	*seize*	sixteen
sept	seven	*dix-sept*	seventeen
huit	eight	*dix-huit*	eighteen
neuf	nine	*dix-neuf*	nineteen
dix	ten		

The number *one* in French changes form to agree in gender with the noun it modifies. *Un* is used before singular masculine nouns. *Une* is used before singular feminine nouns.

un *homme*	***une*** *pomme*
one man	**one** apple

Attention!

The masculine form *un* translates as *one* when counting.

un, *deux, trois ...*
one, two, three ...

Numbers between twenty and sixty-nine are composites made up of the tens digit and the single number, linked by a hyphen.

vingt-deux *couleurs*
twenty-two colors

L'Exception

The numbers *twenty-one, thirty-one, forty-one, fifty-one,* and *sixty-one* take *et* with no hyphen between the components.

vingt et un *lapins*
twenty-one rabbits

The numbers *seventy* through *ninety* derive their name from the sum of the other numbers.

soixante-dix	seventy (literally, sixty and ten)
soixante et onze	seventy-one (literally, sixty and eleven)
soixante-douze	seventy-two (literally, sixty and twelve)
quatre-vingts	eighty (literally, four twenties)
quatre-vingt-un	eighty-one (literally, four twenties and one)
quatre-vingt-deux	eighty-two (literally, four twenties and two)
quatre-vingt-dix	ninety (literally, four twenties and ten)
quatre-vingt-onze	ninety-one (literally, four twenties and eleven)
quatre-vingt-douze	ninety-two (literally, four twenties and twelve)

L'Exception

An *-s* is added to the end of the written form of *quatre-vingts* (*eighty*). The numbers after that do not add the *-s* at the end.

1980 → *mille neuf cent* **quatre-vingts**
1998 → *mille neuf cent* **quatre-vingt-dix-huit**

Cent means *hundred* in French. The numbers 100 to 999 are formed by adding the cardinal before *cent(s)* and the tens digits after, similar to the English construction.

deux cents *pêches*	***quatre cent cinquante*** *pamplemousses*
two hundred peaches	**four hundred fifty** grapefruits

An *-s* is added at the end of *cent* to form numbers between two hundred and nine hundred that are not followed by other numbers. The number *cent* (one-hundred) does not take an *-s,* nor do any numbers that have tens and ones digits. *Mille* never takes an *-s* at the end.

cent *cercles*	**one hundred** circles
trois cents *étoiles*	**three hundred** stars
trois cent quatre-vingts *fraises*	**three hundred eighty** strawberries
deux ***mille***	two **thousand**
trois ***mille*** *cinq cents*	three **thousand** five hundred

Un million (one million) and *un milliard* (one billion) take an *-s* at the end if they are the last unit. They do not take the *-s* if another number follows them.

deux ***millions*** *habitants*	two **million** inhabitants
cinq ***million cinq cent mille*** *habitants*	five **million five hundred thousand** inhabitants

La Langue Vivante

In French, a decimal point or space is used when writing numbers *mille* (one thousand) and higher. A comma is used between a whole number and a decimal.

1.500 or 1 500	→	**1,500**
mille cinq cents		one thousand five hundred
1,5	→	**1.5**
un virgule cinq		one point five/oneand a half

Exercise 2

Write out the numbers that solve each arithmetic problem below.

1. 2.000 + 100 = _____ vaches

2. 90 - 5 = _____ gâteaux

3. 500.000 + 500.000 = _____ parapluies

4. 300 + 24 = _____ anges

5. 12 - 11 = _____ professeur

Exercise 1

Complete the crossword puzzle below with the correct French word for each number.

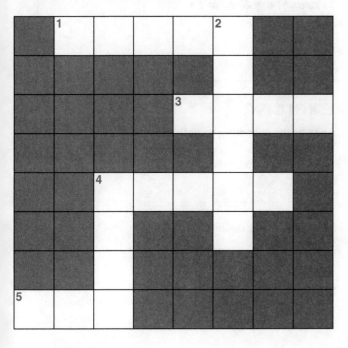

Across
1. 20 ceintures
3. 100 drapeaux
4. 12 stylos
5. 10 tournesols

Down
2. 13 sorcières
4. 2 piscines

Exercise 3

How much do you think the following items cost? Write out your guess in French.

1. une nouvelle voiture

_____

2. une maison dans ta ville

_____

3. des chaussures Adidas

_____

4. une montre Rolex

_____

5. une croisière sur le Nil

_____

83

Ordinal numbers are the adjective form of the cardinal numbers (*first, second, third,* and so on). They are formed by adding the suffix *-ième* to the cardinal numbers after one. Numbers that end in *-e*, drop the *-e* before adding the suffix.

premier première	first	1er (1er) 1ère (1ère)
deuxième	second	2ème (2e)
troisième	third	3ème (3e)
quatrième	fourth	4ème (4e)
cinquième	fifth	5ème (5e)
sixième	sixth	6ème (6e)
septième	seventh	7ème (7e)
huitième	eighth	8ème (8e)
neuvième	ninth	9ème (9e)
dixième	tenth	10ème (10e)
onzième	eleventh	11ème (11e)
douzième	twelth	12ème (12e)

Similar to the cardinal numbers, the ordinals corresponding to the English *twenty-first*, *thirty-first*, and so on include *et* between the tens and ones digits.

vingt **et** unième
twenty **and** first
= twenty-first

trente **et** unième
thirty **and** first
= thirty-first

The ordinal for *un* has both a masculine and a feminine form and must agree with the noun it modifies. The other ordinal do not agree in gender with the noun they modify.

le **premier** mardi
the **first** (masc.) Tuesday

la **première** semaine
the **first** (fem.) week

le **quatrième** mardi
the **fourth** (masc.) Tuesday

la **quatrième** semaine
the **fourth** (fem.) week

All ordinal numbers add an *-s* to the end to agree with a plural noun.

la première cause → **les premières** causes
(**the first** cause) (**the first** causes)

le premier jour → **les premiers** jours
(**the first** day) (**the first** days)

la deuxième cause → **les deuxièmes** causes
(**the second** cause) (**the second** causes)

le deuxième jour → **les deuxièmes** jours
(**the second** day) (**the second** days)

Attention!

There are two different ways of abbreviating ordinal numbers in French. Both are used frequently.

deuxième → **2ème** or **2e**

Exercise 1

Answer the following questions.

1. Quelle est la première lettre de l'alphabet?

   _____

2. Quelle est la deuxième lettre de l'alphabet?

   _____

3. Quelle est la treizième lettre de l'alphabet?

   _____

4. Quelle est la dixième lettre de l'alphabet?

_____

5. Quelle est la vingtième lettre de l'alphabet?

_____

Exercise 2

Use ordinal numbers to label the floors of the apartment building.

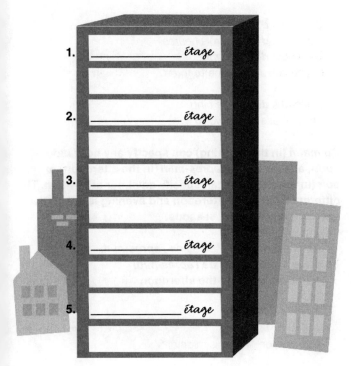

1. _____ _étage_

2. _____ _étage_

3. _____ _étage_

4. _____ _étage_

5. _____ _étage_

Exercise 3

Arnaud is arguing with his brother about channel surfing. Translate their dialogue into French using the correct cardinal and ordinal numbers.

Philippe: —Arnaud, that's the fourth channel you've put on! Please don't change the channel!
Arnaud: —No, it's the third. First I was watching a comedy on Canal Plus, then I was watching the show about the Second World War.
Philippe: —And then you were watching the fifth episode of _Urgence._ And now you're watching this documentary on the French king Louis the Fourteenth. That's four.

_____

_____

_____

_____

_____

_____

_____

_____

_____

_____

_____

_____

_____

84

Even though the hour indicates a point in time rather than a quantity of hours, the French noun *heure* (hour) takes a plural -*s* after a plural number.

*Il est arrivé à **une heure trente.***
He arrived at **one-thirty.**

*Il est arrivé à **deux heures.***
He arrived at **two.**

The 24-hour clock is used in written French. Hours are usually spelled out in literary writing, though not in other writings.

*Le magasin est ouvert de **neuf heures** à **dix-sept heures.***
The shop is open from **nine o'clock** to **five o'clock.**

Attention!

Hours are not usually spelled out in printed schedules. The letter *h* is commonly used as an abbreviation for the word *heure*.

*Le magasin est ouvert de **9h** à **17h.***
The shop is open from **9 A.M.** to **5 P.M.**

The 12-hour system is typically favored in speech, especially when the time of day being referred to is obvious. When expressing multiple hours in spoken French, the first *heure* is sometimes omitted, though the second *heure* is never omitted.

*J'ai cours à **une heure** et à **trois heures.***
*J'ai cours à **une** et à **trois heures.***
I have classes at **one** and at **three.**

Demie (half) and *quart* (quarter) are primarily used in speech and are connected to the hour with the use of *et* after the hour and *moins* (minus) before the hour. When used in writing, the hours and minutes are normally written out.

1:30	*une heure **et demie***	**half past** one
1:15	*une heure **et quart***	**a quarter past** one
12:45	*une heure **moins le quart***	**a quarter to** one

Attention!

A specific time can be expressed many different ways depending on the circumstance or the speaker's preference.

9h45 or 9:45 → *neuf heures quarante-cinq*
(nine forty-five)
dix heures moins le quart
(quarter to ten)

The prepositions *de* and *à* are used to express an interval between two hours, similar to *from* and *to* in English. The word *heure* can be omitted from this construction.

*J'ai cours **d'** une heure **à** trois heures.*
*J'ai cours **d'** une **à** trois heures.*
*J'ai cours **d'** une **à** trois.*
I have class **from** one **to** three.

*J'ai cours **de** deux **à** cinq.*
I have class **from** two **to** five.

Du matin (in the morning) can specify any hour before noon, and either ***de l'après-midi*** (in the afternoon) or ***du soir*** (in the evening) can specify any hour after noon. The difference between afternoon and evening is subjective and can vary with the seasons.

*d'une heure à trois heures **de l'après-midi***
*d'une à trois heures **de l'après-midi***
from one to three **in the afternoon**

Attention!

Midi is noon. *Minuit* is midnight.

Exercise 1

Fill in the arms of the clocks below to indicate the following times.

1. trois heures et demie

2. quinze heures et demie

3. midi

4. sept heures du soir

5. 20h

Exercise 2

Use complete sentences to answer the following questions about your daily routine.

1. À quelle heure est-ce que tu te lèves?

_____

_____

2. À quelle heure est-ce que tu prends ton petit-déjeuner?

_____

_____

3. À quelle heure est-ce que tu te couches?

_____

_____

4. À quelle heure est-ce que tu prends ta douche?

_____

_____

5. À quelle heure est-ce que tu commences l'école?

_____

_____

Exercise 3

Write out each of the following times.

1. 17h

_____

2. 14h15

_____

3. 8h45

_____

4. 12h

_____

85

All days of the week are masculine and begin with a lowercase letter.

lundi	Monday
mardi	Tuesday
mercredi	Wednesday
jeudi	Thursday
vendredi	Friday
samedi	Saturday
dimanche	Sunday

Events or activities that are habitual and occuring on the same day each week are expressed using the masculine singular definite article, *le*.

> *J'ai cours **le mardi** et **le jeudi**.*
> I have class on **Tuesdays** and **Thursdays**.

When referring to something happening this particular week, the definite article before the day is not used.

> *J'ai cours **mardi** et jeudi.*
> I have classes on **Tuesday** and **Thursday**.

When referring to something happening on a specific day not during this week, the adjectives *dernier* (last), *prochain* (next), and *le suivant* (the following) are used.

*J'avais cours **mardi dernier**.*
I had classes **last Tuesday**.

*J'ai cours **mardi prochain**.*
I have classes **next Tuesday**.

*J'ai cours **le mardi suivant**.*
I have classes **the following Tuesday**.

La Langue Vivante

The singular definite article (*le*) is common in written and spoken French. However, the plural definite article (*les*) can be used in formal settings. The meaning of the sentence remains the same.

*J'ai cours **les mardis** et (les) **jeudis**.*
I have class on **Tuesdays** and **Thursdays** (each week).

*J'ai cours **des** (de + les) **mardis aux** (à + les) **jeudis**.*
I have class **from Tuesday to Thursday** (each week).

The months of the year are also masculine and begin with lowercase letters.

janvier	January
février	February
mars	March
avril	April
mai	May
juin	June
juillet	July
août	August
septembre	September
octobre	October
novembre	November
décembre	December

In French, dates are expressed using cardinal numbers (*one, two, three*) not ordinal numbers (*first, second, third*). In a written story or essay, dates are usually spelled out. In a schedule or a news article, dates are seldom spelled out.

> *Il est venu le **deux** mai.*   *Il est venu le **2** mai.*
> He came on May **second**.   He came on May **2**.

The definite article *le* is used to specify certain dates.

> *Il est venu **le** 2 et **le** 4.*
> He came on **the** second and **the** fourth.

La Langue Vivante

In colloquial speech, months are sometimes omitted completely, as long as context makes it obvious which month is being discussed.

*Il est venu **le deux**.*
He came on **the second**.

The phrase *du ... au* (from the ... to the) is used to express duration from a specific start date to a specific end date.

> *Il est resté **du** (de + le) 2 **au** (à + le) 4.*
> He stayed **from the** second **to the** fourth.

Unlike in the United States, where the month usually comes before the day, in French dates are written with the day followed by the month, then by the year. Days, months, and years are frequently separated by a period.

le 2 mai	→	2.5
le 2 mai 1950	→	2.5.1950

Exercise 1

Compose complete sentences, including the full dates, to indicate when each of the following holidays occur.

1. La Saint-Valentin

_____

_____

2. La Toussaint (All Saint's Day)

_____

_____

3. Jour J (D-day)

_____

_____

4. Noël

_____

_____

5. Ton anniversaire

_____

_____

Exercise 2

Match the dates in column A to the way they would be expressed in French in column B.

A	B
_____ **1.** May 1, 1976	a. 2.3.1920
_____ **2.** February 3, 1920	b. 11.12.2006
_____ **3.** November 12, 2001	c. 1.5.1976
_____ **4.** January 5, 1976	d. 3.2.1920
_____ **5.** March 2, 1920	e. 5.1.1976
_____ **6.** December 11, 2006	f. 12.11.2001

Exercise 3

When were the following people born? Write complete sentences using the full dates.

1. ta soeur/ton frère

_____

2. ton père

_____

3. ta tante

_____

4. ton meilleur ami/ta meilleure amie

_____

5. ton chien

_____

86

The interjections discussed in this section are not actual words but sounds represented typographically. Interjections, like the English *wow!*, *oh!*, and *ahh!*, are used to convey emotion and state of mind.

French interjections are different from those used in English. Some of the most common French sound words, along with their approximate pronunciation in parentheses, are included below.

French interjection	Use	English equivalent
Aïe! (Eye!) Ouille! (Oo-ii!)	express pain	Ouch! Ow!
Chout! (Shhoutt!)	make someone be quiet	Shhh ...
Beurk! (Berk!)	express disgust, usually about food	Ew!
Beh ... heu ... alors ... (Bah ... eu ...)	indicates a pause, such as during thought	Ummm ... so ...
Ouf (oof)	signify hard work that has been finished	Ø
Hein? (Heh?)	express confusion	Huh?
Hop-là (Up-la)	signify that a small physical task has been completed	Ø
Boum (Boom)	mimic explosions or a heartbeat.	Boom! Thump thump (for the heart)
Oh-là (O-la)	ask somebody what he or she is doing, if it's a bad idea; also to get someone's attention	Ø
Héhé (Hay-hay)	signify laughing in a humorous situation	Hee hee
Oups (Oops)	signify a mistake	Oops
Zut (Zoot) Mince (Maance)	signify a mistake or express frustration	Darn
Et toc! (Ay tock!)	show satisfaction that someone got something he or she deserved	So there. Serves you right.
Toc, toc! (Tock, tock!)	mimic knocking on a door	Knock, knock
Coucou (Coo coo)	mimic knocking on a door while peeking inside.	Peek-a-boo
Miam miam (Meeyum, meeyum)	express delight while eating	Yum, yum
Bon ... (Bohn ...)	stall, literally meaning *good*	Ummm ... well ...
Oh là là (Oh la la)	express frustration or excitement	Come on! Oh, good!
quoi? (... kwah?)	put at the end of any familiar phrase	right? you know?
Hé! (Hey!)	call someone from across the room, in an informal setting	Hey!

La Langue Vivante

Interjections are often spelled differently across various situations and in various regions where French is spoken.

La Langue Vivante

As in English, interjections are often used in spoken French. They are also seen in print comic books and in informal e-mail messages.

Exercise 1

What French sounds would you use in the following situations?

1. Someone falls and twists her ankle. It hurts a lot.

   _____

2. Someone catches a toddler from falling.

   _____

3. Someone tells a story about watching a building explode by demolition.

   _____

4. A teacher is trying to make his students be quiet on a field trip to a museum.

   _____

5. Someone is stalling and uncomfortable when trying to ask someone out on a date.

   _____

Exercise 2

Fill in the blanks in the following sentences with appropriate French sound words.

1. _____, j'ai fait une bêtise.

2. C'est bien fait pour lui. Ça lui servira de leçon.

_____!

3. _____! Franchement, c'est le meilleur

éclair au chocolat de Paris.

3._____

4. _____! Tu as vu comment il est beau, lui?

5. Achète le nouveau CD, _____.

6. 21h30 _____.

Exercise 3

Caption each of the following drawings with an appropriate French sound word.

4._____

1._____

5._____

2._____

87

175

Specific rules govern when a word can be contracted with an apostophe.

Before a vowel or a silent *h,* the definite articles and personal pronouns *le* and *la* both become *l'.*

le + *ami* = *l'ami* (male friend)
la + *amie* = *l'amie* (female friend)

Il le tue.
He kills **him.**

Il l'a tué.
He killed **him.**

Before a vowel or a silent *h,* the personal pronouns *je, me, te,* and *se* become *j', m', t',* and *s'.*

Il se tue.
He kills **himself.**

Il s'est tué.
He killed **himself.**

L'Exception

When linked to an inverted verb by a hyphen, the personal pronouns *le, la,* and *je* are not shortened with the word following.

J'ai aimé.
I have loved.

Ai-je aimé?
Have **I** loved?

L'Exception

Before a conjunction, the articles *le* and *la* are not shortened.

Les policiers cherchent le ou la coupable.
The police are looking for **the** culprit.

Before a vowel or a silent *h,* the preposition *de* becomes *d'.*

beaucoup de chats
a lot **of** cats

beaucoup d'amis
a lot **of** friends

Before a vowel or a silent *h,* the negative adverb *ne* becomes *n'.*

Il ne veut rien.
He wants nothing.

Il n'a rien.
He has nothing.

Before a vowel or a silent *h,* the relative pronoun *que* becomes *qu'.*

Je dis qu'elle a raison.
I say **that** she is right.

The composite conjunctions *lorsque* (when) and *puisque* (since) become *lorsqu'* and *puisqu'* when used before *un, une, il, ils, elle, elles, on,* and *en.*

Puisque Alex est ton ami ...
Since Alex is your friend ...

Puisqu'il est ton ami ...
Since he is your friend ...

Si* becomes *s'* when used before *il* or *ils.

Dis-moi si elles partent.
Tell me **if** they leave.

Dis-moi s'il part.
Tell me **if** he leaves.

Before an *e,* the demonstrative pronoun *ce* becomes *c'.*

Ce sont des amis.
These are friends.

C'est un ami.
This is a friend.

Exercise 1

Decide whether the following words should form contractions.

1. beaucoup de ail _____

2. nous le avons fait _____

3. le hibou _____

4. ils se entendent bien _____

5. le hérisson _____

6. que elle _____

7. la histoire _____

Exercise 2

In the following sentences, circle the correct form of the word in parentheses.

1. Elles (se/s') apprecient.

2. Je rentre dans (le/l') hangar.

3. (Je/J') habitais à Dijon en 1985.

4. Il travaille à (le/l') hôpital.

5. Je pense (que/qu') avec vous tout se passera bien.

6. (Puisque/Puisqu') Antoine a bu, il ne peut plus conduire.

Exercise 3

Provide a contraction that demonstrates each of the following descriptions.

1. Before a vowel or a silent *h*, *le* and *la* both become *l'*.

   _____

2. Before a vowel or a silent *h*, the adverb *ne* becomes *n'*.

   _____

3. Before a vowel or a silent *h*, the personal pronouns *je*, *me*,

   te, *se* become *j'*, *m'*, *t'*, *s'*. _____

4. Before a vowel or a silent *h*, *que* becomes *qu'*.

   _____

5. *Si* becomes *s'* only before *il(s)*. _____

6. The composite conjunctions *lorsque* and *puisque* become
   lorsqu' and *puisqu'* before *un(e)*, *il(s)*, *elle(s)*, *on*, and *en*.

   _____

88

Though neither the aspirate *h* nor the silent *h* is pronounced in French, there are slightly different rules for each of them. There is a distinct pause in the pronunciation between the article and a word beginning with an aspirate *h*. The article forms a *liason* with a word beginning with a silent *h*, meaning the two words run together. The silent *h* usually follows the same rules as vowels.

In French, an aspirate *h* prevents liaisons, while the silent *h* does not. The pronunciation with the articles depends on whether the *h* is aspirate or silent.

	Example	Pronunciation
Aspirate *h*	*une hache* (an axe)	*une ache*
	la hache	*la ache*
	un hublot (a porthole)	*un ublot*
	le hublot	*le ublot*
Silent *h*	*une habitude* (a habit)	*unabitude*
	l'habitude	*labitude*
	un hébergement (a lodging)	*unébergement*
	l'hébergement	*lébergement*

Attention!

Words that begin with an aspirate *h* retain their definite article (*le* or *la*). Words that begin with a silent *h* follow the same rules as words beginning with vowels. They take the contracted article *l'* and are pronounced beginning with their first vowel sound.

l'humour (the humor)
l'humanité (the humanity)
l'haleine (the breath)

When possessive adjectives modify words that begin with a silent *h*, they follow the rules for words beginning with vowels. In these instances, feminine words take *mon, ton,* and *son* rather than *me, te,* and *se.*

une habitude (feminine)	*une amie* (feminine)
mon *habitude* (**my** habit)	**mon** *amie* (**my** friend)
son *habitude* (**his** habit)	**son** *amie* (**his** friend)

Before a vowel or a silent *h*, the masculine demonstrative adjective *ce* becomes *cet*.

ce + *ami* = **cet** *ami* (**this** friend, masculine)
ce + *homme* = **cet** homme (**this** man, masculine)

Some adjectives change form depending on whether the noun it modifies begins with an aspirate or silent *h*, or a vowel.

beau (beautiful)	un **bel** *homme* (a **beautiful** man)
nouveau (new)	un **nouvel** *ami* (a **new** friend)
vieux (old)	un **vieil** *ordinateur* (an **old** computer)

Attention!

Possessive, demonstrative, or descriptive adjectives do not change form before a noun starting with an aspirate *h*.

le *haricot* (the bean)
ce *haricot* (this bean)
un **beau** *haricot* (a beautiful bean)

La Langue Vivante

Words that begin with an aspirate *h* are usually derived from languages other than French. For example, *le hamac* (hammock) comes from Spanish.

La Langue Vivante

In most French/English dictionaries some distinction will be made between words that begin with an aspirate *h* and those that begin with a silent *h*. For example, all those beginning with an aspirate *h* may have an asterisk (*) before them.

Exercise 1

Place each of the following words into the appropriate bin, along with the correct definite article.

hibou, hiver, homme, haricot, halles, homard, hasard, honte, haine, handicap, harcèlement

Aspirate *h*	Silent *h*

Exercise 2

Correct any errors in the following sentences. Note: Not all sentences include errors.

1. C'est un beau héritage.

_____

_____

2. Ma amie s'appelle Louise.

_____

_____

3. Il a acheté une nouvelle housse pour son iPod.

_____

_____

4. Elle a acheté un nouvel aspirateur pour le salon.

_____

_____

5. Ma habitation est une cabane en bois.

_____

_____

6. Le hippopotame mange la herbe.

_____

_____

Exercise 3

Translate the following sentences into French.

1. It was by chance!

_____

_____

2. I want to eat this lobster.

_____

_____

3. What beautiful oysters!

_____

_____

4. It's a new hybrid.

_____

_____

5. The pilot put the plane in the hangar.

_____

_____

89

Geographic names in French differ from their names in English.

Each geographical name has a gender in French. Most place names that end in -*e* are feminine.

la France	France
la Suisse	Switzerland
l'Irlande	Ireland

All continents end in -*e* and are feminine.

l'Asie	Asia
l'Europe	Europe
l'Amérique du Nord	North America
l'Amérique du Sud	South America
l'Afrique	Africa
l'Antarctique	Antarctica
l'Australie	Australia

L'Exception

The following geographic places end in -*e* but are masculine:

Countries:
le Cambodge (Cambodia)
le Mexique (Mexico)
le Mozambique (Mozambique)
le Zaïre (Zaire)
le Zimbabwe (Zimbabwe)

U.S. states:
le Delaware
le Maine
le New Hampshire
le Nouveau-Mexique (New Mexico)
le Tennessee

When used in a sentence, most geographical place names are accompanied by a preposition, to mean *in, to,* or *from.*

		in, to	from
Masculine	**Singular**	*au*	*du*
	Plural	*aux*	*des*
Feminine	**Singular**	*en*	*de, d'*
	Plural	*aux*	*des*

*Je vais **en** Afrique.*
I'm going **to** Africa.

*Je suis **du** Brésil.*
I'm **from** Brazil.

*Je connais quelqu'un **des** Émirats Arabes Unis.*
I know someone **from the** United Arab Emirates.

As a general rule, articles are not included in the name of cities. For island groups, gender does not affect the preposition because groups of islands are always plural and take the plural article. Cities and islands take the following prepositions:

	in, to	from
city or singular island	*à*	*de, d'*
plural islands	*aux*	*des*

*Je vais **à** Barcelone.*
I'm going **to** Barcelona.

*Je suis **de** Portland.*
I'm **from** Portland.

*Je connais quelqu'un **des** Caraïbes.*
I know someone **from the** Carribean.

Many U.S. states are spelled differently in French than in English:

la Californie	California
la Caroline du Nord	North Carolina
la Caroline du Sud	South Carolina
le Dakota du Nord	North Dakota
le Dakota du Sud	South Dakota
la Floride	Florida
la Géorgie	Georgia
le Hawaï	Hawaii
la Louisiane	Louisiana
le Nouveau-Mexique	New Mexico
la Pennsylvanie	Pennsylvania
la Virginie	Virginia
la Virginie-Occidentale,	West Virginia

Attention!

Most cities in native English-speaking countries retain the English spelling or use a spelling close to it in French. Some notable exceptions include:

le Cap	Cape Town
Londres	London
la Nouvelle-Orléans	New Orleans
Philadelphie	Philadelphia

For cities in non-Anglophone countries, the spelling is nevertheless often quite close to the English.

Athènes	Athens
Bruxelles	Brussels
le Caire	Cairo
Genève	Geneva

Lisbonne	Lisbon
Moscou	Moscow
Pékin	Beijing
Varsovie	Warsaw
Vienne	Vienna

Exercise 1

Fill in the crossword puzzle with the French equivalent of each of the following place names. Do not include the article.

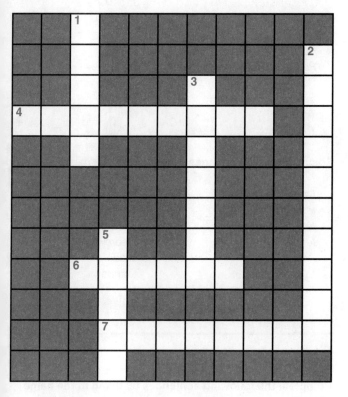

Across
4. Frankfurt
6. Scotland
7. Austria

Down
1. Lebanon
2. Copenhagen
3. London
5. Chad

Exercise 2

Choose the correct preposition to complete each sentence below.

1. Je viens _____ États-Unis.

2. Charlotte viens _____ Canada.

3. Arlette viens _____ Mexique.

4. Nous venons _____ Italie.

5. Il va _____ Bolivie.

6. Je suis _____ Belgique.

7. Sam vient _____ Allemagne.

8. *Le Seigneur des Anneaux* a été réalisé _____ Nouvelle-Zélande.

Exercise 3

Translate the following sentences into French.

1. For two years I lived in Madagascar.

_____

_____

2. I have never been to Germany, but I visited Italy last year.

_____

_____

3. London is the capital of the United Kingdom.

_____

_____

4. I heard New England is nice, especially Maine.

_____

_____

5. I want to go to South America because I have family in Argentina.

_____

_____

90

Nationalities and languages follow specific rules based on how they are used in a sentence.

When nationalities are used as adjectives, they agree in gender and number with the subject.

> ***Jacques* est *français*.**
> **Jacques** is **French**.

> ***Jacqueline* est *française*.**
> **Jacqueline** is **French**.

> *Jacques et Jacqueline sont **français**.*
> Jacques and Jacqueline are **French**.

> *Jacqueline est sa soeur sont **françaises**.*
> Jacqueline and her sister are **French**.

When used as nouns, languages are masculine.

> *Je parle **l'anglais** et **le français**.* (masculine)
> I speak **English** and **French**.

> *Je parle **la langue anglaise**.* (feminine, to agree with feminine noun *langue*)
> I speak **the English language**.

When used as adjectives, nationalities agree with the nouns they modify.

> ***les filles*** anglaises
> **the** English **girls**

> ***Les Anglais*** *sont sympathiques.*
> **The English** are nice.

When used as adjectives, nationalities and languages are not capitalized.

> *Au lycée j'étudie la langue **espagnole** et la langue **anglaise**.*
> In school I study the **Spanish** language and the **English** language.

> *Je ne parle ni **russe**, ni **croate**.*
> I don't speak **Russian** or **Croatian**.

When used as proper names, nationalities are capitalized.

> ***Les Chinois*** *attendent les jeux Olympiques.*
> **The Chinese** are waiting for the Olympic Games.

Some common nationalities include:

Allemand(e)	German
Américain(e)	American
Anglais(e)	English
Brésilien(ne)	Brazilian
Britanique	British
Canadien(ne)	Canadian
Chinois(e)	Chinese
Espagnol(e)	Spanish
Égyptien(ne)	Egyptian
Indien(ne)	Indian
Irlandais(e)	Irish
Italien(ne)	Italian
Japonais(e)	Japanese
Mexicain(e)	Mexican
Néerlandais(e)	Dutch
Polonais(e)	Polish
Portuguais(e)	Portuguese
Russe	Russian
Suisse	Swiss
Tchèque	Czech
Turque	Turkish

Some common languages include:

l'arabe	Arabic
le cantonnais	Cantonese
le flamand	Flemish
le hébreu	Hebrew
l'hindi	Hindi
le mandarin	Mandarin

Exercise 1

Complete the following sentences by filling in the name of the language generally spoken by each nationality.

1. Les Américains parlent_____.

2. Les Belges parlent_____ et

_____.

3. Les Égyptiens parlent_____.

4. Les Brésiliens parlent_____.

5. Les Irlandais parlent_____.

6. Les Australians parlent _____.

7. Les Autrichiens parlent _____.

8. Les Canadiens parlent _____ et

_____.

9. Les Japonais parlent _____.

10. Les Cubains parlent _____.

6. Les Russes sont beaux.

_____

_____

7. J'aime aussi les pizza italiens.

_____

_____

Exercise 2

Correct the errors in the following sentences. Note: Not all sentences include errors.

1. Elle a des origines Polonais, mais elle ne parle pas la langue de ses ancêtres.

_____

_____

2. L'anglais Américain n'est pas pareil que l'anglais Britannique.

_____

_____

3. Les Américains ne sont pas pareils que les Britanniques.

_____

_____

4. J'aime la cuisine italien.

_____

_____

5. Les hommes Russes sont beaux.

_____

_____

Exercise 3

Write a complete sentence providing the nationality and language of the following people.

1. Céline Dion (Canadian: French/English)

_____

_____

2. Jodie Foster (American: English/French)

_____

_____

3. Roger Federer (Swiss: German/French/English)

_____

_____

4. Ingrid Bergman (Swedish: Swedish/English/German/ Italian/French)

_____

_____

5. Gael García Bernal (Mexican: Spanish/English/French/ Italian)

_____

_____

91

Syntax/Other *Faux Amis (False Friends)*

Many words that look the same in French and in English actually have very different meanings. These words are called false cognates, or *faux amis* (false friends). They are important to know in order to avoid confusion.

Some common *faux amis* include:

sensible	= sensitive	≠	sensible ↓ *raisonable*
supporter pas	= to not bear, to not stand (something)	≠	to support ↓ *soutenir*
pas terrible	= not that great	≠	not terrible, not bad ↓ *pas trop mal*
un photographe	= photographer	≠	photograph ↓ *une photographie, une photo*
l'entrée	= appetizer	≠	main dish, entrée ↓ *le plat principal*
le collège	= middle school	≠	college ↓ *l'université, la faculté*
le football	= soccer	≠	football ↓ *le football américain*
un libéral	= a right-leaning politician	≠	a liberal, a leftist ↓ *quelqu'un de gauche*
embrasser	= to kiss	≠	to embrace ↓ *étreindre*
une émergence	= an emergence	≠	emergency ↓ *un urgence*
un enfant	= a child	≠	infant ↓ *un nourisson, un bébé*
avoir envie de	= to feel like doing something	≠	envy ↓ *la jalousie*

exceptionnel	= something unexpected, unusual	≠	exceptional ↓ *extraordinaire, magnifique*
un lac	= a lake	≠	a lack ↓ *un manque*
une librairie	= a bookstore	≠	a library ↓ *une bibliothèque*
une location	= a rental	≠	a location ↓ *un endroit*
actuellement	= currently, right now	≠	actually ↓ *en fait, vraiment*
sympathique	= nice	≠	sympathetic ↓ *compatissant*
assister	= to be present at, to attend	≠	to assist ↓ *aider*
une phrase	= a sentence	≠	a phrase ↓ *expression*
une veste	= a jacket or coat	≠	a vest ↓ *un gilet*
un délai	= a period of time	≠	a delay ↓ *un retard*
le hasard	= chance, luck	≠	a hazard ↓ *un danger, un risque*
une licence	= a bachelor's degree	≠	a license ↓ *un permis*
demander	= to ask	≠	to demand ↓ *exiger, commander*

Attention!

Though the French noun *une occasion* means *an occasion,* the expression *d'occasion* translates as *used.*

184

Exercise 1

Match the English word in column A with its French equivalent in column B.

		A		B
_____	**1.** un résumé		a. a grape
_____	**2.** des soldes		b. a vest
_____	**3.** un gilet		c. a palace
_____	**4.** un raisin sec		d. a luxury hotel
_____	**5.** demander		e. a summary
_____	**6.** le patron		f. to insert
_____	**7.** un raisin		g. sales
_____	**8.** introduire		h. to ask
_____	**9.** une palace		i. a raisin
_____	**10.** un palais		j. the boss

Exercise 2

The following objects are all _faux amis_. Write the French name for the following objects.

1. _____

2. _____

3. _____

4. _____

Exercise 3

Translate the following sentences into French. Note: The italicized words are _faux amis_.

1. Mr. Spielberg is a well-known *director*.

   _____

   _____

2. I *injured* myself during the ice hockey game.

   _____

   _____

3. The *principal* of my elementary school wore bow ties.

   _____

   _____

4. I'm always in a bad *mood* on Mondays.

   _____

   _____

92

The French language found in the Canadian province of Québec is slightly different from French found in France. In some cases, Canadian French resembles archaic aspects of French used at the time the first French settlers arrived. In other cases, Canadian French has been more willing to adopt words with obvious English roots.

La Langue Vivante

The French spoken in the Canadian province of Québec goes by any of the following names: *le québécois, le français québécois, le français canadien,* or *le français du Québec.*

A number of nouns translate differently in Québécois than in standard French.

Standard French	Québécois	English
une fontaine	*un abreuvoir*	a water fountain
mon ami	*mon chum*	my friend
des enfants	*des flots*	children
un film	*une vue*	a movie
un chien	*un pitou*	a dog
l'argent	*le foin*	money
des lunettes	*des barniques*	eyeglasses
une bière	*une broue*	a beer
un pansement	*un plasteur*	a Band-Aid
une voiture	*un char*	a car

A number of adjectives translate differently in Québécois than in standard French.

Standard French	Québécois	English
imbécile, idiot	*cave, niaiseux*	idiotic, stupid
ringard	*matante, mononcle*	old-fashioned, dated
coincé	*jammé*	stuck
vachement	*crissement*	really *(familiar)*

A number of verbs and verb phrases translate differently in Québécois than in standard French.

Standard French	Québécois	English
fermer la porte	*barrer la porte*	to close the door
tomber tête la première	*bêcher*	to fall headfirst
embrasser	*bécotter*	to kiss
conduire	*chauffer*	to drive
faire du shopping	*magasiner*	to go shopping
caresser	*minoucher*	to caress
écraser	*écrapoutir*	to crush
devenir fou	*capoter*	to go crazy

Several *québécois* words are derived from English, and are used in place of the *Français* equivalent.

Standard French	Québécois	English
une arachide, une cacahuète	*une pinotte*	a peanut
une prise	*une plogue*	a plug, an electrical socket
une glacière	*une cooler*	a cooler
une lampe de poche	*une flashlight*	a flashlight
une chanson	*une toune*	a tune, a song
appeler	*caller*	to call

La Langue Vivante

A common tendency in Québécois is to use a brand name to refer to a general object. These names are not generally carried over to standard French.

Québécois	Standard French	English
un Cutex	*le vernis à ongles*	nail polish
un Q-tips	*un coton-tige*	a cotton swab
un Kodak	*un appareil-photo*	a camera

Exercise 1

Classify the following words according to the region in which they are used more commonly.

une plogue, une prise, matante, ringard, une vue, un film, caresser, minoucher, un pansement, un plasteur, jammé, coincé

Standard French	Québécois

Exercise 2

Write in standard French and Québécois what you see Alexandre doing in each picture.

1. French:_____

   Québécois: _____

2. French:_____

   Québécois: _____

Exercise 3

Change the following conversation between Claire and Jean-Pierre from Québécois to standard French.

Claire: —Jean-Pierre, ça te dit d'aller magasiner cet après-midi?
Jean-Pierre: —Oui, pourquoi pas? Viens, monte dans mon char.
Claire: —C'est comme tu veux, si tu veux me chauffer au centre commercial.
Jean-Pierre: —Peux-tu me donner mes barniques dans la boîte à gants?
Claire: —Celles-là? Achètes-en des nouvelles, les tiennes font un peu matante.
Jean-Pierre: —OK! Nous sommes arrivés, pense à bien barrer ta porte.
Claire: —D'accord. Et toi, pense bien à prendre du foin pour les achats.
Jean-Pierre: —T'inquiète pas, mon chum. J'ai tout ce qu'il faut avec moi.

_____

_____

_____

_____

_____

_____

_____

_____

_____

_____

_____

_____

_____

_____

_____

93

94 Syntax/Other *Written French vs. Spoken French*

The French heard on the street is likely to be very different from the French read in a textbook. Just as in English, many common grammatical rules are disregarded in everyday spoken language.

In spoken French, *ne* is almost always left out of the negative construction of a sentence.

	Spoken	Written
I don't know.	*Je sais pas.*	*Je ne sais pas.*
I don't know anymore.	*J'en sais plus rien.*	*Je n'en sais plus rien.*

The pronoun *on* very often replaces the pronoun *nous* in informal situations.

	Informal	Formal
Are **we** going to the movies?	***On** va au cinéma?*	***Nous** allons au cinéma?*
We went to Montpellier.	***On** est allé à Montpellier.*	***Nous** sommes allés à Montpellier.*

Est-ce que **and inversions are not often used to form questions in colloquial speech. Instead, an affirmative statement is stressed differently when forming a question, just as in colloquial English.**

	Informal	Formal
How old are you?	*Tu as quel age?*	*Quel age as-tu?*
Where are you going?	*Tu vas où?*	*Où est-ce que tu vas?*

Emphatic disjunctive pronouns (*moi, toi, elle, lui*, and so on) are much more common in spoken French than in written French.

	Spoken	Written
Where are you going?	*Tu vas où, **toi**?*	*Où est-ce que tu vas?*
I'm not hungry.	*J'ai pas faim, **moi**.*	*Je n'ai pas faim.*

The pronoun *tu* is often used in spoken language, as it is less formal than *vous*. *Tu* is commonly contracted to *t'* when followed by a vowel in informal speech and writing.

	Informal	Formal
Are **you** hungry?	***T'**as faim?*	*Est-ce que **tu** as faim?*
Are **you** crazy?	***T'**es fou, toi?*	*Est-ce que **tu** es fou?*

Many other words are shortened in informal speech.

	Spoken	Written
restaurant	*un resto*	*un restaurant*
nice	*sympa*	*sympathique*
advertisement	*une pub*	*une publicité*
laboratory	*le labo*	*le laboratoire*
okay	*d'ac*	*d'accord*
university	*la fac*	*la faculté*
apartment	*un apart*	*un appartement*
breakfast	*le petit déj*	*le petit déjeuner*

Exercise 1

Match each common spoken abbreviation in column A with the more formal word in column B.

A	B
_____ **1.** un frigo	a. la philosophie (philosophy)
_____ **2.** une récré	b. une compilation (a mix CD, a playlist)
_____ **3.** la cata	c. un apéritif (a before-meal drink)
_____ **4.** la philo	d. un frigidaire (a refrigerator)
_____ **5.** un apéro	e. la catastrophe (a catastrophe)
_____ **6.** impec	f. une récréation (a break, a recess)
_____ **7.** une compil	g. impeccable (impeccable, great, fantastic)

Exercise 2

Each of the following sentences is grammatically correct. Rewrite each to show how it would likely be expressed if heard on the street.

1. Je n'en sais rien.

_____

_____

2. Nous voudrions aller manger au restaurant.

_____

_____

3. Nous trouvons qu'elle est sympathique.

_____

_____

4. Est-ce que tu as déjà dîné?

_____

_____

5. Est-ce que ça ne t'intéresse pas d'aller à l'université?

_____

_____

6. Est-ce que tu as déjà mangé ton petit déjeuner?

_____

_____

Exercise 3

Classify each of the following sentences as more likely to be written (read) or spoken (heard).

1. On y va, d'ac? _____

2. Ça sert à rien. _____

3. Bouge pas. _____

4. Je n'y suis jamais allé. _____

5. Il a amené ses examens au labo. _____

Exercise 4

You've recently taken a vacaction with your French class to Paris. First, using formal French, write a paragraph describing your trip. Then rewrite your description as it might be told to your friends, using informal French.

_____

_____

_____

_____

_____

_____

_____

_____

_____

_____

_____

_____

_____

_____

_____

_____

_____

_____

_____

_____

94

Non is added to the beginning of a negative sentence to emphasize a negative response to a question, similarly to *no* in English.

Est-ce que tu aimes le fromage?	**Non,** *je n'aime pas le fromage.*
Do you like cheese?	**No,** I don't like cheese.

Non can also be placed before a noun or adjective to form the negative, similarly to the *non* prefix in English. When acting as a noun, a hyphen is placed between the *non* and the word it modifies. When the construction functions as an adjective, no hyphen is used.

un **non-**conformiste
a **non**conformist

un étudiant **non** conformiste
a **non**conformist student

Attention!

Before a noun, *non compris* (*not including*) is considered a preposition and remains invariable. When used as an adjective after the noun, *non-compris* agrees with the noun.

dix pages, **non compris** l'introduction
ten pages, **not including** the introduction

dix pages, l'introduction **non comprise**
ten pages, the introduction **not included**

There is no English equivalent to the French *si,* though it is most often translated as *yes. Si* is used to correct a negative statement.

Tu n'aimes pas le fromage, toi?	**Si,** *j'aime le fromage.*
You **don't** like cheese, do you?	**Yes,** I like cheese.
Est-ce que vous n'avez pas de soeurs?	**Si,** *j'ai des soeurs.*
You **don't** have sisters?	**Yes,** I have sisters.
Est-ce que le printemps n'est pas encore arrivé?	**Si,** *le printemps a déjà commencé.*
Spring **hasn't** arrived yet?	**Yes,** spring has started.

Oui is added to the beginning of an affirmative sentence to emphasize a postive response to a question, similarly to *yes* in English.

Est-ce que tu aimes le fromage?	**Oui,** *j'aime le fromage.*
Do you like cheese?	**Yes,** I like cheese.

Non, si, and *oui* are invariable and do not change form when used as nouns.

*J'ai entendu quelques **oui** et beaucoup de **non**.*
I heard a few **yeses** and a lot of **nos.**

La Langue Vivante

In colloquial French, *oui* is often shortened or pronounced in slang as *ouais*. This use is similar to *yeah* or *yep* in English.

Ouais, *c'est génial!*
Yeah, that's cool!

La Langue Vivante

There are a few other very common colloquial expressions with *oui.*

Oui, oui.	Yes, yes
Mais, oui!	But yes!
Je crois que oui.	I think so.

Exercise 1

Use context to complete each response below.

1. Veux-tu du fromage?

_____, je veux bien du fromage.

2. Est-ce que tu es russe?

_____, je ne suis pas russe.

3. Est-ce que tu n'es pas polonais?

_____, je suis polonais.

4. Est-ce que tu n'as pas des frères?

_____, j'en ai trois.

5. Veux-tu y aller à pied?

_____, je ne veux pas y aller à pied.

6. Est-ce que tu ne veux pas y aller en voiture?

_____, pourquoi pas y aller en voiture?

Exercise 2

Respond to the following personal questions using _si_, _oui_, and _non_.

1. Est-ce que tu es américain(e)?

_____

_____

2. Est-ce que tu n'es pas un élève?

_____

_____

3. Est-ce que tu aimes les feux d'artifice (fireworks)?

_____

_____

4. Est-ce que tu n'aimes pas les vacances scolaires?

_____

_____

5. Est-ce que tu regardes souvent des matchs de rugby?

_____

_____

Exercise 3

You're playing a game of Twenty Questions. Your friend is trying to guess the mystery person you are thinking of by asking _yes_ and _no_ questions. Your answer is Napoléon Bonaparte. Use _oui_, _si_, and _non_ to write responses to the ten questions that your friend has asked you.

1. Est-ce qu'il était français?

_____

_____

2. Est-ce qu'il est né à Paris?

_____

_____

3. Est-ce qu'il était soldat?

_____

_____

4. Est-ce qu'il a gagné toutes les guerres?

_____

_____

5. Est-ce qu'il n'a jamais perdu de guerres?

_____

_____

6. Est-ce qu'il a dirigé la France?

_____

_____

7. Est-ce qu'il était marié?

_____

_____

8. Est-ce que sa femme s'appellait Marie-Antoinette?

_____

_____

95

Repetition for certain parts of speech occurs more frequently in French than in English.

The pronoun *on* is usually repeated before each verb in a sentence.

> ***On*** *boit et* ***on*** *mange.*
> **We** drink and (**we**) eat.

After a subject-verb inversion, the pronoun is repeated before another verb.

> *"Non," dit-**il**, et **il** partit.*
> "No," **he** said, and (**he**) left.

Reflexive and reciprocal pronouns are repeated before simple verb tenses. These pronouns are repeated before composite verb tenses only if the auxiliary verb is also repeated.

> *Il **s'aime** et **se hait** tout à la fois.* (simple verb tense)
> He both **loves** and **hates himself.**

> *Il **s'est aimé** et **(s'est) haï** tout à la fois.*
> (composite verb tense)
> He has both **loved** and **hated himself.**

When used in a composite verb tense, the auxiliary verbs *avoir* or *être* do not have to be repeated if there is only one subject and all verbs take the same auxiliary. When the auxiliaries differ, both auxiliaries must be included.

> *J'**ai** bu et j'**ai** mangé.*
> *J'**ai** bu et mangé.* (Both forms are acceptable as they have same auxiliary.)
> I drank and (I) ate.

> *Je **suis** rentré et je **suis** reparti.*
> *Je **suis** rentré et reparti.* (Both forms are acceptable as they have same auxiliary.)
> I came back and (I) left again.

> *Je **suis** rentré et j'**ai** mangé.*
> (The two different auxiliary verbs must both be used.)
> And not: *Je suis rentré et mangé.*
> I came back and (I) ate.

Both auxiliaries in a composite verb tense must be included when one verb is reflexive and the other is not.

> *Je me **suis** levé et je **suis** parti au travail.*
> I got up and (I) went to work.

Both auxiliaries must be included in a composite verb tense when a complement qualifies only one of the verbs.

> *Je **suis vite** rentré et je **suis** reparti.*
> I came back **quickly** and (I) left again.

Attention!

The verbs *avoir* and *être* are not always auxiliaries. They must be repeated in a sentence when they are both not serving as auxilaries.

> *J'**ai bu*** (composite tense), *et j'**ai*** (simple verb) *faim.*
> And not: *J'ai bu et faim.*
> **I drank,** and **I am hungry.**

When a prepositional phrase or indefinite qualifier ends with *à*, *de*, or *que*, only repeat the *à*, *de*, or *que*.

> *Je vis **loin d'**elle et **du** père de Luc.*
> I live **far from** her and **from** Luc's father.

> *Je mange **beaucoup de** pommes et **d'**avocats.*
> I eat **a lot of** apples and avocados.

When the same noun is repeated with two different qualifying adjectives, the noun does not have to be repeated. The second adjective can stand in place of the omitted noun.

> *un gros **chat** et un beau **chat***
> a big **cat** and a beautiful **cat**

> *un gros **chat** et **un beau***
> a big **cat** and a **beautiful one**

When using ordinal numbers as adjectives in a series, several options are available for repetition, all grammatically correct.

> *au **premier** acte et au **deuxième** acte*
> (during the first act and the second act)
> = *au **premier** acte et au **deuxième***
>   (during the first act and the second)
> = *au **premier** et au **deuxième** acte(s)*
>   (during the first and the second act/s)
> = *au **premier** et **deuxième** acte(s)*
>   (during the first and second act/s)
> = *aux **premier** et **deuxième** actes*
>   (during the first and second acts)

Exercise 1

Indicate whether the element being repeated in the sentences below is a pronoun, preposition, noun, or auxiliary verb.

1. Je vais à l'école et à la boulangerie tous les jours.

   _____

2. J'ai déjà vu des belles maisons et des maison laides.

   _____

3. Cet après-midi on fait du vélo et on a prévu d'aller se

   baigner. _____

4. Je me suis couché tard et puis je me suis levé tard le

   lendemain. _____

5. Sophie a mangé un fromage très fort et un fromage très

   doux. _____

Exercise 2

Correct the errors in the following sentences.

1. J'ai soif et chaud.

   _____

   _____

2. J'ai fait mes courses et rentré à la maison.

   _____

   _____

3. Je suis montée et frappé à la porte.

   _____

   _____

4. On se bat et puis se pardonne.

   _____

   _____

Exercise 3

Translate the following sentences into French.

1. She brushed her hair and washed herself.

   _____

   _____

2. I went to the library and studied there.

   _____

   _____

3. Lucie has a new car and and old one.

   _____

   _____

4. I climbed up the stairs and I'm tired.

   _____

   _____

96

C'est and *il est* are very common expressions used when describing people and things.

C'est and its plural form, *ce sont*, are usually followed by a specific noun that may also be modified by an adjective. They generally translate as *it's, it is, that's* or *that is*.

Qui est arrivé? (Who arrived?)

C'est *mon mari.* (**It's** my husband.)
C'est *ma femme.* (**It's** my wife.)
C'est *mon fils aîné.* (**It's** my oldest son.)
C'est *ma petite-fille.* (**It's** my granddaughter.)
C'est *le plombier.* (**It's** the plumber.)

Julie et Catherine? **Ce sont** *des belles filles.*
Julie and Catherine? **They are** beautiful girls.

C'est can be followed by a proper noun (a name) or a disjunctive pronoun.

Qui est arrivé? (Who arrived?)

C'est *Thomas.* (**It's** Thomas.)
C'est *Lauren.* (**It's** Lauren.)
C'est *moi.* (**It's** me.)
C'est *nous.* (**It's** us.)
Ce sont *les enfants.* (**It's** the kids.)

C'est can be followed by an infinitive serving as the subject.

Voyager, **c'est** *profiter de la vie.*
To travel **is** to take advantage of life.

C'est can be used to indicate a date.

À quelle date partiras-tu?
On what date will you leave?

Mon départ, **c'est** *le 13 mai.*
My departure **is** May 13.

C'est can be followed by an adjective when describing qualities of a specific situation or thing.

Tu vois le lait qui est dans le frigo depuis un mois?
C'est *périmé!*
You know the milk that's been in the fridge for a month?
It's expired.

Tu peux porter mon colis? Attention! **C'est** *lourd.*
Can you carry my package? Be careful, **it's** heavy.

C'est can also be followed by an adjective describing an unspecified situation.

C'est *trop tard.* (**It's** too late.)
C'est *difficile à faire.* (**It's** difficult to do.)

When using adjectives to describe people rather than things, the expressions *il est, elle est, ils sont,* or *elles sont* are used.

Il est *beau.* (**He's** handsome.)
Elle est *belle.* (**She's** beautiful.)
Ils sont *beaux.* (**They are** beautiful.)

Because an object in French has a gender, *il est/ils sont* or *elle est/elles sont* are used to describe an implied object.

Mon camion? **Il est** *beau.* (My truck? **It's** beautiful.)
Ma voiture? **Elle est** *belle?* (My car? **It's** beautiful.)
Mes véhicules? **Ils sont** *beaux.* (My vehicles? **They're** beautiful.)

When using a noun to describe a person's profession, nationality, or religion, no article is used with the noun following the expressions *il est, elle est, ils sont,* and *elles sont*.

Il est *plombier.* (**He is** a plumber.)
Elle est *sage-femme.* (**She is** a midwife.)

Il est can be impersonal and may not refer to a specific person or thing. This use is common when discussing time.

Il est *tard.* (**It's** late.)
Il est *deux heures et demi.* (**It's** two-thirty.)

Exercise 1

Determine whether *c'est* or *il est* is appropriate to complete each of the following sentences.

1. _____ Jacques.

2. _____ des épices piquantes.

3. George?_____ un grognon.

4. George?_____ malin.

5. Le 14 juillet,_____ la fête nationale de la France.

6. C'est qui la prochaine? _____ moi.

7. _____ génial comme jeu.

8. _____ bouddhiste.

9. _____ bouddhistes.

10. Louise? _____ grincheuse.

Exercise 2

Translate each of the following sentences into French.

1. To work is to stay in good health.

_____

_____

2. It's time.

_____

_____

3. It's disgusting.

_____

_____

4. It's him.

_____

_____

5. Today it's March 17.

_____

_____

6. It's easy to sew.

_____

_____

7. That's really easy to sew.

_____

_____

Exercise 3

Convert the following sentences from *il est* to *c'est*, making the necessary modifications to each.

1. Il est tôt pour manger.

_____

_____

2. Il est canadien.

_____

_____

3. Il est grand, Patrick.

_____

_____

4. Elles sont étudiantes.

_____

_____

5. Elle est gourmande.

_____

_____

97

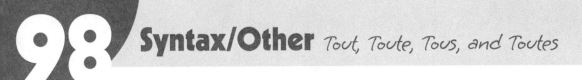

Tout can serve as four different parts of speech: adjective, adverb, noun, and pronoun.

Tout has four different forms, depending on its use.

	Singular	Plural
Masculine	*tout*	*tous*
Feminine	*toute*	*toutes*

As an adjective or adverb *tout* agrees with the noun it modifies.

> **Toute** la journée j'ai écouté la musique.
> The **whole** day I listened to music.

> **Toutes** ces idées sont bonnes.
> **All** these ideas are good.

> Le tramway à Clermont-Ferrand est **tout** nouveau.
> The tram in Clermont-Ferrand is **completely** new.

> Les chansons de Johnny Hallyday sont **toutes** ringardes.
> Johnny Hallyday's songs are **all** old-fashioned.

The masculine singular form of *tout* is used as a noun meaning *the whole thing*. In these cases, *tout* is invariable and does not change form.

> Pour cet exercice, vous devez lire **le tout**.
> For this exercise, you must read **the whole thing**.

The masculine singular form of *tout* is also used as a pronoun meaning *everything* or *all*. In these cases, *tout* is invariable and does not change form.

> J'ai **tout** mangé.
> I ate **everything**.

Tout can also be used as a pronoun to refer back to another noun. In these cases, *tout* changes to agree with the noun it replaces.

> **Julie et ses soeurs** sont belles.
> **Julie and her sisters** are beautiful.

> **Toutes** sont belles.
> **They** are all beautiful.

Several common idiomatic expressions use *tout* in its various forms.

tout le temps	all the time
pas du tout	not at all
tout de suite	right away
tout le monde	everyone (literally, the whole world)
tout à fait	completely
malgré tout	despite everything
tout à coup	all of a sudden
tous les jours	every day
tous (toutes) les deux	both of them
tous les deux jours	every two days
toutes les deux semaines	every two weeks
en tout cas	in any case
tout à l'heure	in a little while, a little while ago
tout droit	straight ahead

> Il faudra **malgré tout** payer vos impôts.
> **Despite everything,** you must pay your taxes.

> **Tout à coup** le vent se mit à souffler.
> **All of a sudden** the wind started to blow.

> Je vais chez mon coiffeur **tous les deux mois**.
> I go to the hairdresser **every two months**.

Exercise 1

Choose the correct form of *tout* to complete each sentence.

1. _____ les invités sont là ce soir.

2. _____ les personnes sont là ce soir.

3. J'ai conduit _____ la journée.

4. On ira _____ au paradis.

5. Les enfants sont _____ contents de leurs cadeaux de Noël.

Exercise 2

Indicate which part of speech *tout* is being used as in each of the following sentences.

1. Tout s'est bien passé. _____

2. Je viens d'acheter une télévision toute neuve.

   _____

3. J'ai dansé toute la nuit. _____

4. Mélangez le sucre et la farine et mettez le tout dans un

   saladier. _____

5. Toute ma famille est là pour mon anniversaire.

   _____

Exercise 3

Fill in the correct idiomatic phrase from the choices below to complete each of the following sentences. Use each phrase only once.

tous les jours, tous les deux, tout à l'heure, en tout cas, pas du tout, tout de suite

1. Ils sont heureux quand ils sont _____.

2. Pierre à Paul: Rendez-vous dans quinze minutes. Paul à

   Pierre: OK, à _____.

3. Avec son travail de guide touristique, c'est comme s'il était

   _____ en vacances.

4. Pierre à Paul: Rendez-vous dans deux heures. Paul à

   Pierre: OK, à _____.

5. _____ tu devrais prendre un parapluie car le temps est menaçant.

6. Je ne vois _____ de quoi tu me parles.

The adverbs *encore* and *toujours* have numerous uses, some of which overlap and can be confusing for most French speakers.

When referring to an action, *encore* can mean *again*.

> *Fais-le **encore**!*
> Do it **again**!

Encore can also mean *another*.

> *Est-ce que tu veux **encore** une boule de glace?*
> Do you want **another** scoop of ice cream?

When used with a comparitive, *encore* can mean *even more*.

> *Shrek le Troisième est **encore meilleur** que le deuxième.*
> *Shrek the Third* is **even better** than the second one.

When modifying an adjective, *encore* can sometimes be an intensifier meaning *even more* or *yet more*. The English translation would often be the comparative adjective + *still*.

> *Larry Bird est **grand**, mais Shaquille O'Neal est **encore plus grand**.*
> Larry Bird is **tall**, but Shaquille O'Neal is **taller still**.

Following negative constructions, such as *ne pas*, *encore* means *yet*.

> *Je **ne** suis **pas encore** prête.*
> I'm **not** ready **yet**.

Attention!

Pas encore can be used as a brief negative response, similar to *not yet*.

> *Est-ce que tu as déjà vu* Shrek le Troisième*? **Pas encore**.*
> Have you already seen *Shrek the Third*? **Not yet**.

Toujours often means *always*.

> *Il est **toujours** souriant.*
> He is **always** smiley.

Toujours can mean *still*, when discussing an action or quality consistent over time.

> *Tu as **toujours** le même sourire.*
> You **still** have the same smile.

Toujours can precede *pas* in the negative construction *ne pas* to mean *not yet*. Though the meaning is the same, the negative construction with *encore* is more common.

> *Je **ne** suis **toujours pas** prête.*
> I'm **not** ready **yet**.

Attention!

Déjà is used to mean *yet*, when forming a question.

> *Est-ce que tu as **déjà** mangé?*
> Have you eaten **yet**?

Toujours can follow the negative *pas* to mean *not always*.

> *Je **ne** suis **pas toujours** à l'heure.*
> I'm **not always** on time.

Exercise 1

Provide the approximate English translation for *encore* in each of the following sentences.

1. Il m'a vu encore une fois. _____

2. Je veux encore un verre de vin. _____

3. Ils ne sont pas encore arrivés. _____

4. Je me trouve ici encore une fois. _____

5. Mes devoirs d'histoire sont encore pires que mes devoirs de biologie. _____

Exercise 2

Provide an English translation for *toujours* in each of the following sentences.

1. Depuis longtemps il a toujours la même attitude.

   _____

2. Il est toujours fâché; ce n'est pas bien pour la santé.

   _____

3. Il me doit toujours une grosse somme d'argent.

   _____

4. Je suis toujours contente quand il fait beau.

   _____

5. Je suis toujours optimiste, malgré tout.

   _____

Exercise 3

Complete each sentence below with either *encore* or *toujours.*

1. Le matin les élèves sont _____

   fatigués.

2. Donne-moi _____ un Fanta. J'ai

   _____ soif.

3. Ma petite-fille est _____ plus belle que

   sa jolie mère.

4. Nous sommes _____ en retard le

   lundi.

5. Même après la passage de la loi, les gens fument

   _____ dans les lieux publiques.

6. La guerre est _____ pire, surtout après

   cinq ans.

Exercise 4

Translate the following sentences into French.

1. She's trying again.

   _____

   _____

2. I still haven't mowed the lawn.

   _____

   _____

3. She is still beautiful.

   _____

   _____

4. Even if I eat, I'm still hungry.

   _____

   _____

5. I am always happy.

   _____

   _____

99

The temporal expressions *il y a, pendant,* and *depuis* have overlapping definitions that can sometimes be confusing.

When followed by an amount of time, *il y a* means *ago*. This meaning of *il y a* is reserved for events that are finished or completed; the verb that accompanies this expression will always be in the past tense.

> *Il y a* deux semaines, j'ai fini mes études.
> Two weeks **ago,** I finished my studies.

Depuis means *since* or *for* when referring to an amount of time. The present tense is used with *depuis* to indicate actions that are still continuing in the present, even when those actions have a connection with the past. In English, the present perfect would often be used, but in French the present is always used when the action is still occurring.

> J'étudie *depuis* trois heures.
> I've been studying **for** three hours.

> Je suis en colère *depuis* mon accident.
> I have been angry **since** my accident.

The expression *il y a ... que* indicates an action that has been going on for a certain period of time. This use is similar to *depuis* but is more informal.

> *Il y a* quatre ans *que* j'ai mon chien.
> **For** four years, I've had my dog.

Verbs in past-tense forms are used with *depuis* to indicate actions ongoing in the past but that have been completed.

> J'attendais *depuis* quinze minutes quand le bus est venu.
> I had been waiting **for** fifteen minutes when the bus came.

Pendant also means *for* but is only used for actions occurring over a period of time in the past.

> J'ai fait de l'équitation *pendant* trois ans.
> I rode horses **for** three years.

Pendant can also mean *while* or *during* to mark something occurring over a period of time in the past but no longer occurring in the present.

> *Pendant* mon voyage aux États-Unis, j'ai vu plein de choses.
> **During** my trip to the United States, I saw many things.

Pendant can mean *while* or *during* in the present tense when referring to events happening in the present but not necessarily at the current moment.

> *Pendant* que tu es au magasin, pense à acheter du lait.
> **While** you are at the store, remember to buy some milk.

Exercise 1

Complete each of the following sentences with *il y a, pendant,* or *depuis.*

1. _____ trois ans j'ai acheté une nouvelle voiture.

2. _____ hier nous avons un nouveau président de la République.

3. _____ ce temps il ne fait pas ses devoirs.

4. _____ deux ans j'ai visité le Mont-Saint-Michel en Bretagne.

5. _____ son augmentation, il est très fier.

6. _____ qu'il pleut nous regardons la télévision.

Exercise 2

Say whether *il y a, pendant, il y a ... que,* or *depuis* should be used for each of the following scenarios.

1. To say something happened during a time period that has

   no relation to now. _____

2. To say *ago*, when an action happened but is entirely

   finished now. _____

3. To say what was occurring when something else

   happened. _____

4. To say when an action that is still happening started.

   _____

5. A less formal way to say when an action that is still

   happening started. _____

Exercise 3

Translate the following sentences into French.

1. I have been studying French for three years.

   _____

   _____

2. I have been studying French since middle school.

   _____

   _____

3. Three years ago I started studying French.

   _____

   _____

4. Did you know the festival started last week?

   _____

   _____

5. Yes, I have been going every day since Wednesday.

   _____

   _____

6. I have been studying French since I was fifteen years old.

   _____

   _____

7. While I was in Morocco, I learned a few Arabic phrases.

   _____

   _____

100

Irregular & Special Usage French Words

Articles

du/de la (doo/duh lah): *some*

le/la/les (luh/lah/lay): *the*

un/une/des (uhn/oon/day): *a/an*

Adjectives

ce/cet/cette (suh/set/set): *this/that*

ces (say): *these/those*

-ci/-là (see/lah): *this/that*

mon/ma/mes (muhn/ma/may): *my*

ton/ta/tes (tuhn/ta/tay): *your (singular)*

son/sa/ses (suhn/sa/say): *his/hers*

notre/nos (NO-trah/no): *our*

votre/vos (VO-trah/vo): *your (formal, plural)*

leur/leurs (luhr/luhr): *their*

vrai (vrey): *true; real*

grand (gron): *great; tall*

premier/première: (pruh-MI-ey/pruh-MI-air): *first; primary*

dernier/dernière: (der-NI-ay/der-NI-air): *final; last*

seul(e): (suhl): *alone/single; lonely*

Pronouns

je (zhuh): *me*

tu (too): *you (singular)*

il (il): *he*

le (luh): *him/it (masculine) (direct object)*

elle (el): *she/it (feminine)*

la (la): *her (direct object)*

on (uhn): *one/you (impersonal)*

lui (lu-ee): *him/her/it (indirect object)*

nous (noo): *we*

vous (voo): *you (formal, plural)*

ils (il): *they (masculine)*

elles (el): *they (feminine)*

les (lay): *them (direct object)*

leur (lur): *them (indirect object)*

le mien/meins (luh ME-en/lay ME-en): *mine (masculine)*

la mienne/meinnes (la ME-en/lay ME-en): *mine (feminine)*

le tien/tiens (luh TEE-en/lay TEE-en): *yours (masculine)*

la tienne/tiennes (la TEE-en/lay TEE-en): *yours (feminine)*

le sien/siens (luh SEE-en/lay SEE-en): *his/hers/its (masculine)*

la sienne/siennes (la SEE-en/lay SEE-en): *his/hers/its (feminine)*

le nôtre/nôtres (luh NO-tra/lay NO-tra): *ours (masculine)*

la nôtre/nôtres (la NO-tra/lay NO-tra): *ours (feminine)*

le vôtre/vôtre (luh VO-tra/lay VO-tra): *yours (masculine)*

la vôtre/vôtre (la VO-tra/lay VO-tra): *yours (feminine)*

le leur/leurs (luh luhr/lay luhr): *theirs (masculine)*

la leur/leurs (la luhr/lay luhr): *theirs (feminine)*

me (muh): *myself*

te (tuh): *yourself*

se (suh): *himself/herself/itself*

nos (no): *ourselves*

vos (vo): *yourself (formal); yourselves*

ses (say): *themselves*

moi-même (mwa mem): *myself (emphatic)*

toi-même (twa mem): *yourself (emphatic)*

lui-même (lu-ee mem): *himself (emphatic)*

elle-même (el mem): *herself (emphatic)*

soi(-même): (swa mem): *itself/oneself (emphatic)*

nous-même (noo mem): *ourself (emphatic)*

vous-même (voo mem): *yourself (formal, emphatic)/yourselves (emphatic)*

eux-même (uh mem): *themselves (masculine, emphatic)*

elles-même (el mem): *themselves (feminine, emphatic)*

moi (mwa): *me (disjunctive)*

toi (twa): *you (disjunctive)*

lui (lu-ee): *him (disjunctive)*

elle (el): *her (disjunctive)*

soi (swa): *it (disjunctive)*

nous (noo): *we (disjunctive)*

vous (voo): *you (formal, plural) (disjunctive)*

eux (uh): *them (masculine) (disjunctive)*

elles: (el) *them (feminine) (disjunctive)*

à laquelle/auxquelles (a la-KEL/oh KEL): *to which*

auquel/auxquels (oh-KEL): *to which*

de laquelle/desquelles (duh la-KEL/day-kel): *of which*

duquel/desquels (do-KEL/day-KEL): *of which*

ce (suh): *it/this/that*

ceci/ça (suh-SEE/sa): *this/that (one) (masculine)*

cela/ça (suh-LA/sa): *this/that (one) (feminine)*

celui/celle (se-luh-WE/sell): *the one/that one/this one*

ceux/celles (suh/sell): *these/those/the ones*

lequel/lesquels (luh-KEL/lay-KEL): *which/which one(s) (masculine)*

laquelle/lesquelles (la-KEL/lay-KEL): *which/which one(s) (feminine)*

que/qu'est-ce que (kuh/KESS kuh): *which/what/that*

qui/qui est-ce qui (kee/kee es-suh kee): *who/whom*

quoi (kwa): *which (after a preposition)*

aucun(e): (oh-KUHN/oh-KOON): *none, not one*

autre(s): (OH-trah): *another, the other(s)*

certain(e)(s): (ser-TEN): *certain ones*

chacun(e): (shak-uhn/shak-oon): *each one*

dont (don): *whose*

en (uhn): *of/from there, some/any of*

n'importe qui (nam-PORT-uh-KEY): *whoever, anybody*

n'importe quoi (nam-PORT-uh-KWA): *whatever, anything, nonsense*

où (oo): *where/when*

personne (pair-SON): *no one, nobody*

plusieurs (PLOO-ze-uhr): *many, numerous, several*

quelqu'un (KEL-kun): *someone, somebody*

quelque chose (kel-kuh SHOZE): *something*

quelques-un(e)s (kel-kuhz-UHN/(kel-kuhz-OON): *a few*

quiconque (key-KONK): *whoever, anybody*

rien (REE-en): *nothing*

tel(le)(s): (tell): *such as, like*

tout (too): *all, everything*

tout le monde (too luh MUHND): *everybody*

y (ee): *there*

Prepositions

à (ah): *at/to/in/away/with*

de (duh): *of/from*

Conjunctions

car (car): *because/since*

comme (kuhm): *as/because/like/since*

donc (donk): *therefore*

et (ay): *and*

lorsque (lorsk): *when (formally)*

mais (may): *but*

ni (nee): *nor*

Irregular & Special Usage French Words

or (or): *and yet*

ou ... ou (oo): *either ... or*

puisque (pweesk): *since/because*

quand (kahn): *when*

que (kuh): *that*

si (see): *if*

Verbs

aller (ahl-ay): *to go*

amener (a-men-AY): *to bring along (referring to people, animals, or vehicles)*

apporter (a-por-TAY): *to bring along (referring to things)*

apprendre (a-PRUHN-druh): *to learn, to teach, to give news, to hear about*

arriver (ar-ee-VAY): *to arr.*

avoir (a-VWAHR): *to have*

boire (bwahr): *to drink*

conduire (con-DWEER): *to drive*

connaître (kon-ET-trah): *to know/to be familiar with*

couvrir (koo-VREER): *to cover*

découvrir (day-koo-VREER): *to discover*

devoir (duh-VWAHR): *to have to*

dire (deer): *to say*

dormir (dor-MEER): *to sleep*

écrire (ay-CREER): *to write*

entendre (en-TUHN-druh): *to hear*

entrer (UHN-tray): *to enter/to come in*

emmener (em-en-AY): *to take along (referring to people, animals, or vehicles)*

emporter (em-por-TAY): *to take along (referring to things)*

enseigner (uhn-sen-YAY): *to teach*

être (ET-truh): *to be*

faire (fair): *to make/to do*

habiter (a-bee-TAY): *to live/to dwell/to reside in*

manquer (man-KAY): *to miss*

mettre (MET-ruh): *to put/to place, to turn on*

lire (leer): *to read*

offrir (off-REER): *to offer*

ouvrir (oo-VREER): *to open*

partir (par-TEER): *to leave/to go away*

porter (por-TAY): *to carry*

poser (po-SAY): *to put down/to get rid of, to install, to pose*

pouvoir (poo-VWAH): *to be able to*

prendre (PRAHN-druh): *to take, to order (food)*

quitter (kee-TAY): *to leave (something or someone)*

rater (rat-AY): *to miss*

rencontrer (ron-con-TRAY): *to meet/to get acquainted/to run into*

rentrer (ren-TRAY): *to go back to/to return to*

retourner (ruh-toorn-AY): *to go back/to go again*

retrouver (ruh-troov-AY): *to meet up (with), to find/to regain*

revenir (ruh-vuhn-EER): *to come back/to return/to come again*

savoir (sa-VWAH): *to know*

sortir (sor-TEER): *to go out/to take out*

souffrir (soo-FREER): *to suffer*

suivre (SWEE-vruh): *to follow*

tenir (ten-EER): *to hold*

venir (ven-EER): *to come*

vivre (VEE-vruh): *to live/to be alive/to exist, to experience*

voir (vwahr): *to see*

vouloir (voo-LWAHR): *to want*

Common Reflexive Verbs

s'approcher de (suh-pro-CHAY): *to approach*

s'asseoir (sas-WAHR): *to sit down*

se baigner (suh ben-YAY): *to bathe, swim*

se brosser (les cheveux, les dents)　(suh bro-SAY): *to brush (one's hair, teeth)*

se casser (la jambe): (suh cas-AY): *to break (one's leg)*

se coiffer (suh kwof-AY): *to fix one's hair*

se coucher (suh koo-CHAY): *to go to bed*

se couper (suh koo-PAY): *to cut oneself*

se déshabiller (se dez-ab-ee-YAY): *to get undressed*

se doucher (suh doo-SHAY): *to take a shower*

se fâcher (se fa-SHAY): *to get angry*

s'habiller (sab-ee-AY): *to get dressed*

se laver (suh lah-VAY): *to wash (one's self)*

se lever (suh lev-AY): *to get up*

se maquiller (suh ma-kee-AY): *to put on make-up*

se marier (avec): (suh mar-ee-AY a-VEK): *to get married (to)*

se moquer de (suh mok-AY duh): *to make fun of (someone)*

se moucher (suh moo-SHAY): *to blow one's nose*

se peigner (suh pen-YAY): *to comb one's hair*

se raser (suh raz-AY): *to shave*

se regarder (suh ruh-gard-AY): *to look at oneself*

se reposer (suh ruh-pohz-AY): *to rest*

se réveiller (suh RAY-vay-ay): *to wake up*

se souvenir de (suh soo-ven-EER duh): *to remember*

Common Verbs with Prepostions

accepter de (ak-sep-TAY duh): *to accept*

aider à (ey-DAY ah): *to help*

apprendre à (a-PRAHN-druh a): *to learn/to teach*

arrêter de (arr-ett-TAY duh): *to stop*

commencer à (ko-men-SAY a): *to start*

continuer à (kon-tin-yoo-AY a): *to continue*

demander de (duh-mahn-DAY duh): *to ask*

dire de (deer duh): *to say*

faire la connaissance (de): (fair la kon-ay-SANSE duh): *to meet (for the first time)/to get acquainted*

inviter à (en-vee-TAY a): *to invite*

manquer de (mahn-KAY duh): *to lack (something)*

regretter de (ruh-gret-AY duh): *to regret*

suggérer de (soo-zher-AY duh): *to suggest*

Interrogatives

Avec qui? (ah-VEK key): *For whom?*

Chez qui? (shay key): *Whose home?*

Combien? (kom-BYEN): *How much?*

Comment? (ko-MAHN): *How?*

Depuis quand? (duh-PWEE kahn): *Since when?*

D'où? (doo)**:** *Where from?*

Où? (oo): *Where?*

Pour combien? (por kom-BYEN): *For how much?*

Pour qui? (por key): *With whom?*

Pourquoi? (por-KWAH): *Why?*

Quand? (kahn/kuhn): *When?*

Qui? (key): *Who?*

Quoi? (kwah): *What?*

Comparatives

autant (de/d'): (oh-TAN duh): *as many (of)*

aussi (oh-SEE): *as*

meilleur(e): (may-YER): *better*

moindre (mwandr): *lesser*

moins (mwahn): *less*

pire (peer): *worse*

plus (ploos): *more*

très (tray): *very/extremely*

Glossary of Grammar Terms

adjectival: A word or phrase that is related to or functions like an adjective and is used to describe a noun. For example: *The woman **who wrote the book** is my sister.* In this sentence, *who wrote the book* is an adjectival phrase that describes the noun *woman*.

adjective: A word that describes the quality or state of a noun. In the example *the **beautiful** dog, beautiful* is an adjective that describes the quality of *dog*.

adverb: A word that describes or enhances the meaning of a verb, adjective, another adverb, or sentence. An adverb answers *How? Where?* or *When?* In English, most adverbs end in *–ly*. For example: s*lowly, hourly, softly.* Other common adverbs include: *there, now, yesterday.*

article: A word used in combination with a noun to indicate if that noun is definite (specific) or indefinite (generic). English has two articles: *the* (definite article) and *a/an* (indefinite article).

auxiliary: A verb that is used in combination with another verb when forming a specific tense or mood. In English, common auxiliary verbs include *to have* and *to be.* For example: *She **is** running, and he **has been** waiting.*

cardinal numbers: Numbers that are used when counting to describe how many of an item are present: *one, two, three ...*

comparative: The form of a word, or the word construction, that is used to compare specific qualities between two things. In English, the comparative is generally formed by adding *-er* or *more/less* to an adjective or adverb. For example: *fast**er**, **more/less** intelligent.*

compound sentence: A sentence that has one main (independent) clause and one or more subordinate (dependent) clauses. *My father is generous* is an independent clause, and can be part of a compound sentence when combined with a dependent clause: *My father is generous **when he gives me an allowance.***

conditional clause: A sentence or clause that describes a situation that is dependent on a condition explained by another clause or sentence. In English, conditional clauses generally begin with *if, unless,* or another conjunction with a similar meaning. For example: *I'll buy the cake **unless you don't want it.***

conditional mood: The form of a verb used when describing an imaginary situation that would happen in the future if a specific condition is met. In English, the conditional mood is formed with the auxiliaries *would* or *could* and a verb. For example: *I **would go** to the movies if you pay for my ticket. If you have enough time and money, we **could see** two movies.*

conjugation: The possible form a verb can take in a given tense to express person, number, and mood. In English, for example, the present tense conjugation of the verb *to be* is *am, are,* and *is.* The past tense conjugation for *to be* is *was* and *were.*

conjunction: A word that joins two or more words, phrases, or sentences. Conjunctions are either coordinating and subordinating, depending on how the two elements relate to each other. *And, but, because, unless,* and *if* are examples of common conjunctions in English.

coordinating conjunction: A conjunction that joins two elements that are on the same grammatical level, such as noun + noun, adjective + adjective, independent clause + independent clause. The coordinating conjunctions in English are *and, but, or,* and *so. The boy **and** the girl are swimming. The house is on fire, **and** the firemen are on the way.*

declarative sentence: A statement of fact or state of being, as opposed to a question, exclamation, or command. For example: *I would like to have pizza. The weather is nice. She has been working hard.*

declension: A group of nouns, pronouns, or adjectives that undergo the same kind of changes according to number, gender, and, in some languages, case.

demonstrative: A word that refers to a noun in terms of its proximity to the speaker. In English, demonstratives include *this, that, these,* and *those.*

dependent clause: See **subordinate clause**

direct object: The direct object in a sentence is usually a noun or pronoun that is directly affected by the action of the verb. The direct object will generally answer the question *what do you do (with the verb)?* In the sentence *I wrote **a letter**,* the noun *letter* is the direct object because it is directly affected by the verb (*wrote*).

disjunctive: A word used to establish a relationship of contrast or opposition between two or more things or events. For example, the preposition *but* is disjunctive: *I am stronger **but** you are faster.*

future tense: A tense used to refer to events that have not yet occurred but will or are likely to happen. In English, the future tense can be formed in two ways: with the auxiliary *will* + a verb (*I **will read** that book tomorrow*) or with the present of *to be* + *going to* + a verb (*I **am going to read** that book tomorrow*).

future perfect tense: The future perfect refers to an event that is either currently in progress and will be finished in the future, or will begin and be finished in the future. In English, the future perfect is formed with the auxiliary *to have* in future tense (*will have*) + the past participle of a verb. For example: *I will have finished my project by the time you come back.*

gerund: A verb in a form ending in *–ing.* For example: *eating, writing, reading.* Gerunds can function as nouns in a sentence (***Smoking*** *is bad for you*). They are also the verb form used after a preposition (*Thanks **for** calling me back*).

imperative: The form of a verb used to give commands or orders. In the imperative form, the subject is often implied and is therefore omitted. The imperative can be either affirmative or negative. For example: *Go! Come! Don't speak! Don't eat!*

imperfect tense: A past tense form used to discuss repeated, habitual, or continued actions in the past. Though considered a separate tense in some languages, the imperfect tense is not considered a separate tense in English, and it is equivalent to the simple past and past progressive tenses. The imperfect is commonly formed using *used to* or *would* (*I **used to** visit my grandparents every Sunday. I **would** visit them every week.*).

indefinite adjective: An adjective that refers to an undefined or inexact number or quantity. Common indefinite adjectives in English are: s*ome, all, many, few, more, most,* and *several.*

independent clause: See **main clause**

indicative mood: The verb form used in declarative sentences or questions. The indicative is the most commonly used mood in most languages. For example: *She bought a cake. Are you OK?*

indirect object: The indirect object of a verb expresses who or what has been affected indirectly by the action of the verb. The indirect object is the receiver or beneficiary of the action, and answers the question *To/for whom?* In the sentence *I wrote you a letter,* the pronoun *you* is the indirect object because it benefits from the action (the written letter).

infinitive: The base form of a verb. In English, the infinitive is expressed with the particle *to* + the verb. The infinitive is the form of the verb defined in a dictionary. For example: *to go, to eat, to come, to dance.*

interjections: A single word or phrase that conveys a strong emotion or an attitude, such as shock, surprise, delight, or disgust. Common interjections include *Ouch! Wow! Oh! Yuck!*

interrogative adjective: An adjective used in forming a question, asking for definition or clarification, and distinguishing among various choices. In English, interrogative adjectives include *what, which, who, whom,* and *whose.*

invariable: A word that never changes form, regardless of tense, number, or person. In English, prepositions are invariable. Verbs, however, are not, because they change form depending on the tense and, occasionally, subject.

main (independent) clause: A sentence that expresses a complete thought on its own and does not depend on another clause to create meaning. For example: *I like cake. They have been traveling. Math is difficult.*

modal verb: In English, modal verbs are auxiliary verbs that express an attitude (doubt, desire, need) about the event expressed by another verb. Modal verbs are also used to make requests and ask permission. Modal verbs include *can, could, may, might, must, have to, should, shall, will,* and *would.* For example: *I **would** like to go to the movies. I **can** speak French.*

modify/qualify: To use a word or group of words to give further information about another noun or phrase, sometimes resulting in a change of meaning and/or form. Words are considered **modifiers** when they come before the word they alter. Words are considered **qualifiers** when they come after the word they alter. In the sentence *The **yellow** taxi **from New York**,* the adjective *yellow* modifies *taxi* and *from New York* qualifies it.

mood: All sentences are said to be in a specific mood, depending on the attitude and intentions of the speaker. The specific form of a past, present, or future tense verb in a given sentence indicates the mood.

nominal: A word or phrase that is related to or functions like a noun. For example: *I liked **what she gave me**.* In this sentence, *what she gave me* is a nominal phrase or clause because it functions like a noun describing *what I liked.* This nominal phrase is a direct object and can be replaced by a pronoun: *I liked **it**.*

noun: A word referring to a person, an animal, a thing, a place, or an abstract idea. For example: *Steve, dog, teacher, book, California, love, freedom.*

object pronoun: Words used in place of the direct object in a sentence. The object pronouns in English are *me, you, him, her, it, us,* and *them.* In the sentence *I like cake,* the noun *cake* is the direct object and can be replaced by the direct object pronoun *it*: *I like **it**.*

ordinal numbers: Numbers used when designating the place of items listed in a sequence: *first, second, third, fourth,* and so on.

Glossary of Grammar Terms

participle (past and present): A verb form used as an adjective. The present participle is used in progressive tenses with the verb to be (*I am **reading***). The past participle is used in perfect tenses and in the passive voice with the verb *to be* (*the homework was **made***). In English, the present participle is formed by adding -*ing* to the verb (*I am **dancing**, they are **walking***) and the past participle is formed by adding either -*ed* to the verb (*danc**ed**, walk**ed***), or -*en* instead (*writt**en**, brok**en***). Some past participles are irregular (*sing/**sung**, eat/**ate***).

partitive adjective: A phrase used to express quantity when distinguishing a piece from the whole or when referring to an uncountable noun. For example: *a piece of cake, a slice of bread, a bunch of grapes, a pinch of salt.*

past tense: The verb tense used to describe events that occurred in the past. For example: *She **walked** to the store. He **ran** to the house.*

past perfect (pluperfect) tense: A past tense form that refers to an event completed in the past, prior to the beginning of another event that also occurred in the past. In English, the pluperfect tense is formed with the auxiliary *to have* in past tense (*had*) + the past participle. For example: *I **had read** the book before you told me the ending.*

possessive adjective: An adjective that indicates ownership or possession. In English, the possessive adjectives are *my, your, his, her, its, our, their.*

possessive pronoun: A pronoun that replaces a possessive adjective and its noun. In English, the possessive pronouns are *mine, yours, his, hers, its, ours, yours, theirs.* For example: *I bought my house. It is **mine.***

preposition: A word used to join nouns, adjectives, and pronouns with other words to indicate ownership, physical location, direction, or time. Prepositions are invariable, meaning they never change form. Some common English prepositions include *about, before, but, for, from, in, at, of,* and *on.* For example: *She sat **on** the bench. I left **before** you got there.*

present tense: The tense that describes an action taking place in present time or an action that is habitual. Present tense can also be used to describe facts or states of being in the present. For example: *She **reads** a book. I **go** to the movies every day. Madrid **is** the capital of Spain.*

present perfect tense: A past tense form that refers to an action that has been completed, occurred within a specific time period, or has results that continue up to a specific point in time. In English, the present perfect is formed with the auxiliary *to have* in present tense (*have, has*) + the past participle. For example: *I **have been** to New York twice. She **has finished** her homework.*

preterite tense: A past tense form used to discuss an action completed in the past, an action that happened only once, or an action that interrupted another in the past. For example: *I **saw** the movie yesterday. I **ran** into you while you were walking.* The preterite is also known as the simple past in English, though in some languages there is a distinction between the preterite and other past tenses.

progressive tenses: A progressive tense expresses an action that is in progress or is developing at a given time. Progressive tenses in English are formed with the auxiliary *to be* + the present participle (-*ing* form of a verb). A progressive action can be expressed in present tense (*I **am reading** a book now*), past (*She **was taking** notes during class*), and future (*We **will be eating** pizza next Saturday*).

pronoun: A word that replaces a noun or a noun phrase. English pronouns come in three forms: subject pronouns (for example, *I* and *we*), object pronouns (*me* and *us*), and possessive pronouns (*my/mine* and *our/ours*).

qualify: See *modify*.

reflexive verb: A verb used to imply that the subject is performing an action on itself. In English, reflexive verbs are expressed with the pronoun -*self* (*myself, herself, themselves*, etc.) or are implied by the verb alone. For example: *I **hurt myself**. I was **shaving.***

relative pronoun: Relative pronouns introduce a sentence or clause that gives additional information about a noun. The relative pronouns in English are *who, whom, whose, which,* and *that.* In the sentence *The man **who** called was my father,* the clause *who called* provides additional information about the noun *man.*

subject pronoun: Pronouns that replace the subject of a sentence. Subject pronouns have the same gender and number as the noun they replace. The subject pronouns in English are *I, you, he, she, it, we, you, they,* and *one.* In the sentence *My mother is nice,* the noun phrase *my mother* can be replaced by the subject pronoun s*he:* ***She** is nice.*

subjunctive mood: The verb form used to express wishes, desires, emotions, and uncertainty, and hypothetical or nonfactual situations. For example: *If I were you, I wouldn't go.*

subordinate (dependent) clause: A clause that does not express a complete idea on its own. A subordinate clause must be used with another clause or sentence (called a **main clause** or **independent clause**). In the sentence *They told me that she was not coming, that she was not coming* is the subordinate clause, since it does not form a complete idea on its own.

subordinating conjunction: A conjunction that joins an independent clause with a dependent clause. Common subordinating conjunctions in English include *after, before, because, since, although, if, unless, until, while,* and *even if. I am going outside **even if** it is cold.*

superlative: The form of a word or the word construction used to show the most or the least in quantity, quality, or intensity. In English, the superlative is formed by adding –*est* or *most/least* to an adjective or adverb. For example: *tall**est**, **most** difficult.*

tense: Tense conveys when in time an event happened, how long it lasted, and whether the event has been completed. All tenses can be divided into one of three groups: present, past, and future. The specific form of a verb in a given sentence indicates the tense.

verb: A word that refers to an action or a state of being. For example: *to eat, to write, to read.*

voice: Voice indicates whether emphasis is placed on the person or thing causing the action, or the person or thing receiving the action. The voice of a sentence is either **active** or **passive**. In the **active voice**, the subject is the person or thing performing the action: ***She visited** the school.* In the **passive voice**, the subject is receiving the action of the verb: ***The school is visited** by her.* Two sentences can be written in different voices, but still carry the same meaning. For example: *I ate the cake* (active voice). *The cake was eaten by me* (passive voice).

Answer Key

Workout 1 .... p. 2

Exercise 1
1. la, les
2. le, les
3. l', les
4. l', les
5. la, les
6. l', les

Exercise 2
1. Les filles sont canadiennes.
2. (correct)
3. J'ai grillé le poisson.
4. Les oreilles sont très sensibles.
5. Nous avons vu le nouveau film de Luc Besson.

Exercise 3
1. J'ai rencontré le président.
2. La poste est fermée.
3. Ma mère a fait les biscuits.
4. L'actrice est belle.
5. Il a nagé à la piscine.
6. J'ai mangé au restaurant.

Workout 2 .... p. 4

Exercise 1
1. une, des
2. un, des
3. un, des
4. un, des
5. une, des
6. un, des

Exercise 2
1. des
2. une
3. des
4. un
5. un

Exercise 3
1. J'habite dans une maison.
2. Elle a un chat.
3. Je voudrais un café au lait.
4. Ils ont acheté une chemise at un cadeau.
5. Nous avons acheté des vêtements et des cadeaux.
6. J'ai des problèmes.

Exercise 4
1. des
2. le
3. une
4. la

5. une, des

Exercise 5
1. Je ne suis pas une pessimiste.
2. Je n'ai pas de voiture.
3. Il n'a pas d'amie.
4. Il n'a pas d'amis.
5. Ce n'est pas une sorcière.

Workout 3 .... p. 6

Exercise 1
1. de, du
2. de la
3. de
4. de l'
5. de l'

Exercise 2
1. Je ne vais pas acheter de café.
2. Qui ne boit pas d'eau?
3. Il n'a pas commandé de pâté.
4. Ce soir je ne mange pas de thon.
5. Vous ne faites pas de sport demain.
6. Il n'a pas mangé de fromage.

Exercise 3
1. La
2. les
3. des
4. un, au
5. du

Workout 4 .... p. 8

Exercise 1
1. F
2. F
3. M
4. N
5. M
6. F
7. M
8. N
9. F
10. M

Exercise 2
masculine: prince, fils, taureau, garçon, jumeau, homme
feminine: cousine, nièce, jumelle, duchesse, étudiante

Exercise 3

1. un
2. un
3. un
4. une
5. une
6. une
7. une
8. un
9. un
10. une

Workout 5 .... p. 10

Exercise 1

masculine: genou, cyclisme, hibou, cerf, renard
feminine: chance, natation, ambiance, cerise, tendresse

Exercise 2
Possible answers:

1. un trottoir
2. un oracle
3. un escroc
4. un chameau
5. un caillou
6. un bâtiment

Exercise 3
Possible answers:

1. la nature
2. une cité
3. la couronne
4. la glace
5. la fête
6. une discussion

Exercise 4

1. une serveuse
2. une lionne
3. une coiffeuse
4. une directrice
5. une laitière

Workout 6 .... p. 12

Exercise 1

1. genoux
2. souris
3. drapeaux
4. festivals
5. journaux
6. messages

Exercise 2

1. main
2. mademoiselle
3. clou
4. récital
5. corail
6. bijou

Exercise 3

			P			D	
V	A	C	A	N	C	E	S
			T			V	
			E			O	
	C		S			I	
	H					R	
D	E	C	H	E	T	S	
	V						
	E	C	H	E	C	S	
	U						
	X						

Workout 7 .... p. 14

Exercise 1

1.

porte-	avions
verb	masc. pl. noun

Answer Key

2.

arc-	en-	ciel
masc. sing. noun	preposition	masc. sing. noun

3.

sourd-	muet
masc. adjective	masc. adjective

4.

station-	service
fem. sing. noun	masc. sing. noun

5.

oiseau-	mouche
masc. sing. noun	fem. sing. noun

6.

après-	midi
preposition	masc. sing. noun

7.

chou-	fleur
masc. sing. noun	fem. sing. noun

8.

haut-	parleur
adjective	masc. sing. noun

9.

contre-	offensive
preposition	fem. sing. noun

10.

cessez-	le-	feu
verb	article	masc. sing. noun

Exercise 2
1. masculine
2. masculine
3. masculine
4. feminine
5. masculine

Exercise 3
1. des porte-avions
2. des oiseaux-mouches
3. des haut-parleurs
4. des contre-offensives
5. des cessez-le-feu

Workout 8 . . . . p. 16

Exercise 1
1. fière
2. magnifique (*same*)
3. réelle
4. vieille
5. excellente
6. folle
7. pâle (*same*)
8. inquiète

Exercise 2
1. belle
2. grand
3. délicieuse
4. belle
5. léger

Exercise 3
Possible answers:
1. belle, vieille
2. douce, gentille
3. grand, petit
4. méchant, discret
5. magnifique, folle

Workout 9 . . . . p. 18

Exercise 1
1. ces
2. cette
3. ce
4. cette
5. ces
6. ces
7. cet

Exercise 2
Le fromager: Bonjour. Que désirez-vous?
Le client: Quel est **ce** fromage-**ci**? (*Pointing directly to the cheese in front of him.*)
Le fromager: **Ce** fromage-**ci** est un Époisses de Bourgogne.
Le client: Et quel est **ce** fromage-**là**? (*Pointing to a cheese farther away.*)
Le fromager: **Ce** fromage-**là** est un Ami du Chambertin.
Le client: Lequel me conseillez-vous?
Le fromager: Entre l'Époisses et le Chambertin je vous recommande **ce** fromage-**ci** à **ce** fromage-**là**.
Le client: Bon, je prends 500g d'Époisses. Merci de votre conseil.

Exercise 3
1. Ce matin il a plu.
2. Cet après-midi il y avait du soleil.
3. Ce soir le temps est nuageux.

4. Ces phrases sont difficiles.

5. Est-ce que tu préfères cette chemise-ci ou ce débardeur-là?

6. Entre les deux je préfère ce débardeur-là.

Workout 10 .... p. 20

Exercise 1
1. d
2. f
3. g
4. c
5. a
6. e
7. b

Exercise 2
1. appartement, livre
2. chemise, règle, gomme, jupe
3. scooters, devoirs
4. idées, colliers, chambres
5. fourchette, mère
6. ordinateur, cahier, maison, pitié

Exercise 3
1. ma
2. son, son
3. ta *or* votre
4. leurs, leur
5. mon, ma
6. Vos, ses

Workout 11 .... p. 22

Exercise 1
1. (correct)
2. une valise noire
3. (correct)
4. (correct)
5. le bruit affreux

Exercise 2
1. l'école catholique
2. des veaux jeunes
3. un grand coeur
4. l'eau chaude et salée
5. les hommes gros

Exercise 3
Possible answers:
1. une jeune petite fille mignonne
2. un vieux homme grand et malade
3. une vieille femme élégante et chic

4. un jeune homme fatigué, studieux, et sérieux
5. une jeune fille mince, heureuse, et sportive

Workout 12 .... p. 24

Exercise 1
1. lentement
2. probablement
3. fréquemment
4. amoureusement
5. suffisamment

Exercise 2
1. J'aime vraiment Camus.
2. (correct)
3. Elles sont absolument correctes.
4. Nicolas et Jacques chantent merveilleusement.
5. (correct)

Exercise 3
1. Oui, elle est extraordinairement jolie.
2. Oui, j'aime énormément la glace.
3. Je mange ma glace lentement.
4. Elle m'a invité gentiment.
5. Oui, il va sûrement à Dijon.

Exercise 4
Adverbs: crissement, uniquement, apparemment, finalement, franchement, honnêtement, justement	**Nouns:** un appartement, un traitement, un équipement, un bâtiment

Workout 13 .... p. 26

Exercise 1
1. b
2. d
3. c
4. g
5. h
6. i
7. f
8. e
9. a

Exercise 2
1. debout
2. loin
3. précisement
4. derrière
5. ainsi
6. apparemment

Answer Key

Exercise 3

1. Tu devrais plutôt faire tes devoirs.
2. Ici il fait toujours beau.
3. Il vaudrait mieux partir maintenant.
4. Je préfèrerais vivre ailleurs.
5. Je l'aime bien.

Workout 14 .... p. 28

Exercise 1

1. c
2. e
3. h
4. a
5. b
6. f
7. g
8. i
9. d

Exercise 2

1. assez
2. trop
3. après
4. autrefois
5. bientôt

Exercise 3

1. J'en ai eu assez de tes bêtises.
2. Tu me demande encore de t'aider.
3. J'ai trop chaud!
4. Il ne faut jamais dire que c'est impossible.
5. Ne rentrez pas trop tard!

Workout 15 .... p. 30

Exercise 1

1. vrai
2. vrai
3. faux
4. vrai
5. faux

Exercise 2

1. Il parle très fort.
2. Il parle beaucoup.
3. Ce livre est vraiment intéressant.
4. Cette fille est très fatiguée.
5. Ce jeu est super passionnant.

Exercise 3

1. J'ai un chien qui est parfois méchant.
2. Il a roulé trop vite et, bien sûr, s'est fait arrêter par la police.
3. J'ai une maison qui est parfois cambriolée.

4. Il ronfle souvent en dormant.
5. Mon nouveau voisin fait beaucoup plus de bruit que l'ancien.

Workout 16 .... p. 32

Exercise 1

1. Nous allons au café.
2. Les enfants vont à la piscine.
3. Madame Dumont va à la poste.
4. Oscar va au travail.
5. Sylvie et Cynthia vont aux États-Unis.

Exercise 2
Possible answers:

1. Des vêtements aux couleurs vives.
2. Une femme/un homme au charme incroyable.
3. Une pizza au fromage.
4. Une confiture aux cerises.
5. Un tableau aux lignes fortes.

Exercise 3

1. Ses soeurs vivent à cinq minutes d'ici.
2. J'aimerais être à Madagascar.
3. Mon collègue m'a invité(e) à jouer au golf avec lui.
4. Je vais au lit à dix heures.
5. Donnons cet ananas à Nadège.

Workout 17 .... p. 34

Exercise 1

1. Cette voiture vient d'Italie.
2. Ce chocolat vient de Belgique.
3. Ce champagne vient de France.
4. Ce saké vient du Japon.
5. Cet ordinateur vient de Chine.
6. Cette fusée vient des États-Unis.

Exercise 2
Possible answers:

1. Un bonbon est fait de sucre.
2. La Tour Eiffel est faite de métal.
3. Une table ancienne est faite de bois.
4. Un verre est fait de plastique.
5. Une feuille est faite de papier.

Exercise 3

1. Un monstre de trois pieds de long était là.
2. Il a arrêté de fumer l'année dernière.
3. Le gâteau de ma grand-mère est la fierté de ma famille.
4. J'ai regretté de ne pas avoir assisté au spectacle.
5. De ma fenêtre, j'ai tout vu.

Workout 18 p. 36

Exercise 1
1. il
2. je
3. elle
4. tu
5. nous
6. vous
7. ils
8. elles
9. vous
10. ils

Exercise 2
1. je
2. il
3. tu
4. vous
5. ils
6. vous

Exercise 3

Tu: younger cousin, your father, a classmate,   **Vous:** your professor, the bus driver, your elderly neighbor

Exercise 4
Possible answers:
1. Oui, tu es en retard.
2. Non, je n'aime pas chanter.
3. Elles vont à l'école à sept heures tous les jours.
4. Elle a mangé un sandwich au thon.
5. Non, nous sommes les anciennes élèves.

Workout 19 p. 38

Exercise 1
1. b
2. e
3. f
4. a
5. c
6. d

Exercise 2
1. b
2. c
3. a
4. c
5. a

Exercise 3
1. Le mien
2. La mienne

3. Les miennes
4. Les miens
5. Les nôtres

Workout 20 p. 40

Exercise 1
1. direct-object pronoun
2. reflexive pronoun
3. subject pronoun
4. reflexive pronoun
5. emphatic reflexive pronoun

Exercise 2
1. Je me regarde (moi-même) dans le miroir.
2. Elles s'observent (elles-mêmes).
3. Ils s'interrogent (eux-mêmes).
4. Je me donne la permission (moi-même).

Exercise 3
1. Faites vos photocopies vous-mêmes!
2. Ils font le ménage eux-mêmes.
3. Elle cuisine elle-même.
4. J'apprend le karaté moi-même.

Workout 21 p. 42

Exercise 1
1. c
2. a
3. d
4. b

Exercise 2
1. C'est celle dans le placard.
2. (correct)
3. C'est celui-ci qui s'est fait arrêter par la police.
4. (correct)
5. (correct)

Exercise 3
1. Je les aime, surtout ceux qui puent.
2. C'est celle que j'aime.
3. J'aime celui-ci.
4. Je prends la petite.
5. Veux-tu celui-ci ou celui-là?

Answer Key

Exercise 1
Possible answer:
Ceci and *cela* are both possible, though they are more formal. *Ça* is the option most likely to be heard in spoken French because it is less formal and easier to say. *Ce* is usually only used before the verb *être*. Because the verb in this sentence is *sembler*, *ce* is not used.

Exercise 2
1. Ce sont des amis fidèles.
2. C'est le jour de paie.
3. C'est l'hiver.
4. C'est une bonne idée.
5. C'est fou.
6. Ce sont de bons chanteurs.
7. C'est moi.

Exercise 3
1. Dans l'avenir il faudra penser à ça.
2. À propos de ce cartable, ça me semble un peu trop lourd pour toi.
3. Ça me plaît.
4. Ça va bientôt faire quatre ans que je suis au collège.
5. Ça commence à être difficile.

Exercise 1
1. c
2. a
3. f
4. e
5. d
6. b

Exercise 2
1. Qu'est-ce qui
2. Qui
3. Qu'est-ce qui
4. Qu'est-ce que
5. quoi
6. Qui est-ce que
7. qui

Exercise 3
1. Qu'est-ce que tu as fait?
2. Avec qui est-ce qu'ils étudient?
3. Qui est-ce que vous connaissez?
4. Qu'est-ce que tu veux manger?
5. Qu'est-ce qui ne marche pas?
6. Qu'est-ce qui se passe?
7. Qui est le premier ministre du Canada?

Exercise 1
lequel: un lecteur DVD, un mouchoir, un radio-réveil
lesquels: des savons, des portefeuilles
laquelle: une pomme, une brosse, une chaise
lesquelles: des serviettes, des chaussures, des portes, des poires, des lunettes

Exercise 2
1. Lequel est-ce que tu veux louer?
2. Laquelle veux-tu prendre pour partir en vacances?
3. Lesquels souhaites-tu acheter?
4. Lesquelles t'ont fait un cadeau pour ton départ en retraite?
5. Lequel souhaites-tu acheter pour ton neveu?
6. Auquel penses-tu pour ce soir?
7. De laquelle parlez-vous?

Exercise 3
Possible answer:
Pierre: Okay, Paul. Va me chercher des gateaux apératif.
Paul: Lesquels veux-tu que je prenne?
Pierre: Les crackers, les Apéricubes, ceux pour lesquels j'ai une faiblesse.
Paul: Et quoi d'autre?
Pierre: Pense à prendre également du jus d'orange.
Paul: Entre toutes les marques de jus d'orange laquelle préfères-tu?
Pierre: La marque la moins chère me va très bien.
Paul: OK, mais à laquelle penses-tu?
Pierre: Prends une marque Acme.
Paul: OK, mais pense au foie gras. Tu sais, la boîte verte.
Pierre: Lequel?
Paul: Celui qui est tout au bout du rayon, et prends-en deux boîtes.
Pierre: Très bien. À tout à l'heure.

Exercise 1
1. c
2. b
3. d
4. e
5. a

Exercise 2
1. Je les encourage.
2. (correct)
3. Il s'ennuie.
4. Écoutez-moi!
5. Marine nous invite.
6. (correct)
7. Je l'ai mangé.

Exercise 3
Possible answers:
1. Oui, je l'aime.
2. Non, je ne l'ai pas vu.
3. Oui, elle l'a bu.
4. Oui, ils la font souvent.
5. Non, je ne vais pas la voir.

Exercise 4
1. Mange les!
2. Embrassez-moi!
3. Dépêche-toi!
4. Dépêchez-vous!
5. Ne le fais pas!

Workout 26 .... p. 52

Exercise 1
1. faux
2. vrai
3. vrai
4. vrai
5. faux

Exercise 2
1. leur
2. me
3. nous
4. lui
5. moi

Exercise 3
1. Tu me donnes la télécommande.
2. Je lui parle deux fois par semaine.
3. Marie y a répondu.
4. Stéphane lui a téléphoné.
5. Nous lui avons donné un cadeau.

Workout 27 .... p. 54

Exercise 1
1. moi
2. Lui
3. elle
4. soi
5. toi
6. moi
7. nous

Exercise 2
1. In a short answer, without a verb.
2. In a sentence with a compound subject.
3. For emphasis.

4. Used after *c'est*.
5. To form an emphatic reflexive pronoun.
6. With the negative conjunction *ne ... ni.*
7. In a comparison, after *que.*
8. For emphasis in asking questions.
9. After a preposition to indicate possession.
10. With the adverb *ne ... que.*
11. After a preposition.

Exercise 3
1. Eux, ils vont faire des courses.
2. Lui, il a décidé de faire de la peinture.
3. Moi, j'ai envie de te parler.
4. Nous, nous pensons qu'il fera beau demain.
5. Tu te compliques trop la vie, toi.

Workout 28 .... p. 56

Exercise 1
1. tout
2. Plusieurs
3. Tout le monde
4. Chacun
5. quelque chose
6. Les autres

Exercise 2
1. Je n'ai vu personne.
2. Je n'ai rien prévu.
3. Elle n'a invité personne.
4. Elle n'a rien mangé.
5. Aucune fille n'est contente.

Exercise 3
1. Tout est prêt?
2. Je n'ai rien préparé.
3. Plusieurs candidats sont venus pour le débat.
4. Tout le monde est parti au centre commercial.
5. Quelques-uns vont faire du jogging plus tard.

Workout 29 .... p. 58

Exercise 1
1. que
2. qui
3. qui
4. que
5. que

Exercise 2
1. Ce que
2. Ce que
3. ce qui
4. ce que

Answer Key

5. ce qui

6. Ce que

Exercise 3

1. Christine est très intelligente, ce qu'elle étudie sont les mathématiques.

2. Elle a envie de dépenser les dix euros qu'elle a trouvés.

3. J'ai une belle moto, ce qui me déplace vite en ville.

4. Ce qui m'énerve le plus, c'est le café.

5. J'ai un cousin qui s'appelle Michel.

6. J'ai une belle moto que tu peux acheter.

Workout 30 .... p. 60

Exercise 1

1. a

2. b

3. d

4. a

5. d

6. b

Exercise 2

1. auquel

2. auxquels

3. Lesquelles

4. laquelle

5. duquel

Exercise 3

1. Ce dont j'ai besoin, c'est un taille-crayon.

2. C'est ce à quoi ils rêvent.

3. La France est un pays où il fait bon vivre.

4. L'Olympique Lyonnais est une équipe dont les Lyonnais sont très fiers.

5. Tu lui demandes ce à quoi elle réfléchit?

Workout 31 .... p. 62

Exercise 1

1. en

2. en

3. y

4. y

5. en

6. y

7. en

Exercise 2

1. Allons-y! *or* On y va!

2. J'y vais ce weekend.

3. J'en ai assez.

4. Profites-en!

5. Je n'y crois plus.

Exercise 3
Possible answers:

1. Non, je n'y suis jamais allé(e).

2. Oui, je m'y intéresse beaucoup.

3. Non, c'est ma mère qui s'en occupe.

4. Oui, j'en ai beaucoup.

5. Non, je n'y fais pas trop attention.

Workout 32 .... p. 64

Exercise 1

1. On est contente.

2. On n'aime plus cette série, *Lost.*

3. S'il fait froid, on mange de la soupe.

4. On y va!

5. On est descendues les escaliers.

Exercise 2
Possible answers:

1. a. Nous aimons chanter. b. Des gens, en général, aiment chanter.

2. a. Nous aimons danser. b. J'aime danser.

3. a. Nous chantons et dansons. b. Je chante et danse.

4. a. Nous jouons souvent le hockey sur glace. b. Des Canadiens jouent souvent le hockey sur glace.

5. a. Nous nous habituons. b. Je m'habitue.

Exercise 3

1. On parle italien ici.

2. Si on ne mange pas, on a faim.

3. On est sérieux/sérieuse.

4. On est des filles sérieuses.

5. On est arrivé(e)(s) hier.

6. On ne sait jamais.

7. On m'a dit de venir.

Workout 33 .... p. 66

Exercise 1

1. Mangez les!

2. (correct)

3. (correct)

4. Il les a posés.

5. (correct)

6. J'en ai assez.

Exercise 2

1. Elle lui parle d'elle-même.

2. La mienne est la meilleure.

3. Je me suis coupé(e) les cheveux moi-même.

4. Je me les suis coupés (moi-même).

5. Est-ce que tu préfères celui-ci ou celui-là? (*masculine object*)

6. J'aime ça.

7. Ne l'oublie pas! C'est important.

8. Après quinze minutes, j'en ai eu assez.

Exercise 3

1. elle s'est débrouillée elle-même

2. je n'en ai pas

3. il ne les a pas lus

4. je me débrouille moi-même

5. vous les avez vus

Workout 34 .... p. 68

Exercise 1

Group 1	Group 2	Group 3	Other Irregular Verbs
manger avancer	finir	faire	être avoir

Exercise 2

1. (correct)

2. Nous avançons

3. Vous avancez

4. (correct)

5. Je bougeai

Exercise 3

					T				A
	M	A	N	G	E	R			L
					A				L
	F				D		T		E
	I		P	O	U	V	O	I	R
	N		E		I		M		
	I		R		R		B		
P	R	E	N	D	R	E		E	
			R				R		
		V	E	N	I	R			

Workout 35 .... p. 70

Exercise 1

1. m'appelle, j'étudie

2. paie/paye, m'aide

3. lève

4. mangeons, étudions

5. J'aime

6. préfère, communiquent

7. s'ennuye/ennuie, apprécions

Exercise 2

1. Les restaurants au centre-ville ouvrent normalement à septe heures trente du soir et ferment à minuit.

2. Le professeur parle très rapidement et souvent je lui demande de répéter.

3. Regardez le menu, mais je suggère de prendre quatre plats différents, ainsi on les partage.

4. Chaque jour mon frère achète son journal préféré.

Exercise 3

1. Chaque vendredi je nettoye/nettoie la maison et j'achète du pain.

2. Didier regarde mes photos et il pense qu'elles sont belles.

3. Mes amis et moi ne voyageons jamais, mais cet été on decide de partir ensemble.

4. Joséphine appelle sa mère chaque jour.

5. Tu aimes bien ta copine et lui envoies un beau cadeau pour son anniversaire.

Workout 36 .... p. 72

Exercise 1

1. Marie ne dort pas bien.

2. Mes parents partent à la campagne chaque vendredi.

3. Tu haïs aller avec eux.

4. Nous choisissons toujours les chaussures les plus chères.

5. Les enfants ouvrent leurs cahiers et écrivent une dictée.

Exercise 2

1. Mon frère dort beaucoup.

2. (correct)

3. Quand il se couche, il ouvre la fenêtre.

4. (correct)

Exercise 3
Possible answer:

Mon grand-père a une mémoire exceptionnelle. Il se souvient de tout. Quand il commence un de ses contes de jeunesse parfois il doit s'interrompre et reprendre après quelques temps, mais il reprend d'où il a laissé et il finit tout ce qu'il veut dire. Il réussit à reproduire exactement des conversations qu'il a eues il y a quarante ans, et à décrire des lieux qu'il a vus une fois de sa vie. Quand il veut me raconter quelque chose, il m'appelle et me dit de m'asseoir près de lui. J'obéis et je ne pars de chez moi que quand il a terminé. Mon grand-père est un homme rare et charmant. Mais, en fait, il pourrait même tout inventer, n'est-ce pas? Mais peu importe ... tout ce qu'il raconte est fabuleux!

Workout 37 . . . . p. 74

Exercise 1
1. corrompent
2. reprend
3. remets
4. abattez
5. remets

Exercise 2
1. Chaque jour tu m'attends au café.
2. Il prend le train à six heures.
3. Nous vous entendons parler.
4. Ces artistes peignent de tableaux magnifiques.

Exercise 3
Possible answer:

Cher Didier,

Comment vas-tu? Alors, tu es prêt pour ton voyage? On va faire un tas de choses ensemble et ça sera super! Je suis désolée que je ne puisse pas venir te chercher à la gare, je travaille jusqu'à sept heures et ça serait trop tard. En fait, ce n'est pas du tout difficile de venir à ce café TouTou dont je t'ai parlé. Quand tu descends du train, tu prends un ticket pour le métro. Il y a des trucs qui vendent les tickets juste à la sortie de la gare, tu ne peux pas les manquer. Puis tu cherches le métro rouge direction centre-ville. Normalement je n'attends que quelques minutes. Tu descends au quatrième stop. Tu peux m'appeler, mon portable est toujours allumé, mais si je ne réponds pas, c'est parce que je travaille. Dans ce cas-là, rappelle-moi. Si tu te perds, demande à quelqu'un de t'aider, mais je confie te voir au café à huit heures. Francine, la fille dont je t'avais parlé, sera là ...

Bisous,

Camille

Workout 38 . . . . p. 76

Exercise 1

	A									
	P		C							
	P	A	Y	O	N	S				
	E			N				J		
	L			S				E		
	L			I				T		
	E			D		P		T		
		P	R	E	F	É	R	E		
				R		L		N		
N	E	T	T	O	I	E		T		
				N		S				
				S						

Exercise 2

Lucie: Mais c'est pas vrai!

Claudine: Mais si! Il m'a laissée là, toute seule.

Lucie: Et qu'est-ce que tu vas faire maintenant?

Claudine: J'appelle mon analyste!

Lucie: Il est où, ton analyste?

Claudine: Rue des Moulins. C'est pas mal du tout.

Lucie: Et combien tu le payes?

Claudine: 100 euros la séance.

Lucie: Tu sais, parfois j'ai l'impression que tu jettes ton argent par les fenêtres.

Claudine: Pourquoi?

Lucie: Je ne sais pas, pourquoi tu ne t'achètes pas quelque chose de joli?

Claudine: Parce que je ne m'appelle pas Paris Hilton et je préfère dépenser mon argent pour quelque chose d'utile!

Exercise 3
1. e
2. c
3. a
4. d
5. b

Workout 39 .... p. 78

Exercise 1
1. ont/a envahi
2. sera
3. participé
4. souhaitent
5. suffiront

Exercise 2
Possible answers:
1. Un tas de gens visitent la Tour Eiffel chaque année.
2. Une multitude de touristes admirent Mona Lisa chaque année.
3. Milliers d'étudiants prennent des photos du David de Donatello à Florence.

Workout 40 .... p. 80

Exercise 1
1. Partir
2. m'appeler
3. Tourner
4. reprocher
5. Pleurer

Exercise 2
1. Eating, drinking, and sleeping are simple but essential pleasures.
2. It must be admitted that reading Proust is not easy.
3. If you have anything to say, it is necessary to do it now.
4. I don't like playing tennis, but I love watching it.
5. Dancing? No, thank you, I prefer to sit down.

Exercise 3
1. Éteindre les portables.
2. Mettre toujours la ceinture de sécurité.
3. Couper l'oignon très fin.
4. Remettre les livres à leurs places.
5. Ne pas parler au conducteur.

Workout 41 .... p. 82

Exercise 1
1. Ça y est, je rentre.
2. C'est le 30 avril.
3. Est-ce que vous étudiez le français à l'université?
4. Je pense qu'on se connaît, n'est-ce pas?

Exercise 2
1. est
2. sommes
3. es
4. êtes
5. suis

Exercise 3
Je suis étudiante à la Sorbonne. J'ai vingts ans. Je suis française, mais mes parents sont russes. Ils sont deux personnes très intéressantes: mon père est sculpteur, ma mère est avocat. Ils sont tous les deux passionnées de l'opéra, mais moi, je suis plutôt intéressée au cinéma. Je suis une fan de Carax, tu le connais? Il est un vrai génie, n'est-ce pas? Quoi encore ... je suis assez jolie. Je suis maigre mais pas étique. Mes cheveux sont blondes et mes yeux sont verts. Et toi? Comment es-tu? Je suis curieuse, moi aussi ...

Workout 42 .... p. 84

Exercise 1
1. Le petit Nicolas a peur des rats.
2. Ce chien a toujours sommeil!
3. Louis a mal à la tête.
4. Joseph a faim, donne-lui un steak.

Exercise 2
1. Marie a toujours froid et son petit frère a toujours chaud.
2. "Tu as faim?" "No, j'ai seulement un peu soif."
3. Quelle âge as-tu?" "J'ai trente ans."

Exercise 3
1. Charles a onze ans.
2. Nous avons envie de jouer à tennis.
3. J'ai besoin d'acheter de la viande.

Workout 43 .... p. 86

Exercise 1
1. Hier j'ai lu ton livre.
2. Puis j'ai fait mes devoirs.
3. Vers midi j'ai vu David.
4. Il a voulu manger à un nouveau café près de l'université.
5. À trois heures, j'ai appelé Carole pour étudier ensemble.

Exercise 2
Possible answers:
1. Elle a pris le soleil à la plage.
2. Elle a mangé dans des restaurants très chic.
3. Elle a écrit des cartes postales à ses amis.

Exercise 3
Possible answer:
J'ai pris un avion le matin et j'ai dormi pendant tout le vol. Quand j'ai ouvert mes yeux, nous étions arrivés à Venise! J'ai laissé ma valise à l'hôtel et j'ai commencé à explorer cette ville extraordinaire ... Pendant mon séjour, qui a duré cinq jours, j'ai connu un tas

Answer Key

de personnes intéressantes que j'ai à inviter chez moi pour les prochaines vacances. Aldo, un vieil homme de quatre-vingts ans en retraite, m'a fait connaître tous les endroits les plus mystérieux de Venise, et m'a accompagnée voir des expositions de verre magnifiques ... Il arrive dans un mois, et je lui ai préparé une belle surprise ...

Workout 44 .... p. 88

Exercise 1
1. Hier je suis arrivé(e) chez moi à quatre heures.
2. Je me suis préparé(e) un toast et je suis allé(e) dormir un peu.
3. Quand je me suis levé(e), je me suis souvenu(e) d'appeler Annie.
4. Vers six heures, je me suis promené(e) au centre-ville.
5. Quand je suis rentré(e), je me suis mis(e) une jolie veste et je suis sorti(e) encore avec ma copine.

Exercise 2
La semaine dernière, je me suis amusé(e) en lisant un article très intéressant qui parlait des relations d'amour, et j'ai appris que, pour être heureux, il faut garder une certaine distance vis-à-vis de son copain. Je suis immédiatement allé(e) voir mon/ma copain(e) au café puisque j'ai trouvé ce sujet plutôt intéressant, mais il/elle m'a dit: "Si tu veux garder une distance, permets-moi de t'aider: ce matin j'ai déménagé." Je suis retourné(e) au bureau et j'ai jeté l'article.

Exercise 3
1. sommes allés
2. avons vu, sommes amusés
3. s'est approché, est sorti, couru, a commencé
4. ai acheté, est redevenu
5. n'a pas eu peur, a posé
6. a ris, a mis
7. a pris
8. sont venus, me suis senti

Workout 45 .... p. 90

Exercise 1
1. J'étais juste rentré des vacances quand j'ai reçu ton coup de fil.
2. Elle a acheté plusieurs livres d'art qu'elle avait étudié à l'université.
3. L'hôtel avait perdu nos réservations.
4. Marthe et toi aviez déjà nettoyé toute la maison avant mon retour.
5. Le petit Paul était déjà né quand son père arriva à l'hôpital.

Exercise 2
Possible answers:
1. J'avais acheté une nouvelle jupe, contrôlé mon passeport, et réservé une place côté couloir sur l'avion.
2. Non, je ne l'avais jamais visité. J'avais déjà été au Maroc, en Angleterre, en Inde, et en Argentine.
3. Oui, j'étais déjà parti à l'aventure une fois, quand j'étais parti pour le Caire avant d'y trouver un logement. La première nuit j'ai dormi chez un homme que j'avais rencontré en avion. J'ai toujours préféré dormir chez les gens.
4. J'avais projété de tout voir!
5. Oui, ça m'était arrivé une fois, au Maroc. Ce lieu était si mystérieux et fascinant que j'avais presque décidé d'y rester.

Exercise 3
Possible answer:
1. Jean-Louis avait déjà appelé sa mère.
2. Il avait déjà arrosé les plantes.
3. Il avait déjà acheté et lu le journal.
4. Il avait déjà payé ses factures à la poste.
5. Il avait déjà fait une petite somme.

Workout 46 .... p. 92

Exercise 1
1. Tu ne crus jamais à ce que te dis.
2. Tu pensas que ton point de vue fut le seul qui compta.
3. Et puis tu finis toutes nos conversations en haussant les .. épaules.
4. Tu n'y crus pas, mais c'est ce que je fis.

Exercise 2
Possible answers:
1. Pépé Pierre se marria.
2. Pépé Pierre devint père.
3. Pépé Pierre parta faire la guerre.

Workout 47 .... p. 94

Exercise 1
Possible answers:
1. Non, je viendrai demain.
2. Non, j'y irai la semaine prochaine.
3. Non, je les appellerai ce soir.
4. Non, je le finirai dimanche.
5. Non, je ne la ferai plus jamais.

Exercise 2
1. Tu liras un bon livre quand tu retourneras du bureau.
2. Sophie finira d'écrire un e-mail quand la petite Berthe dormira.

3. Joseph et Marie regarderont un film quand ils arriveront à la maison ce soir.

4. Nous serons chez nous tout le soir.

5. Est-ce que vous prendrez l'avion quand vous partirez pour l'Allemagne?

Exercise 3
Possible answer:

Ta vie commencera à changer quand tu rencontreras une personne qui te demandera de la suivre dans une aventure merveilleuse. Tu attendras cette occasion et elle arrivera. Tu rencontreras cette personne à une fête, tu la fréquenteras quelques temps, et puis tu comprendras que tu feras quoi qu'elle te demande. Vous partirez faire un voyage dans un endroit exotique, où vous démarrerez une petite activité ensemble. Vous deviendrez très riches, ce qui vous permettra d'aider beaucoup de gens. Mais ce n'est pas tout ...

Workout 48 .... p. 96

Exercise 1
1. Dans le passé, je me levais à neuf heures et j'allais au bureau.

2. Je venais chez toi pour un café et j'achetais un croissant pour Pierre.

3. Quand j'arrivais, il y avait toujours beaucoup de travail qui m'attendait.

4. Avant de commencer, je passais un coup de fil à ma mère et je bavardais avec mes collègues.

Exercise 2
1. avait, était
2. était, avait
3. avait, n'était, était, n'étaient
4. avait, était
5. avait, avait
6. n'était, était, avait

Exercise 3
1. Hier il faisait vraiment froid.
2. Quand j'étais jeune, je ne l'aimais pas.
3. Chaque hiver ma famille allait à la campagne.
4. Nous faisions beaucoup de promenades et nous dormions beaucoup.

Workout 49 .... p. 98

Exercise 1
1. Chaque matin je dormais jusqu'à dix heures.
2. Quand j'étais petit, en été nous allions à la mer.
3. Quand l'école se terminait, je faisais des voyages merveilleux.

4. L'hiver dernier, chaque après-midi je prenais un café avec Sylvain.

5. Je ne mentais jamais.

Exercise 2
1. habitait, était
2. faisait, pleuvait, savait
3. a rencontré, étudiait
4. sont devenus, ont commencé
5. allaient, se promenaient, aimaient
6. a grandi, ont continué, ont quitté, sont retournés

Exercise 3
Possible answers:
1. Mercredi il faisait très beau, par conséquent je suis sortie pour me promener dans le parc.

2. J'étais en train de marcher dans le parc quand j'ai vu une personne que je ne pensais jamais revoir: mon premier amour!

3. C'était la première fois que je le voyais après qu'on s'est quittés en 1998.

4. Après avoir échangé quelques mots vagues et gênés, on a commencé à marcher ensemble sans savoir où aller.

5. Et enfin on a décidé de se revoir. Ce soir.

Workout 50 .... p. 100

Exercise 1
Possible answers:
1. À dix heures, Martine sera dèjà venue.
2. Quand tu arriveras, j'aurai perdu mon train.
3. Il aura appelé quand j'arriverai au bureau ...

Exercise 2
1. serai marié
2. aurons terminé, irons
3. passerons
4. aurons perfectionné, partirons
5. serons devenus, retournerons

Exercise 3
Possible answers:
1. ... j'aurai dèjà beaucoup travaillé.
2. ... j'aurai mangé avec un ami.
3. ... je serai allé voir mon oncle.
4. ... j'aurai déjà bu un verre de vin.
5. ... j'aurai déjà beaucoup rêvé!

Exercise 4
1. a
2. c
3. c
4. d
5. a

Answer Key

Workout 51 p. 102

Exercise 1
1. Anne aurait préparé un bon dîner si elle avait fait les courses.
2. Laure irait au cinéma mais elle est toute seule.
3. Robert promènerait son chien, mais il est malade.

Exercise 2
1. Je lui ferais faire le tour du monde.
2. Je le vendrait et donnerait les recettes aux pauvres de ma ville.
3. Je l'amènerais au parc avec moi.

Exercise 3
1. Pourriez-vous m'apporter la carte, s'il vous plaît?
2. Je voudrais savoir quel est le meilleur vin.
3. Je préfèrerais du blanc.

Workout 52 p. 104

Exercise 1
Possible answers:
1. Si j'avais du talent comme architecte, j'aurais fait comme André.
2. Je serais retourné(e) immédiatement skier pour vaincre la peur.
3. Oui, j'aurais quitté un travail qui ne me plaisait pas et je serais devenu un pianiste exceptionnel.

Exercise 2
1. Hier soir j'aurais pu aller dormir à dix heures, mais j'ai vu . un film magnifique.
2. Ce matin j'aurais voulu prendre l'autobus, mais je me suis réveillé trop tard.
3. Enfant, j'aurais dû comprendre que la vie n'aurait plus été si facile.
4. L'été dernier j'aurais voulu partir en Afrique, mais j'ai eu un terrible accident.
5. Il y a une minute j'aurais voulu te donner un bisou, mais tu n'étais pas à la maison.

Exercise 3
1. Sonia a dit qu'elle aurait porté du vin.
2. David a dit qu'il aurait pensé à la musique.
3. Marc a dit qu'il aurait acheté de la bouffe.
4. Sylvie a dit qu'elle serait retournée de la mer à temps.
5. Sabine a dit qu'elle aurait dansé comme une folle.

Workout 53 p. 106

Exercise 1
1. Il faut que les citoyens aillent voter aux élections politiques.
2. Je ne pense pas qu'aujourd'hui les femmes soient plus protégées qu'autrefois.
3. Je crois que les travailleurs veuillent protester pour leurs droits.
4. Je ne suis pas sûr/e que tu t'informes avant de voter.
5. Il est important que les politiciens fassent face aux problèmes de leur électorat.

Exercise 2
1. aies confiance dans les jeunes
2. fasses un effort pour ta communauté
3. dises ton opinion
4. ailles aux débats politiques

Exercise 3
1. respectons
2. n'ayons, n'utilisons, abîmons
3. soit, peut
4. redécouvrent, modifierait

Workout 54 p. 108

Exercise 1
1. Ayant appelé à l'avance, elle est arrivée à huit heures du matin.
2. Gérard ayant été en retard, on n'a pas pu partir.
3. Elles sont des filles très aimantes.
4. Ces filles, ayant du talent, donnent beaucoup de concerts.
5. Ils les a vus arrangeant leur rendez-vous.

Exercise 2
1. étudiant
2. finissant
3. ayant
4. étant
5. venant

Exercise 3
1. N'étudiant pas chaque jour, il a raté son examen.
2. Finissant ses cours, il est retourné chez soi.
3. Luc, n'ayant pas d'argent, ne peut pas louer un appartement.
4. Les choses étant claires, il ne nous reste plus rien à discuter.
5. Venant de Russie, elle aime le froid.

Workout 55 . . . . p. 110

Exercise 1
1. Ayant écouté cette chanson, chante avec moi.
2. Ayant écris ces questions, je reponds.
3. Ayant trouvé les lettres, je m'en vais.
4. Ayant considéré tes résultats, je dis que tu n'as pas étudié.
5. Ayant mangé tous le bonbons, on se sent mal.

Exercise 2
1. eu
2. allée
3. montée
4. Arrivée, connu, vendu

Exercise 3
1. b
2. b
3. a
4. c

Workout 56 . . . . p. 112

Exercise 1
1. Paul a entendu un enfant crier en sortant de chez lui.
2. Il a couru vers lui en appelant la police.
3. En lui parlant, Paul a compris la situation.
4. Paul a commencé à rire en raccrochant.
5. Il lui a tapoté doucement la tête en lui promettant de lui acheter un nouveau ballon.

Exercise 2
Possible answers:
1. Je parle au téléphone avec mon ami en écrivant mes mails.
2. Je fais la cuisine en lisant un dossier important.
3. Je prends ma douche en étudiant les verbes irréguliers.
4. Je fais mes courses en finissant mon café.
5. Je dîne en te regardant dans les yeux.

Exercise 3
Possible answers:
1. Je ne bouge pas en voyant un film.
2. Je ne peux pas m'asseoir en répétant mes leçons.
3. Je n'arrive pas à me concentrer en écoutant la musique.
4. Je ne bois jamais en conduisant la voiture.
5. Je ne dîne pas au restaurant en travaillant.

Workout 57 . . . . p. 114

Exercise 1
1. Chaque jour Christine se lève à sept heures.
2. Elle prend sa douche, s'habille et prend son petit déjeuner.
3. Puis elle se prépare pour sortir, mais seulement après un café bien fort.
4. Quand elle arrive au bureau, elle s'assied à son bureau et commence à téléphoner.
5. Le soir, elle retourne chez elle très fatiguée et d'habitude s'endort à dix heures.

Exercise 2
1. se contenter
2. se relaxer
3. s'amuser
4. s'endormir
5. se sécher

Exercise 3
Possible answer:
Chaque jour je me réveille à sept heures; je me lève et je prends une douche. Puis je me prépare un bon petit déjeuner, je m'habille, et je sors. Je prends le métro pour aller à l'université, là où je me donne rendez-vous avec mes copines pour le premier café de la journée. Nous nous asseyons à une table près de la fenêtre et nous nous amusons à nous moquer des gens qui passent. Ce n'est pas très gentil, je sais ... Puis on entre dans nos cours jusqu'à treize heures, quand nous prenons le déjeuner dans la cafétéria de l'université. Là-bas, on s'ennuie: il n'y a aucun beau garçon à connaître et la bouffe est épouvantable. Alors ...

Workout 58 . . . . p. 116

Exercise 1
1. Martine s'est levée à huit heures.
2. Elle s'est acheté une belle veste.
3. Elle s'est dépêchée pour prendre le train.
4. Elle s'est endormie dans le train.
5. Et elle s'est réveillée à Amsterdam!

Exercise 2
1. souvenue
2. mise
3. dit
4. regardée
5. trompée

Exercise 3
Possible answers:
1. Elle s'est assise dans le métro à côté d'un homme très élégant.
2. Quand elle est arrivée au bureau pour son entretien, elle s'est présentée à M. Boulot.
3. Ils se sont serré la main et ils ont bavardé pendant une heure.
4. À la fin de l'entretien, M. Boulot lui a dit, "Bienvenue dans notre société," et ils se sont dit au revoir.

Answer Key

Exercise 1
1. They have just moved into their new house.
2. They have installed a new TV set in the living room.
3. Jeanne put all her books on the shelf in her room.
4. Christine began to clean the kitchen.
5. Christine and Jeanne had fun preparing their first dinner.

Exercise 2
1. elle s'est dirigée
2. ils s'en sont allés
3. je perds
4. il s'arrête
5. elles se sont débrouillées
6. je me demande
7. ils se fâcheront
8. tu t'es mis à
9. tu entends
10. elle s'est trompée

Exercise 3
1. s'appelle
2. se lève, se lave, s'habille, se promène
3. se sont succédés, se sont envolées

Exercise 1
1. Le sud de la France est aimé des touristes.
2. Ce roman ne se vend pas bien en ce moment.
3. Le mari et sa maîtresse ont été vus par ta tante au parc.

Exercise 2
1. Est-ce que le pop-corn est vendu ici?
2. Est-ce que le pourboire est inclus dans l'addition?
3. Est-ce que les Gitanes sont encore fumées de tous les peintres français?
4. Est-ce que les Américains seront toujours considérés des cowboys criards?

Exercise 3
1. P
2. A
3. P
4. A

Exercise 1
Possible answers:
1. Tais-toi! Tu n'as plus d'excuses! Tu m'entends?
2. Ah, non, mon cher. J'ai entendu ça trop souvent. Maintenant lève-toi du lit et commence.

3. Absolument. Prends brosse et balai et vas-y!
4. Allez, et n'oublie pas qu'après ça tu devras ...
5. Non, je n'attends plus. Nettoie le loyer et fais la cuisine.
6. Avant six heures.
7. Tu as neuf heures pour faire tout, c'est assez de temps. Aller, commence.
8. Tais-toi et travaille. Garde ton énergie pour le parquet.

Exercise 2
1. Achète du lait!
2. Dormez!
3. Sortons!
4. Fais tes devoirs!
5. Aie confiance!

Exercise 3
Possible answers:
1. Justin, écris au maire!
2. Albert, appelle le studio!
3. Monique et Lucien, lisez ce fax!
4. Lola, envoie un e-mail aux partenaires!
5. Frank, sois ponctuel!

Exercise 1
1. a
2. avez
3. ont
4. avons
5. a

Exercise 2
Possible answers:
1. J'ai vingt-deux ans.
2. J'ai les yeux gris, les cheveux noirs.
3. J'ai peur des vampires et des fantômes.
4. Il y a des peintures.
5. J'ai envie d'aller à la plage.

Exercise 3
1. Nadia a les cheveux très courts; elle a de petits pieds; elle a l'air heureuse.
2. À cinquante ans, on a besoin de s'amuser comme à vingt ans.
3. À qui est ce chien? Il est à Magalie?
4. Ils ont peur de regretter leur décision.
5. Les nuages ont l'air d'annoncer de la pluie, et je n'ai pas mon parapluie avec moi.

Workout 63 .... p. 126

Exercise 1
1. je connais, on connaît, vous connaissez, elles connaissent
2. tu sais, ils savent, nous savons, il sait

Exercise 2
1. sait
2. Connaissez
3. sais
4. connais
5. sait

Exercise 3
Possible answers:
1. Amélie sait jouer la comédie.
2. Christo et Jeanne-Claude connaissent Central Park.
3. Daniel Auteuil sait chanter.
4. Tu ne connais pas ma grand-mère.
5. Je ne sais pas parler chinois.

Exercise 4
1. a *or* b
2. a *or* c
3. a *or* c
4. b *or* c

Exercise 5
1. Elle connaît cette musique
2. George a rencontré sa femme quand il avait vingt ans.
3. Ils ne savent pas où aller.
4. Je ne sais pas choisir les ananas.

Workout 64 .... p. 128

Exercise 1
Possible answers:
1. Il fait gris et il fait frais.
2. Il fait 18 degrés Celsius.
3. Ma mère fait la cuisine chez moi.
4. Oui, je fais du sport. Je fais du volley. *or* Non, je ne fais pas de sport.
5. Oui, je fais de la musique. Je fais du piano. *or* Non, je ne fais pas de musique.

Exercise 2
Possible answers:
1. Claude Debussy fait du piano.
2. Thierry Henry fait des exercices.
3. Je ne fais pas de discours.
4. Vous ne faites pas de volley.
5. Je fais du volley.

Exercise 3
1. Je me fais masser aujourd'hui!
2. Il s'est fait arrêter par la police hier.
3. Fais laver ta voiture.

Workout 65 .... p. 130

Exercise 1
1. b
2. a *or* b
3. a
4. a *or* b

Exercise 2
1. j'ai manqué *or* j'ai raté
2. manquer
3. manquent
4. manque
5. ratent

Exercise 3
1. Cet appartement manque de lumière.
2. Les deux soeurs ne manquent jamais une occasion de chanter.
3. Les beaux pommiers de son jardin lui manquent.
4. Gérard n'échoue jamais à rien.
5. Tu leur manques tous les jours.

Exercise 4
1. Nous n'avons pas réussi notre examen hier.
2. Ne manque pas ton train! *or* Ne manquez pas votre train!
3. Je suis arrivé au cinéma en retard et j'ai manqué le début du film.
4. Elle ne réussit pas ses gâteaux à chaque fois.
5. Dommage! Tu as encore manqué la sortie d'autoroute!

Exercise 5
Possible answers:
1. Les fruits me manquent.
2. Ma famille me manque.
3. Les forets et les lacs me manquent.

Workout 66 .... p. 132

Exercise 1
1. sortir
2. quittent
3. sortent
4. sort, quitte
5. pars

Answer Key

Exercise 2
1. a sorti
2. êtes parti(e)(s)
3. avez-vous quitté
4. sont partis
5. es sorti(e)

Exercise 3
1. Si ce crocodile ne part pas, je ne sors pas de cette cabane.
2. Armelle a quitté son travail; elle a quitté sa maison; et elle a quitté le pays.
3. Si tu sors après moi, n'oublie pas de fermer la porte.
4. Bonjour Mr. Sabatier. Ne quittez pas.
5. Depuis quand est-ce que mes deux colègues sortent ensemble?

Workout 67..................................... p. 134

Exercise 1
1. rentre
2. retourne
3. revenir
4. revient
5. retournons *or* revenons

Exercise 2
1. Chantal est rentrée à midi le samedi.
2. Les ouvriers ne sont pas retournés au travail.
3. Les enfants sont revenus de vacances en août.
4. Valentin a rentré les chaises.

Exercise 3
Possible answers:
1. Mon oncle et ma tante retournent en Alsace.
2. Tu rentres seul.
3. Tu rentres dans trois jours.
4. Merlin retourne à la forêt.

Exercise 4
1. Si tu es malade, ne retourne pas au travail.
2. Quand rentres-tu ce soir?
3. Ils ont retourné leurs T-shirts.
4. Il y a trop de vent. Rentrons les plantes.

Workout 68 .... p. 136

Exercise 1
1. vivez
2. ont vécu
3. vivent, vivent
4. avons vécu
5. vis-tu

Exercise 2
1. a *or* b
2. b
3. *all three choices are correct*

Exercise 3
1. Where do you see yourself living in ten years?
2. This is a fish that lives in fresh water.
3. You live on boulevard Raspail in Paris, right?
4. She's alive; that's wonderful.
5. You had a bad experience during that transition.

Exercise 4
1. Laissez-moi vivre!
2. Elle vit/habite dans un petit appartement avec son frère.
3. Dis-moi, où à Paris habites-tu/habitez-vous?
4. Nous vivons aujourd'hui.
5. Il a vécu au Moyen-Âge.

Workout 69 .... p. 138

Exercise 1
1. c
2. d
3. a
4. e
5. b

Exercise 2
1. faire connaissance
2. retrouvent
3. retrouve
4. suis tombée sur
5. a rencontré

Exercise 3
1. Il va se retrouver sans sa voiture.
2. Retrouve ton sourire, mon cher.
3. Tu as retrouvé ta montre?
4. J'aimerais faire leur connaissance. *or* J'aimerais les rencontrer.
5. Ils sont tombés sur leur comptable à la soirée.

Exercise 4
Possible answers:
1. J'ai rencontre José.
2. J'ai perdu une facture et je ne l'ai pas retrouvée.
3. J'ai retrouvé mon ami Max.
4. Je suis tombé(e) sur une ancienne collègue.
5. Je me suis retrouvée à travailler tard la nuit.

Workout 70 .... p. 140

Exercise 1
1. Tu prends le taxi
2. Les sportifs ne prennent pas d'alcool
3. Les sportifs prennent une douche froide.
4. Juliette Binoche prend le taxi.
5. Vous prenez des vacances.
6. Je ne prends pas de cours de piano.
7. Je prends une douche froide

Exercise 2
Possible answers:
1. D'habitude, je prends un jus d'ananas.
2. Je prends le bus et le métro.
3. Je prends trente jours de vacances par an.
4. J'aimerais prendre un cours de film.
5. Je prends quarante minutes pour me préparer le matin.

Exercise 3
1. Prends les livres avec toi.
2. Prenons un sandwich au fromage.
3. Ils ont pris deux mois de congé.
4. Tu prendras ton vélo ou ta voiture?
5. Mon oncle passera nous prendre ce soir.

Workout 71 .... p. 142

Exercise 1
1. b
2. b
3. b
4. a

Exercise 2
1. avons appris
2. enseigne, enseigne
3. apprends
4. apprendre
5. apprenez

Exercise 3
1. Ils m'ont appris à danser le tango.
2. Il enseignait les maths au lycée.
3. J'ai appris la nouvelle: félicitations!
4. Tu vas apprendre comment il a survécu.
5. Enseigner est une profession difficile.

Exercise 4
Possible answers:
1. J'ai appris à explorer.
2. J'ai appris qu'il faut être patient.
3. J'ai appris à apprécier.
4. J'ai appris la grammaire à des élèves.
5. Je vous ai appris un nouveau verbe.

6. J'ai appris un jeu à Victor.

Workout 72 .... p. 144

Exercise 1
1. amener
2. emporte
3. apporte
4. emmenons
5. amène

Exercise 2
1. Les fourmis emportent du gâteau.
2. Monsieur Hulot amène sa vieille voiture.
3. Tu emmènes du gâteau
4. Xavier et moi apportons mon poisson rouge.
5. Xavier et moi apportons du gâteau.

Exercise 3
1. En Martinique: J'emmène mon amoureux et j'emporte des lunettes de soleil.
2. Dans les Alpes: J'emmène ma mère et j'emporte un gros pull.
3. A Paris: J'emmène mon frère et j'emporte mon appareil photo.

Exercise 4
1. Je n'emporte pas mon parapluie.
2. Apporte la table.
3. Laure n'est pas venue te chercher?
4. Nous emmenons mes parents au concert.
5. Amenez vos maris.

Workout 73 .... p. 146

Exercise 1
1. mettez
2. met
3. mets
4. mettons
5. mettent

Exercise 2
Possible answers:
1. Non, je ne mets jamais la radio.
2. C'est moi qui mets la table chez moi.
3. Oui, j'aimerais poser pour un artiste.
4. Je le pose sur mon lit.
5. Je mets dix minutes pour arriver au travail.

Exercise 3
1. a *or* c
2. a *or* b
3. a *or* c

Answer Key

Workout 74

Exercise 1
1. Est-ce qu'il aime les asperges?
2. Est-ce qu'il est de Lyon?
3. Est-ce qu'elle a fini ses devoirs?
4. Est-ce que tu as étudié la Deuxième guerre mondiale?
5. Est-ce que tu voyages beaucoup?
6. Est-ce que tu as mangé un sandwich au jambon?

Exercise 2
1. Avez-vous vu le match de football?
2. Aime-t-il les asperges?
3. A-t-elle un professeur préféré?
4. Voyages-tu beaucoup?
5. As-tu mangé un sandwich au jambon?
6. Etudies-tu la Deuxième guerre mondiale?

Exercise 3
1. Tu voyages beaucoup, n'est-ce pas?
2. Il aime les asperges, n'est-ce pas?
3. Il a fini ses devoirs, n'est-ce pas?
4. Tu étudies la Deuxième guerre mondiale, n'est-ce pas?
5. Jack parle espagnol, n'est-ce pas?
6. Il est de Lyon, n'est-ce pas?

Workout 75
p. 150

Exercise 1
1. c
2. d
3. b
4. a
5. e

Exercise 2
1. Pourquoi
2. Où
3. Quand
4. Comment
5. Qui

Exercise 3
1. "Mon frère étudie à l'étranger." "Lequel? Vous avez beaucoup de frères."
2. Combien est-ce que ça coute?
3. Quel crayon est le tien?
4. Pourquoi est-ce que vous partez?
5. Quelle est la sortie pour l'aéroport?
6. Quand est-ce que le magasin sera ouvert?
7. Qui a mangé la dernière part de la tarte?

Workout 76
p. 152

Exercise 1
1. Quoi?!
2. Quand?
3. Comment?

Exercise 2
1. c
2. a
3. d
4. b

Exercise 3
1. Pour qui?
2. Combien?
3. Comment?
4. Chez qui?
5. Depuis quand?

Workout 77
p. 154

Exercise 1
1. e
2. f
3. a
4. b
5. g
6. c
7. d

Exercise 2
1. Je ne mange jamais de boeuf.
2. Je n'ai envie de rien faire.
3. Il n'a qu'une soeur.
4. Je n'ai vu personne cet après-midi.
5. Elle n'aime ni son cousin ni sa cousine.

Exercise 3
1. Je ne mange que du poulet.
2. Personne n'est venu au théâtre ce soir.
3. Le week-end nous n'allons nulle part.
4. Je n'en ai aucune.
5. Il ne voyage plus.

Workout 78
p. 156

Exercise 1
1. Non.
2. Jamais.
3. Personne.
4. Personne.
5. Rien.
6. Jamais.

Exercise 2

1. noun (subject)
2. preposition
3. noun (subject)
4. noun (direct object)
5. noun (indirect object)

Exercise 3

1. "Qu'est-ce que tu fais?" "Rien."
2. Les bonbons que j'ai goûtés? Je n'en ai aimé aucun.
3. "Qui est-ce que tu as invité dîner chez toi ce soir?" "Personne."
4. Il n'était pas à l'heure non plus.
5. Le printemps arrive sans aucun doute.

Workout 79... p. 158

Exercise 1

1. mais
2. ou
3. car
4. et
5. ni, ni

Exercise 2
Possible answers:

1. Il pleut mais il ne fait pas froid.
2. J'ai oublié mes clés et je veux rentrer.
3. Nous avons faim or nous avons déjà mangé.
4. Elle est en retard car il y a des embouteillages.
5. Ils ont des examens donc ils ne viendront pas.

Exercise 3

1. Muriel déteste le froid, or elle vit à la montagne.
2. Je ne vais pas dire non car j'aimerais essayer.
3. Et je pensais que j'étais seule!
4. Ni toi ni elle ne m'avez convaincu(e).
5. Mais pourquoi Jeanne est-elle sortie?

Workout 80 .... p. 160

Exercise 1

1. lorsque
2. que
3. puisque
4. comme
5. si

Exercise 2

1. c
2. e
3. a
4. b
5. d

Exercise 3
Possible answers:

1. le sport est bon pour la santé.
2. je ferme la fenêtre.
3. mon frigo est vide.
4. je ne suis pas fatigué(e).
5. je termine un exercice.

Exercise 4

1. Puisque tu as acheté ce vélo, tu n'as pas besoin de marcher.
2. Écris-lui que tu acceptes.
3. Comme tu veux!
4. Si tu t'inquiètes, parle-lui.
5. Comme j'arrivais, j'eus une idée incroyable

Workout 81.. p. 162

Exercise 1

1. pire
2. meilleur
3. plus

Exercise 2

1. plus
2. meilleure
3. pire
4. plus
5. meilleure

Exercise 3

1. J'ai mangé autant de pizza qu'elle.
2. Elle parle espagnol aussi bien qu'elle parle italien.
3. Jessica a autant de frères que de soeurs.
4. Je mange autant de viande que de poisson.

Exercise 4
Possible answers:

1. Fabien est plus petit que Charlotte. Charlotte est plus grande que Fabien.
2. La femme est plus vieille que le bébé. Il est plus jeune qu'elle.
3. La fleur est plus jolie que l'arbre. L'arbre est plus grand que la fleur.

Workout 82 .... p. 164

Exercise 1

1. le plus
2. le plus
3. la plus
4. le pire
5. la plus
6. la plus

Answer Key

Exercise 2
Possible answers:

1. David Beckham est le footballeur le plus talentueux.
2. L'Amazone est la fleuve la plus longue.
3. Sarah est l'élève la plus studieuse de cette classe.
4. La Chine devient l'économie la plus importante.
5. L'Auvergne est la plus jolie région de France.

Exercise 3

1. Entre les trois, Fabien est le plus petit. Entre les trois, Charlotte est la plus grande.
2. Entre les trois, la femme est la plus vieille. Entre les trois, le bébé est le plus jeune.
3. Entre les trois, la pastèque est la plus grande. Entre les trois, la fraise est la plus petite.

Exercise 4

1. Elle est très intelligente.
2. L'examen de maths était très difficile.
3. Je suis très malin(e).
4. Franchement, je crois qu'il est très arrogant.

Workout 83 .... p. 166

Exercise 1

	V	I	N	G	T		
					R		
				C	E	N	T
					I		
		D	O	U	Z	E	
		E			E		
		U					
D	I	X					

Exercise 2

1. deux mille cent vaches
2. quatre-vingt-cinq gâteaux
3. un million parapluies
4. trois cent vingt-quatre anges
5. un professeur

Exercise 3

1. quinze mille dollars
2. cent mille dollars
3. quatre-vingt-dix dollars
4. neuf cents dollars
5. huit cent cinquante dollars

Workout 84 .... p. 168

Exercise 1

1. La lettre *a.*
2. La lettre *b.*
3. La lettre *m.*
4. La lettre *j.*
5. La lettre *t.*

Exercise 2

1. dixième
2. huitième
3. sixième
4. quatrième
5. deuxième

Exercise 3

Philippe: —Arnaud, c'est la quatrième chaîne que tu as mise! S'il te plaît, ne change pas de chaîne!

Arnaud: —Non, c'est la troisième. D'abord j'ai regardé une comédie sur Canal Plus, puis j'ai regardé l'émission sur la Deuxième guerre mondiale.

Philippe: —Et puis tu as regardé le cinquième épisode d'*Urgence*. Et maintenant tu regardes ce documentaire sur le roi de France Louis Quatorze. Ça c'est quatre.

Workout 85 .... p. 170

Exercise 1

1.

2.

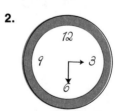

3.

4.

5.

Exercise 2
Possible answers:
1. Je me lève à sept heures du matin.
2. Je prends mon petit-déjeuner à sept heures.
3. Je me couche à dix heures du soir.
4. Je prends ma douche à huit heures et demie.
5. Je commence l'école à huit heures.

Exercise 3
1. dix-sept heures
2. deux heures et quart, quatorze heures et quart
3. neuf heures moins le quart, huit heures quarante-cinq
4. midi, douze heures
5. vingt et une heures trente, neuf heures et demie

Workout 86 . . . . p. 172

Exercise 1
1. La Saint-Valentin est le 14 février.
2. La Toussaint est le 1 novembre.
3. Jour J (D-day) est le 6 juin 1944.
4. Noël est le 25 décembre.
5. Mon anniversaire est le ____.

Exercise 2
1. c
2. d
3. f
4. e
5. a
6. b

Exercise 3
Possible answers:
1. Ma soeur est née le ____.
2. Mon père est né le ____.
3. Ma tante est née le ____.
4. Elle est née le ____.
5. Mon chien est né le ____.

Workout 87 . . . . p. 174

Exercise 1
1. Aïe! *or* Ouille!
2. Hop-là!
3. Boum!
4. Chout!
5. Bon ... ben ... alors ...

Exercise 2
1. Oups
2. Et toc
3. Miam miam
4. Oh là là
5. quoi

Exercise 3
1. Toc, toc!
2. Coucou!
3. Hein?
4. Beurk!
5. Miam miam!

Workout 88 . . . . p. 176

Exercise 1
1. beaucoup d'ail
2. nous l'avons fait
3. (correct)
4. ils s'entendent bien
5. (correct)
6. qu'elle
7. l'histoire

Exercise 2
1. s'
2. le
3. J'
4. l'
5. qu'
6. Puisque

Exercise 3
Possible answers:
1. l'eau
2. N'écoutez pas!
3. Tu t'es fait mal.
4. Qu'attendez-vous?
5. Demain s'il demande d'emprunter ta voiture, dis non.
6. Puisqu'il n'est pas là nous reviendrons.

Answer Key

Workout 89 .... p. 178

Exercise 1

Aspirate h: le hibou, le haricot, les halles, le homard, le hasard, la honte, le handicap

Silent h: l'hiver, l'homme, l'haine, l'harcèlement

Exercise 2

1. C'est un bel héritage.
2. Mon amie s'appelle Louise.
3. (correct)
4. (correct)
5. Mon habitation est une cabane en bois.
6. L'hippopotame mange l'herbe.

Exercise 3

1. C'était par hasard!
2. J'ai envie de manger ce homard.
3. Quelles belles huitres!
4. C'est une nouvelle hybride.
5. Le pilote a mis l'avion dans le hangar.

Workout 90 .... p. 180

Exercise 1

Exercise 2

1. des
2. du
3. du
4. d'
5. en
6. de
7. d'
8. en

Exercise 3

1. Pendant deux ans j'ai vécu à Madagascar.
2. Je ne suis jamais allé(e) en Allemange, mais j'ai visité l'Italie l'année dernière.
3. Londres est la capitale du Royaume-Uni.
4. On m'a dit que la Nouvelle Angleterre était bien, surtout le Maine.
5. Je veux aller en Amérique du Sud parce que j'ai de la famille en Argentine.

Workout 91 .... p. 182

Exercise 1

1. l'anglais
2. le français, le flamand
3. l'arabe
4. le portuguais
5. l'anglais
6. l'anglais
7. l'allemand
8. l'anglais, le français.
9. le japonais
10. l'espagnol

Exercise 2

1. Elle a des origines polonaises, mais elle ne parle pas la langue de ses ancêtres.
2. L'anglais américain n'est pas pareil que l'anglais britannique.
3. (correct)
4. J'aime la cuisine italienne.
5. Les hommes russes sont beaux.
6. (correct)
7. J'aime aussi les pizzas italiennes.

Exercise 3

1. Céline Dion est canadienne. Elle parle le français et l'anglais.
2. Jodie Foster est américaine. Elle parle l'anglais et le français.
3. Roger Federer est suisse. Il parle l'allemand, le français, et l'anglais.
4. Ingrid Bergman était suédoise. Elle parlait le suédois, l'anglais, l'allemand, l'italien, et le français.
5. Gael García Bernal est mexicain. Il parle l'espagnol, l'anglais, le français, et l'italien.

Workout 92 .... p. 184

Exercise 1

1. e
2. g
3. b
4. i

5. h

6. j

7. a

8. f

9. d

10. c

Exercise 2

1. une casserole

2. une bande d'amis

3. un médecin

4. une veste

Exercise 3

1. M. Spielberg est un réalisateur bien connu.

2. Je me suis blessé(e) pendant le match de hockey sur glace.

3. Le directeur de mon école primaire portait des noeuds papillons.

4. Je suis toujours de mauvaise humeur le lundi.

Workout 93 .... p. 186

Exercise 1

Standard French: une prise, ringard, un film, caresser, un pansement, coincé	**Québécois:** une plogue, matante, une vue minoucher, un plasteur, jammé

Exercise 2

1. French: Alexandre regarde un film.

Québécois: Alexandre regarde une vue.

2. French: Alexandre caresse un chien.

Québécois: Alexandre minouche un pitou.

Exercise 3

Claire: Jean-Pierre, ça te dit de faire du shopping cet après-midi?

Jean-Pierre: Oui, pourquoi pas? Viens, monte dans ma voiture.

Claire: C'est comme tu veux, si tu veux me conduire au centre commercial.

Jean-Pierre: Peux-tu me donner mes lunettes dans la boîte à gants?

Claire: Celles-là? Achètes-en des nouvelles, les tiennes font un peu ringard.

Jean-Pierre: OK! Nous sommes arrivés, pense à bien fermer ta porte.

Claire: D'accord. Et toi, pense bien à prendre de l'argent pour les achats.

Jean-Pierre: T'inquiète, pas mon ami. J'ai tout ce qu'il faut sur moi.

Workout 94 .... p. 188

Exercise 1

1. d

2. f

3. e

4. a

5. c

6. g

7. b

Exercise 2

1. J'en sais rien.

2. On veux aller manger au resto.

3. On trouve qu'elle est sympa.

4. T'as déjà dîné, toi?

5. Ça t'intéresse pas d'aller à la fac?

6. T'as déjà mangé ton petit déj?

Exercise 3

1. spoken

2. spoken

3. spoken

4. written

5. spoken

Exercise 4
Possible answers:

Nous sommes parties à Paris avec mes parents. Nous avons dormi dans un bel hôtel. Nous avions une très belle chambre avec une vue sur la Tour Eiffel. Nous avons visité l'Arc de Triomphe mais nous n'avons pas eu le temps de faire du bateau-mouche. J'ai adoré visiter Paris. Je pense que c'est une ville magnifique.

On est partis à Paris avec mes parents. On a dormi dans un bel hôtel. On avait une super chambre avec une vue géniale. On a visité l'Arc de Triomphe mais on a pas eu le temps de faire du bateau-mouche. Moi, j'adore Paris. Je pense que c'est une ville géniale.

Workout 95 .... p. 190

Exercise 1

1. Oui

2. Non

3. Si

4. Si

5. Non

6. Si

Exercise 2
Possible answers:

1. Oui, je suis américain(e).

2. Si, je suis un élève.

Answer Key

3. Oui, j'aime les feux d'artifice.

4. Si, j'aime les vacances scolaires.

5. Non, je ne regarde pas souvent les matchs de rugby.

Exercise 3
Possible answers:

1. Oui, il était français.

2. Non, il est né en Corse.

3. Oui, au début de sa carrière il était soldat.

4. Non, il n'a pas gagné toutes les guerres.

5. Si, il a perdu des guerres.

6. Oui, il était empereur des Français.

7. Oui, il était marié.

8. Non, sa femme s'appellait Joséphine.

Workout 96 .... p. 192

Exercise 1

1. preposition

2. noun

3. pronoun

4. subject pronoun, reflexive pronoun, auxiliary verb

5. noun

Exercise 2

1. J'ai soif et j'ai chaud.

2. J'ai fait mes courses et je suis rentré à la maison.

3. Je suis montée et j'ai frappé à la porte.

4. On se bat et puis on se pardonne.

Exercise 3

1. Elle s'est brossée les cheveux et elle s'est lavée.

2. Je suis allé(e) à la bibliothèque et j'y ai étudié.

3. Lucie a une nouvelle voiture et une vieille.

4. Je suis monté(e) et je suis fatigué(e).

Workout 97 .... p. 194

Exercise 1

1. C'est

2. Ce sont

3. C'est

4. Il est

5. C'est

6. C'est

7. Il est

8. Il est or Elle est

9. Ils sont or Elles sont

10. Elle est

Exercise 2

1. Travailler, c'est rester en bonne santé.

2. C'est l'heure.

3. C'est dégueulasse.

4. C'est lui.

5. Aujourd'hui c'est le 17 mars.

6. Il est facile de coudre.

7. C'est très facile à coudre.

Exercise 3

1. C'est trop tôt pour manger.

2. C'est un canadien.

3. C'est un grand homme, Patrick.

4. Ce sont des étudiantes.

5. C'est une gourmande.

Workout 98 .... p. 196

Exercise 1

1. Tous

2. Toutes

3. toute

4. tous

5. tous

Exercise 2

1. pronoun
2. adverb
3. adjective
4. noun
5. adjective

Exercise 3

1. tous les deux
2. tout de suite
3. tous les jours
4. tout à l'heure
5. En tout cas
6. pas du tout

Workout 99 .... p. 198

Exercise 1

1. again
2. another
3. yet
4. again
5. even

Exercise 2

1. still
2. always
3. still
4. always
5. still

Exercise 3

1. toujours
2. encore, toujours
3. encore
4. toujours
5. toujours

Exercise 4

1. Elle essaie encore.
2. Je n'ai pas encore tondu la pelouse.
3. Elle est toujours belle.
4. Même si je mange, j'ai toujours faim.
5. Je suis toujours content(e).

Workout 100 .... p. 200

Exercise 1

1. Il y a
2. Depuis
3. Pendant
4. Il y a
5. Depuis
6. Pendant

Exercise 2

1. pendant
2. il y a
3. depuis
4. depuis
5. il y a ... que

Exercise 3

1. J'étudie le français depuis trois ans.
2. J'étudie le français depuis le collège.
3. Il y a trois ans j'ai commencé mes études de français.
4. Est-ce que tu savais que le festival a commencé la semaine dernière?
5. Oui, j'y vais tous les jours depuis mercredi.
6. J'étudie le français depuis que j'ai quinze ans.
7. Pendant que j'étais au Maroc, j'ai appris quelques phrases arabes.